SOCIAL MOVEMENTS IN LATIN

Also by Ronaldo Munck and published by Agenda

Rethinking Global Labour: After Neoliberalism

SOCIAL MOVEMENTS IN LATIN AMERICA

Mapping the Mosaic

RONALDO MUNCK

agenda
publishing

First published in 2020 by Agenda Publishing

Agenda Publishing Limited
The Core
Bath Lane
Newcastle Helix
Newcastle upon Tyne
NE4 5TF
www.agendapub.com

ISBN 978-1-78821-242-7 (hardcover)
ISBN 978-1-78821-243-4 (paperback)

British Library Cataloguing-in-Publication Data
A catalogue record for this book is available from the British Library

Typeset by Newgen Publishing UK
Printed and bound in the UK by TJ International

CONTENTS

ACKNOWLEDGEMENTS

I first need to thank Alison Howson, my editor at Agenda, for never saying "I would not start from there" or anything other than totally helpful critical advice. I was also helped incredibly to deal with my concerns around the methodology chapter by my very own focus group of excellent social movement researchers and teachers, namely Sam Halvorsen, Cathy McIlwaine, Sarah Radcliffe, Sara Motta, Sian Lazar, Ana Dinerstein, Pablo Pozzi, Leandro Vergara-Camus, Mo Hume, Jenny Pearce, Gerardo Munck and Kyla Sankey. In Ecuador, where I finished this book, Pascual García and Karina Ponce were a great help in terms of introducing me to local social movements. Finally, I would like to mention Peter Waterman (1936–2017), my sparring partner since the 1970s, who would, I hope, have liked this book.

Ronaldo Munck

PREFACE

Latin American social movements have often been romanticized. Emiliano Zapata, Che Guevara, Mothers of Plaza de Mayo, the *piqueteros* and Zapatistas: all well publicized, if not necessarily well understood. There is a sense – not entirely misplaced – that Latin America has been a laboratory of social mobilization and struggles for a better life. While state politics change political complexion and their policies, the social movements are always there in the background and on the streets.

There have been many interpretations put forward to explain the seeming "rise and fall" of the progressive or left-of-centre governments in Latin America since 2000. There has been much talk about "tides" (pink or other colours), which supposedly ebb and flow according to the phases of the Moon, and of "cycles", which also come and go according to some underlying mechanism, never fully explained. Concrete political analysis gives way to some sort of natural rhythm acting in mysterious ways.

What has also prevailed is a rigid analytical distinction between the various types of progressive movements/governments that is less than helpful, as it is based on binary oppositions. From a conservative perspective we have seen a persistent bid to distinguish between a "good" left – respectful of liberal democracy and not seeking radical change – and a "bad" left – "populist", undemocratic and often articulating irresponsible objectives. Ironically, some left commentators mirror this binary scheme, positing a "hard" left that seeks radical change, builds socialism and confronts imperialism, and a "soft" left that respects liberal democracy too much, does not make ambitious promises and lives within the international rules of the game. Even at a quick glance, we can see these are impoverished schemas that do not help us understand the complex interplay of political and social struggles over the last 20 years.

In the chapters that follow, I will not assume any model along these lines. I will foreground, instead, concrete politics and not assume a position of exteriority that interprets, judges and corrects the actions of others. Against any schema that posits binary oppositions, we will see that politics is always complex and certainly cannot be analysed the way meteorologists analyse the tides around our coasts (and, even here, complexity rules). The period from around 1998 in Latin America cannot be understood in terms of any schema in which mysterious mechanisms are foregrounded above the day-to-day political struggles to construct a people *(pueblo)*, develop political alliances and maximize the articulation of social forces contesting the dominant order.

There is a general consensus in Latin America that the 1990s were a period when neoliberal economic policies were hegemonic, but these were also contested by the labour and other social movements. A signal of what was to come was the 1989 Caracazo in Venezuela, which saw a semi-insurrectional situation emerge in a previously stable country. The breakdown of the previous political order led to the dramatic rise of Hugo Chávez as president in 1998. This event marked the start of an unprecedented rise of left-of-centre governments across much of Latin America and ushered in a new post-neoliberalism agenda. The collapse of Argentina's iconic neoliberal model in 2001 was another cataclysmic event that marked the start of a new era.

The post-2000 turn to the left was swift and widespread, to a degree that is quite unprecedented globally. Progressive, post-neoliberal governments came into office in Bolivia, Ecuador, Argentina, Brazil, Uruguay and, arguably, Chile, as well as the controversial return of the Sandinistas in Nicaragua. The "golden era" of this left governmental swing ran from approximately 2003 to 2011, when a boom in commodity prices helped provide the resources for increased public spending. The social and political movements associated with the left were clearly oriented towards the state as the means to secure change, and they often had charismatic leaders: Hugo Chávez, Evo Morales, Lula de Silva, Rafael Correa, Néstor and Cristina Kirchner, and so on. They were redistributive in their policies, but they did not seek, on the whole, to restructure the relations of production, except through nationalizations. Although they sometimes carried out constitutional reform processes, they did not, in the main, promote the politicization of the subaltern masses.

The fate of the progressive governments began to change in the wake of the 2008/9 global financial crisis. At first its impact in Latin America was muted, but it slowed the growth of China, which had generated much of the demand for raw materials in the previous era. Social tensions began to mount and the social and political wings of the left-of-centre governments began to diverge. Symbolically, we can date the turn in fortunes to the death of Chávez in 2013, which had a direct impact on the plans for regional integration under an anti-imperialist banner. His death also led to the deconstruction of the Venezuelan political order and encouraged the mobilization of a hard right opposition, in Venezuela and beyond. The dominant classes saw an opportunity to fight back, after having to some extent acquiesced while the left held power, so long as their fundamental interests were not threatened, as was the case in Brazil.

In 2015 a right-wing business leader, Mauricio Macri, swept to power in Argentina, by effectively labelling the previous Kirchner regime corrupt and inefficient. He inaugurated a new phase of "post-political" anti-left politics dubbed "populist", with a focus on effective economic management. It is significant that he did not openly try to roll back the social gains of the previous era. In a different way, Lula's successor in Brazil was overthrown through a constitutional coup in the country in 2016, again with corruption as a major theme. This ushered in the election of the far right Jair Bolsonaro. In Chile, after a long period of stable centre-left governance, another millionaire, Sebastián Piñera, swept into power at the 2017 elections, gaining an unprecedented 55 per cent of the popular vote. The conservatives were electable again, it seemed, and did not need to rely on the army to seize power. It was not a change in the ebb and flood of the tide that caused this shift but, simply, the play of politics.

In seeking to explain this dramatic sequence of events, often described simply as the "rise and fall" of progressive governments, some critics sought to blame these governments for not being radical enough. Now, some failings were glaringly obvious, such as the rise of the "Boli[varian]bourgeoisie" in Venezuela, enriched by Chavista control of the state. The failings in terms of economic management and good governance were serious in some cases, but not in others (such as in Bolivia). Some criticisms were less realistic, however, such as accusing these governments of not moving beyond the extractivist economic model or, even, of not having built socialism (as though the Russian debate on socialism in one country had not happened).

In a sense, governments can be criticized only in terms of not meeting what they promised. Correa in Ecuador said he would promote a "Citizens' Revolution", and in that his government was reasonably successful. Chávez promised a lot more, and the fall from grace is thus more dramatic in Venezuela. Álvaro García Linera, in Bolivia, always referred to a long period of building "Amazonian capitalism" and ex-Tupamaro Pepe Mujica, in Uruguay, always said there was "a lot to be done" before we could think of socialism. Bolivia and Uruguay, under very different political banners, have actually been reasonably consistent in terms of delivering what they promised. In both these countries, however, the right wing is now in power.

What we see in some of the left critiques, especially international ones, is a discourse from a position that is external and superior in relation to the mass social and political struggles that led to and ran through the progressive governments. We do not choose the conditions under which we govern. We are not permanently mobilized, constantly being radicalized by struggle. Sometimes we need to slow down, compromise; we even need to accept defeat on some fronts. That is the nature of politics when not in a position of exteriority, with its claim of a privileged lens. In reality, this politics, not least in the last 20 years in Latin America, has been about constructing political alliances and articulating, in as broad a way as possible, the democratic demands of the people. Elections also had to be fought and won, something not always obvious to some critics, who seem to assume a free hand for the left in office.

One of the arenas in which the international left beyond Latin America, in particular, criticized the progressive governments was in relation to the role of the social movements that, in many cases, helped them gain high office. For some left critics, the first decade of the 2000s was another "lost decade" for social movements, which would, supposedly, have been better off had this shift to the left not happened. Presumably their innate radicalism would have won out and they would have not been co-opted by these governments. Certainly, many social movements were demobilized during this period: often their leaders were brought into government and divisions emerged. But we also must note that many of their demands were met, so that the pressure was off to some extent. Álvaro García Linera only stated the obvious, perhaps, when he said there were "creative tensions" between the progressive governments and some social movements. There have always been tensions, and even conflict, between the political and social wings of transformative movements. The demands of elections are real and cannot just be put down to reformism. It is never just a case of virtuous social movements confronting morally suspect progressive governments always programmed, as it were, to "sell out".

Recent events confirm the primacy of politics over seemingly theological debates in parts of the left or the tides/cycles paradigms. In Mexico, in 2018, we witnessed the election of Andrés Manuel López Obrador, which, despite all the predictable criticisms about his political timidity and temporizing with existing structures, represents a landmark shift away from the clientelist and bureaucratic politics that have dominated Mexico since the revolution. Often a weathervane for the rest of Latin America, Argentina in 2019 saw the dramatic defeat of Macri by a reconfigured Kirchnerist movement, signalling the ability of Peronism to renew itself and offer a unifying transformative programme in a period of economic crisis. This event showed, yet again, that politics is in command and that the construction of a people (*pueblo*) is central to a transformative movement. This dramatic defeat for the right-wing anti-politics message of Macri will have regional repercussions, as will the return of Kirchnerism, too often written off by right and left alike.

The construction of a *pueblo* to win elections and transform society cannot be achieved from a position of absolute exteriority (for example, by criticizing Kirchnerism for its national-popular rather than explicitly socialist politics) and not understanding the political horse-trading that constructs political alliances and the successful connection to labour and other social movements, which has helped forge a new – potentially hegemonic – political force.

In 2019 there were a series of semi-insurrectionary events that brought social movements centre stage once again. In Ecuador what began as a transport strike against an International Monetary Fund (IMF) package of measures, including a rise in fuel prices, was soon transformed into an indigenous uprising, the likes of which had not been seen for over 20 years. The government was forced to withdraw the IMF measures, and the indigenous movement emerged once again with a huge capacity to inspire students, workers and sectors of the middle class to confront neoliberalism. In Chile, around the same time, a movement that began as students protesting against transport costs was rapidly generalized into an unprecedented mass movement for social change and for the end of the continuity between the democratic regimes and the disdained Pinochet military dictatorship. The "Chilean model" of markets plus democracy lay in tatters, and the very end of neoliberalism as a development strategy loomed large. The government was forced to agree to a referendum on a new constitution. Millions of people in the streets in a prolonged mobilization created a virtual dual-power situation despite the state of emergency and brutal repression. The trade unions were forced out of their quiescence and neighbourhood assemblies gathered to debate and plan a new future. Chile may be the face of the future for social movements and the struggle for a dignified life in Latin America.

The purpose of this text is to carry out a preliminary political mapping of the wide range of social movements that have impacted on Latin American society. It seeks to develop a specifically Latin American theoretical lens and not just replicate or "apply" the dominant theories developed in the very different situations of the North Atlantic. As part of the decolonial turn, I will seek to develop a theoretical frame that is based not just on the best of international social theory but also on indigenous social actions and thinking in Latin America, as the best way to provide a suitable lens for further study of the region's long-lasting and innovative social movements.

I select some of the main social movements that have historically and currently composed the mosaic of protest and contestation in Latin America. The case studies chosen are the workers' and peasant movements, the array of community-based or territorial movements, the women's and indigenous movements and, finally, some of the most important environmental movements. I will foreground the importance of agency: that people chose their destiny, and commitment.

Although each case is examined in its own right, in practice there are a range of cross-fertilizations occurring between the various social movements. There are fascinating interactions between the indigenous and environmental movements, for example, and women, of course, are a key part of the workers' and peasant movements. The final chapter seeks to develop a dynamic mapping of the overall mosaic and show how the whole is greater than the sum of its parts, which can be taken as complex but unified social phenomena.

A methodological appendix provides the researcher with some insights into how best to deploy and combine research methods, including discourse analysis and the comparative approach as well as a range of ethnographic and participatory methods. The text also contains an annotated list of further reading around the main social movements the text introduces.

Source: Peter Hermes Furian / Alamy stock photo.

1

INTRODUCTION

We first need to ask ourselves: *what is a social movement?* An often cited definition is that of Mario Diani, for whom "social movements are defined as networks of informal interactions between a plurality of individuals, groups and/or organizations, engaged in political or cultural conflicts, on the basis of shared collective identities".[1] Social movements are not necessarily progressive, as some analysts assume; they can be revolutionary, reformist and, indeed, reactionary, as I have shown elsewhere.[2] Furthermore, social movements cannot, in my view, be reduced to a bland category of "civil society", sometimes conflated with NGOs (non-governmental organizations) or placed in a generic basket called "social protest". The question of human agency will loom large in this account of social movements.

I then move on to answer the question: *why Latin America?* As a continent that lies betwixt and between the global North and South, it has generated internationally significant social movements, and it may provide global lessons, not least, on how we should approach the study of social movements. By grounding the studies in a particular region, I hope to avoid the tendency to seek universal validity for what is sometimes known as "social movement theory", seen as a self-contained discipline.

Finally, I propose *an open paradigm*, which will serve as a backdrop to the chapters that follow on specific social movements in Latin America. Although I agree in general with the "grounded theory" approach (basically, that theory needs to be based on experience), I will argue that two opening sensitizing concepts will serve us well: Michel Foucault's intuition that "where there is power there is resistance", and Karl Polanyi's vision of history as a "double movement" of market expansion and societal reaction for self-protection. It is the practice of the social movements in Latin America, however, that will help us build and refine a grounded framework subsequently.

What is a social movement?

The first thing we need to recognize is the complexity and fluidity of social movements. Anyone who has been part of a social movement will understand that there is a degree of unknowability about such movements, something that cannot be captured by sociological theory alone. My own understanding of this developed when rereading Julio Cortázar's early Latin American "literary boom" text, *Rayuela* (*Hopscotch*), which had first appeared in 1963, when I read it without much interest at school in Buenos Aires. The main character, Horacio Oliveira, is a well-read bohemian who participates in life intellectually rather than actively. His obsession is to attain a centre, a unifying concept of life he can be contented within. His interlocutor, Lucía (known as "La Maga"), has a love of life and spontaneity that Horacio finds beguiling but also threatening to his peace of mind. As with the novel itself, Horacio is torn between order and chaos as he switches jobs, countries and lovers. He states that

> once again I imposed the false order that hides chaos ... There are meta-physical rivers, she swims in them like that swallow swimming in the air ... I describe and define and desire those rivers, but she swims in them. I look for them, find them, observe them from the bridge, but she swims in them. And she doesn't know it, any more than the swallow. It's not necessary to know things as I do, one can live in disorder without being held back by any sense of order. That disorder is her mysterious order, that bohemia of body and soul which opens its true doors wide for her. Her life is not disorder except for me, buried among the prejudices I despise and respect at the same time.[3]

Horacio, in his nomadic existence, seeks to find a sense of order in the world's chaos. In his statement above he expresses openly and lyrically what his conundrum is and his differences with La Maga. We can take these thoughts as an opening gambit for the study of social movements. We will seek theoretical frameworks that will assist in our task of analysis and understanding but we will not force them on a recalcitrant reality. We will seek to "know things" but also accept that we cannot "impose a false order" on complex phenomena with a degree of unknowability.

Another way of expressing the limitation of social theory in terms of understanding social movements would be in terms of what motivates people to join or follow them. Frances Fox Piven and Richard Cloward wrote a neglected classic on poor people's movements and "why they succeed, how they fail". They reinsert the question of agency and the vital role – for good or ill – that leadership plays in creating, sustaining and sometimes failing social movements.

A particular contribution they make – and one we need to bear in mind – is that people experience deprivation and oppression in concrete settings and not through abstract categories. As they put it: "Workers experience the factory, the speeding rhythm of the assembly line, the foreman, the spies and the guards, the owner and the pay-check. They do not experience monopoly capitalism."[4] Our analysis needs to be concrete and our social theories need to be grounded.

A further layer of understanding that we need to develop is in terms of the way social movements do not obey other people's rules: try to think like La Maga. They have their own logic, which cannot be discerned through a simple focus on structural conditions. Structuralism – in its Marxist as much as Durkheimian variants – has always been twinned with functionalism. It leads to a form of determinism – in which such and such structural conditions lead to this or that social movement outcome. We thus lose any sense of contingency (things can always turn out differently) and the vital role of human agency. In social movements – possibly above all other forms of human association – the roles of agency and of leadership are absolutely vital. It is the historians of social movements who have most clearly shown how structural conditions may set the parameters of social action, but they do not determine the outcome – that is the product of spirit and struggle – and there are always alternative historical outcomes.

In a study of the social bases of obedience and revolt based on a close study of the failed German revolution of 1918–20, Barrington Moore Jr challenges what he understood to be the Marxist theory of revolution, arguing against the tendency to "overemphasize the underlying long-run social trends" that do not determine history but, rather, "provide opportunity for political leaders and set outer limits on what is possible in terms of thought and action".[5] Workers being brought into large factories to work did not, in and of itself, create stable union organization, let alone "socialist consciousness". Pain and suffering alone do not create a social movement. In response to the brutal treatment of workers in the Industrial Revolution, what the workers had to learn, argues Moore, "was not to feel pain, but how to stop feeling that the pain was just an inevitable aspect of their existence".[6] For orthodox Marxists, it was as if it was simply a question of demonstrating exploitation for consciousness to emerge. We know now that the equation is much more complex and involves understanding, as Moore does, the "moral economy" of injustice and protest, for example.

Although the discussion above points us towards what a social movement might be, there are two current forms of analysis that present obstacles to this understanding, in my view. The first is the civil society frame, which first emerged in Latin America in the 1970s, to be followed in Eastern Europe in the 1980s. Defined as the territory between the state and the economy, the concept gained considerable purchase during the democratization wave of the 1980s. "Civil society" became a slogan for social movements and international organizations alike. It thus became part of the vocabulary of the World Bank, serving its mission of "good governance", whereby civil society guarded against the state, seen as the source of all problems. As we moved into the 1990s there was a marked "NGOization" of social movements in Latin America, to the extent that this frame now dominates (even when it is being criticized) in the North American literature on social movements.

We also began to see a slippage in language, with social movements increasingly being called CSOs (civil society organizations). The NGOs began to fill the gap in social provision created by the dismantling of the state in the 1990s under the neoliberal pro-market economic policies. At the same time, they gave political cover to the World Bank, which could claim it supported "empowerment" and "bottom-up" development. This is not the place to carry out a balanced evaluation of NGOs and the civil society discourse. Suffice it to say it is not the same thing as social movements and the struggle for social transformation. A separate but related discourse is that of human rights, another Western liberal notion that has gained near-universal acceptance as the new paradigm for both development and social movements. Although we might rhetorically argue that "labour rights are human rights", the reality is that social gains have historically been made through struggle, and today the main priority for labour and other social movements lies in organizing even when demands are posed in terms of rights.[7]

The second contemporary approach to social movements I would view as problematic is the one that merges them with a broader "social protest" genre. Protests of various types – from boycotts to marches, from sit-ins to rent strikes, from petitions to wildcat strikes – are seen to be part of the "repertoire of action" of social movements. Although other actors, such as political parties and pressure groups, also engage in protest actions, they are seen as the privileged tool of the social movements. There has been much emphasis on protest as "performance" and also the role of the mass media in relation to protests. Reflecting on this approach, we can, of course, agree that social movements engage in protests. It is a quite different proposition, however, to replace the social movement problematic by that of social protest. I would argue that protest is certainly an activity that social movements engage in, but it cannot be seen as their *raison d'être*, which would amount to reducing their specificity and diluting them within a much broader frame of analysis.

In Latin America the "protest" lens came to the fore in the 1990s, around the same time as the civil society frame mentioned earlier. With the decline of mass social movements, such as the trade unions, in the 1980s, there was a shift towards direct action: local uprising, mass looting and road blockages. It became widely believed that traditional social movements were in terminal decline and their capacity to articulate alternatives severely compromised. As stable collective identities crumbed – or at least appeared to – the disarticulated masses would respond through a more incoherent social protest modality. Direct action could be disruptive but could never lead to the creation of a new historical subject leading social transformation. Driven by the academic sector, and supported by international research funders, this perspective became hegemonic across Latin America to some extent. This changed after the turn of the century with the rise of the left governments, which only goes to show that "social protest" can never replace "social movements" as an adequate theoretical lens or paradigm.

In this section I have reviewed some basic preliminary matters before entering our full study of social movements in Latin America. I have argued that social movements cannot be reduced to social protest, a much broader and less specific concept. Likewise, I have argued that our enquiry into social movements needs to be concrete. If we start with abstract or general theories, there will be an inevitable tendency to cut the facts to suit the theory. We also need to understand that people take action and join movements on the basis of their concrete personal experience. Although capitalism and its contradictions retain great explanatory power, they remain abstract categories if we do not seek out and develop the mediations between them and concrete lived experience. Finally, I take from Julio Cortázar – and the broader Latin American experience – a refusal to constantly seek order and rational explanations for the sometimes inexplicable outbursts of the desire for freedom.

Why Latin America?

We need to consider why Latin America might provide interesting and relevant case studies for a global study of social movements. Latin America is present in global social movement discourse through iconic examples such as the Zapatistas, Argentina's *piqueteros* and the Brazilian landless movement. These are often taken out of their historical and national contexts and sometimes glamorized. In the chapters that follow I will seek to contextualize these struggles and ground them in Latin American reality. For now, I will argue that Latin America offers a true laboratory for the study of social movements for two main reasons: the first is that Latin America can be seen to be in a liminal position between the global North and the South, and thus provides lessons for both; the second is that we have in Latin America a set of historical phases that allow us to make chronological as well as cross-country comparisons. These phases are a national-popular developmental phase (1930–70), a neoliberal authoritarian market dominant phase (1970–2000) and a post-neoliberal left-of-centre phase (2000–15).

Antonio Gramsci famously remarked that "in Russia the state was everything, civil society was primordial and gelatinous; in the West, there was a proper relationship between state and civil society".[8] This distinction can be taken as a rough measure of East/West, or (more aptly for our purposes) South/North differences. It can then be used to "place" Latin America, which does not easily fit into either category alone. Gramsci did (practically in passing) refer to "peripheral" Western societies that might have a closer parallel in Latin America.[9] The Latin American nation states were often weak but their civil society was relatively well developed. These were also, like their European counterparts, "late" developing countries, with only a few beginning an integrated or organic development process before 1930. These late peripheral societies were marked by their colonial origins, not least in their unequal trading patterns. One of the main characteristics of these "in-between" societies – partly Western but also partly of the South – was that the construction of hegemony was a never-ending task of ephemeral success at best. This provided an opening for contestatory social movements, of course.

We could argue that Latin America has experienced mixed temporalities, leading to multiple modernities. The expansion of capitalism in Latin America led to a process of uneven development whereby old social-economic pattern coexisted with new ones. Modernization was never a smooth, linear process, so, for example, unfree labour relations persisted to the present day. This was not a "dual" society, however, as the mainstream argued, but, rather, a case of uneven and combined development. Thus, we might see the introduction of the most up-to-date technologies in rural areas while also observing the persistence of coerced labour in the new industries. This new-in-the-old and the old-in-the-new pattern was a socio-economic process, but it was also characteristic of the political and cultural domains. Identity and culture are neither fixed nor homogeneous from this "liminal" perspective. This would naturally impact on the social movements that confronted this setting, being torn between modern and traditional modes of organizing and identity formation.

In recent years it is the concept of hybridity that has gained most purchase in Latin America to make sense of this particular setting, and it will inform our specifically Latin American perspective on social movements. As an analytical category it takes us beyond binary oppositions between tradition and modernity, for example, but also the First World/Third World distinction. Latin America is part of a transnational cultural political economy, with its flows of migrants, money and images that defy simplistic nationalist and cosmopolitan projects alike. Nation building in the traditional European sense is no longer seen as viable in the era of global integration and development. Yet globalism (and its implicit cosmopolitanism) is seen to reproduce hierarchies and inequalities at all levels. Certainly, globalization does not produce a racism-free, sexism-free and sustainable world, whatever its self-image might be. In fact, it is a powerful generator of social movements at global, national, regional and local levels.

The first phase of hybrid modernization in Latin America that framed the development of social movements began to emerge after 1930 as the previous agro-export model faltered because of the global economic recession. Despite some industrialization in some countries, the agro-export model prevailed up to the 1930s, and it was only after the Second World War that a new regime of accumulation emerged, which set the context for a flourishing of social movements in the 1950s and 1960s.

In the postwar period most of Latin America moved towards a state-led industrializing regime of accumulation and some form of national-popular state. This was a national development model with import substitution industrialization displacing – with greater or less success – the agro-export model of the oligarchic state. Social actors were based in the workplace, on social class belonging or political affiliation. The institutions of the state were often weak and the state was based on a fundamental class compromise between the dominant and subaltern classes. In some countries the pre-existing level of industrialization was too weak, or the oligarchic class bloc was too strong, to allow for transition to a new *desarrollista* (developmentalist) regime of accumulation. Where it was successful – in the Southern Cone countries, Brazil and Mexico in particular – there was a considerable increase in employment, both in industry and in the new white-collar sectors. There was some degree of income redistribution and the widening of consumption patterns as a mass market emerged. This generated tangible popular support for the state and the emergence of nationalist-populist social movements.

The paradigmatic social movement of the national-popular era was undoubtedly the labour movement, often viewed as irredeemably statist, subjecting the working class to a neo-corporatist straitjacket and class collaboration. In reality, the labour movement was more complex, and its corporatist dimension has often been overstated. As labour became "nationalized" – that is, as its immigrant status dissolved in a new national-popular discourse – it became quite influential in many countries. We need only recall the role of rural and urban workers in the Mexican Revolution of 1910, the role of workers and trade unions in the rise of the national-popular Peronist movement in Argentina after 1945 and the dramatic role of workers, unions and a workers' party in Brazil from the 1980s to the present. These are social movements that have had a dramatic and durable impact on society and the cultural domain.

The other main arena of social mobilization during this era was in the urban domain, as urbanization increased dramatically through internal migration to the cities. The urban movements that emerged were very diverse in nature and cannot be reduced to Manuel Castells's theory of urban movements as a response to "urban contradictions",[10] which some analysts tried to transpose to the very different Latin American context. A rich associational, place-based life and social networks developed, addressing the many issues of urban living, such as housing in particular. Based on a sense of neighbourhood and communalism, these associations or movements could sometimes develop beyond the defensive mode and were a key element in popular class formation. Women were particularly active in these grass-roots organizations, all committed to community building through demands on the state for the necessities of life such as nurseries, schools, health care centres and adequate transport.

The second phase emerged under the twin pressures of the national-popular development model faltering and the global turn towards neoliberalism from the 1980s onwards. The contradictions of the national-popular period were internal – such as a relative exhaustion of "easy" import substitution industrialization – but they were also "external", in the sense that social movements, particularly the urban and rural labour movements, were threatening the stability of the class compromise model. This resulted in a wave of military interventions in the 1970s and the gradual emergence of a new regime of accumulation, which came to be known as neoliberalism. The new development model was market-driven, it advocated an open economy and it was pledged to achieving a minimal role for the state. Civil society was henceforth to be conceived of not as organized groups, let alone social classes, but as individuals and, above all, as consumers. An authoritarian state sought to disarticulate society and break up corporatist groups – such as trade unions – that might advocate collective views. The market would, henceforth, allocate resources rationally, the state would withdraw from economic affairs, and society would be atomized to prevent the re-emergence of populism.

During this period the so-called "new" social movements came to the fore, responding to the closure of democracy by military and civilian neoliberal regimes alike. They were not necessarily new in a literal sense, with church-based community groups, self-help networks and human rights organizations having a long history. They were different from movements in the past in that they recentred democracy as a political category – natural enough in the authoritarian context in which they emerged – and in the way they were presented as non-class, single-issue campaigns, such as in the emblematic Madres de Plaza de Mayo. The free market economy was, to some extent, successful in disembedding the economy from social relations. As the emergency period of the neoliberal offensive came to an end, however, then, inevitably, social issues came to the fore again and social movements formed in the indigenous communities, among women, over environmental issues and around land issues, with a new/old landless peasant movement emerging.[11]

One of the notable features of this period was the changing role of the NGOs once seen as the epitome of global civil society. The notion of civil society came to the fore in Latin America during the 1980s, as military regimes began a process of decompression and as the left began to break with previous conceptions of armed struggle against the state as the only path to socialism. It was also part of the international turn towards the NGOs as creators/drivers of a "civil society" that would counter the economism of the neoliberal strategy. From a social transformation perspective, we see a shift from the NGO as a contestatory presence allied with social movements to the NGO as a service delivery agent for the international financial institutions. Behind the language of empowerment and professionalization lay the reality of depoliticization and an acceptance of the dominant order, albeit with local participatory initiatives.[12] Nowhere was this process clearer than in what Sonia Alvarez has referred to as "the 'NGOization' of Latin American feminism",[13] which created a new layer of feminist leaders and movements increasingly divorced, socially and politically, from the grass roots. Too often the literature on social movements conflates them with NGOs, when, in fact, they are quite distinct.

During the neoliberal period a whole range of transnational social movements were formed within Latin America and with some wider global linkages. One of the most significant movements of the 1990s was that forged across the Americas contesting their proposed US neoliberal free trade project. As Marisa von Bülow notes, "Never before had so many CSOs [civil society organizations] from the region come together to debate and mobilise transnationally around a hemispheric agenda."[14] Although transnational NGOs were the visible front of this campaign, it is noteworthy that the workers' and peasant organizations provided much of the organizational weight. It is important to note at this stage that we should not conflate these movements with the wider alter-globalization movement, which came to the fore after the World Trade Organization (WTO) protests in Seattle in 1999. The social composition of the latter and its politics differ significantly from those of social movements on the ground in Latin America, even though there can be overlaps, as, for example, between the national peasant movements and the transnational Vía Campesina.

The rise of left-of-centre governments in Latin America after 2000 was based, at least to some extent and in some countries, on mass mobilizations and protests.[15] This way, arguably, a post-neoliberal political order emerged even if the extractivist economic model still prevailed, and was even accentuated in some cases. Neoliberalism had emerged in Latin America as a response to hyperinflation, on the one hand, and increased social contestation, on the other. Having achieved its immediate economic objectives, its own internal contradictions emerged as many sectors of the dominant classes were marginalized. There was also sustained contestation by old and new social movements alike. The post-neoliberal era can be said to have begun with the collapse of Argentina's neoliberal model in 2001/2, with the global crisis of 2008/9 consolidating that paradigmatic crisis. The election of left-of-centre governments across the region was both symptom and cause of a new wave of social movement activation, which called for a new analytical lens in so far as it was quite distinct from both the old and new social movements of the past.

In the years after 2000, after some 20 years of neoliberal hegemony, a new wave of critical thought arose in the region, revisiting and updating the legacy of the dependency school. It entailed not only a Southern and critical perspective on the development process but a rethinking of its dynamics "from below", as it were, based on ideas advanced by and from within the social movements. The main features of the development project envisaged in this new wave of critical thought was not simply an abstract model of socialism or postcapitalism. The sources of inspiration for the social transformation project pursued were diverse and based on a wide range of experiences derived from the practice – and theory – of social movements in the region. This included a recovery of indigenous values such as social solidarity and harmony with nature, the envisaging of new modes of communal systems of production and consumption, the recovery and preservation of the commons, and the construction of a non-homogeneous and non-hegemonizing new world.

My stress below will be on the diversity of social movements during this period, rather than on iconic movements, such as the Zapatistas, that have captured the imagination globally to the extent that the online myth is sometimes quite divorced from the on-the-ground reality. Another global myth is that of the "*Qué se vayan todos*" ("Let them [the politicians] all go") in Argentina following the collapse of the US-dollar-linked economy at the end of 2001. Behind the international inflation of the *piqueteros* and occupied factories into models of best practice lay a more prosaic social reality. The unemployed workers' movement that organized flying pickets (hence *piqueteros*) to cut highways to protest was never as "autonomous" as some commentators claimed.[16] They were most often groups organized by far left political parties and others that also developed clientelist relations with the state to deliver social benefits. The recovered factories, likewise, took many different forms but many were defensive moves by workers when their employers went bankrupt and abandoned the premises. What is noticeable in these and other movements of the period, as a unifying strand, is that they were mainly reacting against the failings of the capitalist market and not the state, as was previously the case.

An open paradigm

The next chapter of this book deals specifically with the theories available to the social movement researcher in Latin America. Outlined here are some background or sensitizing concepts that should be borne in mind when approaching the study of social movements in general.

To develop this open paradigm, as I call it, I would start with Foucault's dictum: "Where there is power, there is resistance, and yet, or rather consequently, this resistance is never in a position of exteriority in relation to power."[17] It is not a question of resistance just responding to power, but of understanding how power and resistance exist in a reciprocally integrated fashion and are perpetually in movement. Power does not just react to resistance, nor is it just preceded by it; rather, resistive tensions constitute power at its very core. Foucault's approach lent itself to the understanding of the new social movements in Europe in the 1970s and the growth of "identity politics". Oppressions are not always linked to economic class divisions and are perpetuated by a range of structures, including the family, the media, civil society and language itself. Foucault directed us towards a new political economy of power relations that can be studied empirically. It leads us to take the forms of resistance to different types of power as our starting point.

For Foucault, "between a relationship of power and a strategy of struggle there is a reciprocal appeal, a perpetual linking and a perpetual reversal".[18] Power and resistance do not exist in separate domains; they are always linked, but always in flux. Resistance is never external to power, in so far as power as a system of domination does not have a separate "inside" and "outside". Joseph Rouse puts it that, in Foucault, "power is not something possessed or wielded by powerful agents, because it is co-constituted by those who support and resist it".[19] A system of domination, in other words, cannot simply impose its rules on those it governs. The rules of governance are always at issue, always the subject of struggle. Society, as we know it, does not pre-exist struggle; rather, it is shaped by constant and ongoing struggles. Points of resistance are ever-present and the network of power relations is cut through by these at every point.

Where Foucault further illuminates the analysis of social movements is in his insistence that power and knowledge "are not just superimposed on the relations of production but, rather, are very deeply rooted in what constitutes them".[20] The appropriation of wealth in a feudal society and under capitalism is based on different forms of the power–knowledge relationship. Foucault refuses to "simply accept the traditional Marxist analysis that, labour being man's concrete essence, the capitalist system is what transforms that labour into profit, into hyper profit or surplus value".[21] Rather, we need to consider, according to Foucault, the techniques of power through which people's bodies and time became labour power. We need to direct our attention to the infra-power (*sous-pouvoir*) – that "web of microscopic, capillary political power"[22] – that bound people into production and made them workers. It is these "little powers" that social movements must often contest in practice.

Bringing a Foucauldian perspective to bear does not mean we must reject Karl Marx's insights into the operation of capitalism and resistance to it. I would agree with Jacques Bidet that the two theorists work on different but, arguably, complementary planes. Specifically, the dominant class works on two planes: that of the market, where capitalist power rules; and that of the organization, where knowledge-power dominates.[23] Foucault, who focuses on the second element, can allow us to extend, expand and complete Marx's analysis of capitalism, focused on the first element. Or, put more simply, a "class society" is complemented by a "disciplinary order". In addition, we might say that, whereas Marx directs us to focus on the "power of exploitation", Foucault directs our attention to the "power of control". For the analysis and understanding of contemporary social movements, these insights are absolutely critical. To keep insisting on a "class perspective" against the supposed evils of "postmodernism" is not, I would argue, a mark of radicalism but, rather, represents a failure to engage with contemporary society in all its complexity.

To further develop our new open paradigm, we should also bring in Karl Polanyi's problematic, which poses the possibility that history advances through a series of "double movements". Market expansion leads to the "one big market" that we call globalization today but – as Polanyi argued in his day, and we could argue today – "simultaneously a counter-movement was afoot". Taken in its broadest sense, Polanyi's notion of a social counter-movement could be seen as an incipient theory of counter-hegemony. Challenging the movement towards commodification, these counter-movements seek to "decommodify" society and reassert moral and cultural values. Against materialism and market-determined values, the social counter-movement generated by neoliberal globalization brings to the fore democracy and the social value of all we do.

At its most basic, the Polanyian problematic was based on the notion of a "great transformation" at the start of the nineteenth century, leading to the dominance of free market principles. But this social transformation led to a counter-movement through which society protected itself from the effects of untrammelled free market expansion. History thus advances in a series of "double movements", according to Polanyi, whereby market expansions create societal reactions. We can posit that the emergence of "globalization" in the last quarter of the twentieth century represented the belated fulfilment of the nineteenth-century phase of human history, characterized by "an attempt to set up one big self-regulating market".

According to Polanyi, who was writing during the cataclysm of the Second World War, "the fount and matrix of the [capitalist] system was the self-regulating market". Polanyi traces the birth of market society as we know it to Britain's Industrial Revolution of the nineteenth century. Previous societies had been organized on principles of reciprocity or redistribution or householding; now exchange would be the sole basis of social and economic integration. Markets were previously an accessory feature in a system controlled and regulated by social authority. Henceforth the market ruled unchallenged and changed society in its image: "A market economy can exist only in a market society."[24] Economic liberalism was the organizing principle of the new market society, in which economics and politics were, for the first time, split up. What is remarkable about this economic discourse is that "[t]he road to the free market was opened and kept open by an enormous increase in continuous centrally organized and controlled interventionism".[25] As with neoliberalism in the 1980s, laissez-faire economics was nothing if not planned.

Polanyi goes further than Marx to argue that "labour power" is but an "alleged commodity", precisely because it "cannot be shoved about, used indiscriminately, or even left unused without affecting also the human individual who happens to be the bearer of this peculiar commodity".[26] This is more than a moral critique of capitalism, however, because Polanyi goes on to argue that trade unions, for example, should be quite clear that their purpose is precisely "that of interfering with the laws of supply and demand in respect of human labour, and removing it from the orbit of the market".[27] Any move from within society to remove any element from the market ("decommodification") thus challenges the market economy in its fundamentals.

The "double movement" consisted of economic liberalism driving the extension of the self-regulating market, on the one hand, and the principle of "social protection", on the other hand, defending social interests from the deleterious action of the market. Today, as Stephen Gill puts it, "we can relate the metaphor of the 'double movement' to those socio-political forces which wish to assert more democratic control over political life, and to harness the productive aspects of world society to achieve broad social purposes on an inclusionary basis, across and within different types of civilisation".[28] Movements struggling for national or regional sovereignty, those seeking to protect the environment and the plethora of movements advancing claims for social justice or recognition are all part of this broad and diverse counter-movement. In different, but interrelated, ways, they are bids to re-embed the economy in social relations. Challenging the movement towards commodification, they seek to "decommodify" society and reassert moral and cultural values.

Against all forms of economic determinism and the "class reductionism" of classical Marxism, Polanyi stresses that social class is not always determinant. This critique resonates with the contemporary transition towards "new" social movements mobilized around non-class issues. For Polanyi, "class interests offer only a limited explanation of long-run movements in society. The fate of classes is more frequently determined by the needs of society than the fate of society is determined by the needs of classes."[29] The critique of economism implicit in Polanyi's work has a contemporary ring, as when he stresses the "cultural" element in social dislocation and resistance. Cataclysmic events, such as the Industrial Revolution in the nineteenth century or the "Globalization Revolution" today, are, in Polanyi's words, "economic earthquakes" that transform the lives of vast multitudes of peoples; but "actually, of course [argues Polanyi], a social calamity is primarily a cultural phenomenon that cannot be measured by income figures or population statistics".[30] When peoples are dispossessed of their traditional means of livelihood, when customs and ways of life are disrupted and "alien" cultural values are imposed, this affects the very way in which people ascribe meaning to their condition. So, argues Polanyi, it is "not economic exploitations, as often assumed, but the disintegration of the cultural environment of the victim that is then the cause of the degradation".[31]

There is a fundamental problem from my perspective, however, in that both Foucault's and Polanyi's conceptions of resistance would need to be corrected or expanded on if their very inventive and radical ideas are to serve our purposes. With Foucault there is a quasi-anarchist faith in an all-embracing and sometimes quite vague "resistance". We rarely learn where resistance comes from, how it is constituted or how it is productive of social transformation. In other words, beyond some episodic comments in regard to the anti-prison movements he supported, we do not get much on the concrete mechanics of resistance. With Polanyi it is a different but related problem, because he sees "society" reacting but does not specify who in society – which social groups – resist the encroachment of the self-regulated market and how these counter-movements are formed. With Foucault, in the way he connects power with knowledge through discourse, and posits that knowledge and power are continually reproduced through both formal and informal institutions, there is, ultimately, little space for wilful agents to escape the choking grasp of their culture without reproducing the same forms of oppression they are trying to overcome. Polanyi, for his part, does tell us that "[t]he 'challenge' is to society as a whole [but] the 'response' comes through groups, sections and classes",[32] but that is still quite under-specified in terms of a political sociology for a globalized complex era. Which "groups" or "sections" of society are likely to respond to the encroaching marketization and commodification of life? What is the role of social movements in the process, a set of actors rather absent in Polanyi's narrative? This is where, following Bob Jessop, "the role of specific economic, political and social projects, of hegemonic visions, and of associated capacities become crucial".[33] If the fightback by "society" is to go beyond dispersed, and possible contradictory, struggles, this perspective needs to be built on to generate a transformative politics.

With these provisos in mind, we move in the next chapter to the various competing theories specifically seeking to explain social movements in Latin America with a clear understanding of the broad principles of domination and resistance. From Polanyi we take a broad-brush understanding that the "one big market" (*aka* globalization) continuously generates counter-movements from within society, including what I would call social movements. These might be reactive, seeking to counteract the disembedding of the economy from society; proactive, articulating another globalization; or a combination of both forms. From Foucault we take an understanding that with power comes resistance; they are inextricably intertwined. Against all forms of structuralism – which see "objective" conditions structuring protest – Foucault offers us the possibility of writing a history from the viewpoint of the resistances of the oppressed. Foucault is on the same page as Polanyi when he refuses the attempt by neoliberalism to separate the economy from the social. The Polanyian "counter-movement" and Foucault's "resistance" are basic underlying concepts for the analysis of Latin American social movements.

2
THEORIES

Theoretical frameworks can be enabling, or they can be straitjackets. If I seek to fit the facts to suit my chosen theoretical frameworks, then both my theory and my research outputs are impoverished. In the philosophy of science, it is well known that it is quite normal for theoretical paradigms to persist even when reality shows them wanting.[1] We should, instead, be flexible about our theoretical frameworks and not try to impose them on recalcitrant facts. I am mindful, of course, that these "facts" are constructed by our theoretical frames and our methodologies. The research terrain is fluid, and we need to be prepared to say when something is not working. Finally, I think we should bear in mind Foucault's challenge to normative understandings of what makes critique legitimate: "Critique doesn't have to be the promise of a deduction which concludes: this then is what needs to be done. It should be an instrument for those who fight, those who resist and those who refuse what is."[2] There has been a tendency in engaged research on social movements to conflate the role of analysis with what Foucault refers to as preaching "this is what needs to be done".

The theoretical frameworks considered here are the largely dominant North American social and political science perspectives developed since the 1950s, the European post-1968 "new social movement" (NSM) approach and, finally, the various Latin American options developed to overcome the shortcomings of both these external perspectives.

North American

Orthodox Marxist and socialist theorists had long occupied themselves with social movements in their own particular way, but in the academic milieu they were somewhat under-studied until the 1970s. The socialist tradition was, on the whole, quite instrumental in its approach and it largely looked at why the working class had not fulfilled its allotted historical role. In the first half of the twentieth century the main academic frame related to what we would now call social movements studies, focused on "collective behaviour", whereby individuals were seen to react emotionally to situations outside their control. Another variant was the "relative deprivation" thesis, which saw people joining movements through a sense of deprivation in relation to others, or in terms of their own expectations. Functionalist accounts stressed the irrational and unorganized nature of collective action, as though it simply responded to an individual sense of alienation or frustration. A positive turn occurred in the mid-1960s in North American mainstream political science with Mancur Olson's emphasis on rational actors making choices to join movements based on instrumental and strategic reasoning.[3] The utilitarian logic of the rational choice model – with its emphasis on the individual and a Western model of rationality – had a huge influence on North American social movement theorizing even while it was being critiqued and surpassed.

Resource mobilization (RM) theory starts from the premise that, although social discontent may be universal, collective action is not, and it therefore needs to be explained in some way. Against the previously dominant US theory of "mal-integration" – which posed collective actions as mindless eruptions by people not integrated properly into society – the RM approach stressed the continuity between these collective actions and what we might call "normal" or routine social life. Basically, RM theory took the insights of the fairly well-developed US organizational theory and applied them to collective action. The underlying premise was a form of "methodological individualism" that posited an economically rational model of human agency. The tools that RM advanced have been under constant revision since they were first developed, but they still largely focus on the gaining of resources in a timely, cost-effective manner to implement an organization's goals. Thus, studies of social movements would include research around how the core professional group organizing them brought in money, supporters, media interest and political alliances to help deliver its goals. From this perspective, it is not therefore grievances that explain social movements but, rather, the success or otherwise of the entrepreneurial model that the promoters of collective action advance.

A variant of RM is the "political opportunity structure" (POS) model, which focuses on political rather than economic factors but is still premised on rational choice theory assumptions. Collective social behaviour is based on the calculus of individual actors making individual choices. The POS approach shares the organizational approach of RM theory but then adds the variable of political opportunities. These could take the form of divisions in the ranks of the political elite, a decline in the levels of political repression or an increase in political pluralism, for example. These openings might allow activists to recruit members and mobilize them in pursuit of their objectives. Although the original POS model was quite structuralist in its approach, further refinements focused instead on how the political context affects the strategic choices of political actors.[4] The role of social networks is now also recognized within this approach, and the limits of instrumental means–ends calculation are also acknowledged, allowing for the moral language of "solidarity" to be incorporated into the theoretical frame.

The resource mobilization approach and its variants are firmly grounded in US social and political reality, and, for this reason alone, perhaps, they do not travel well. There is an element of ethnocentrism in assuming that a theoretical model developed at a particular time and place can have universal applicability. The internal critiques of the older theories of collective behaviour are quite restrained and do not, on the whole, question the epistemological assumptions of the theory. This reflects the perceived lack of social class determinants of politics in the United States. Its hegemonic position in orthodox political science – just as that of modernization theory in sociology – reflects US power-knowledge and power rather than any broader applicability, particularly in Latin America.

The RM theoretical frame has been severely criticized since its inception. The underlying cost–benefit analysis is clearly inadequate to account for why activists emerge and people join movements even when there is no direct material benefit to be gained. It can become an unwieldy conceptual apparatus, quite often overwhelming the concrete case study, with facts being squeezed into the model. It is quite ethnocentric, being based unreflexively on North America case studies. Finally, its constant revisions and updating show the classical pattern of paradigm adaptation when it is clearly failing both in theory and in practice. The US academy, given its considerable power/knowledge weight, can perhaps afford to ignore these problems, but that is not a good enough reason to support its dissemination in Latin America.

The underlying assumption of the RM approach that collective behaviour is a "normal" part of political life was welcomed at first, because it was an advance on previous theories based on notions of mal-integration. But it was then questioned by the likes of Piven and Cloward, who, while they recognize that protest is indeed a form of politics, argue that it needs to be understood as outside, or against, "normal" politics, "in the sense that people break the rules defining permissible modes of political action".[5] So, for example, labour movement historians have referred to early forms of collective protest as "collective bargaining by riot". This may help us understand the moral economy of protest but, even so, a riot is not the same as an electoral rally. RM analysts typically de-emphasize the role of violence and coercion by protestors while emphasizing that of the elites. Yet we cannot understand the role of social movements without recognizing the role of force (for example, against strike breakers), which cannot be "normalized" by subsuming the whole world of protest under the rules and moral codes of an idealized Western liberal democracy.

Both the RM and POS approaches often tended to dilute the notion of social movement in the "strong" sense (of a collective movement seeking fundamental social change) with the vague, somewhat apolitical, notion of "repertoires of contention". Even in the one case study in which the RM approach had some purchase – the US civil rights movements – its limited political grammar led it to simply ignore the role of the inner city riots in the emergence and development of the civil rights movements. In Latin America in the 1990s the language of "protest" and "contention" gained some currency, but both largely evaporated in practice after 2000 with the re-emergence of social movements in the classical sense having clear normative goals. The RM approach is, ultimately, "disciplining" in its paradigmatic vision of social movements in that it seeks to fit recalcitrant social reality and rebellious social groups into its theory. In many ways, as Piven and Cloward put it, "like many malintegration analysts before them, resource mobilization analysts have also reduced lower-stratum protest politics to irrational and apolitical eruptions".[6]

There is no doubt that the RM approach has been hugely influential despite these critiques, even if less so in Latin America. In an early review of Latin American social movement theory, Joe Foweraker, however, stated that, "in my view, this rejection is short-sighted, since this theory may have much to offer the analysis of Latin American social movements, especially the analysis of their relationship to the state".[7] There has been some increased influence of this approach in the years since then, not least through the cultural power of the US graduate schools in Latin America. Influential figures such as García Linera have also argued that, compared to the "new social movement" approach, the US theorists "are more useful for studying events in Bolivia, as they focus on the movements' effects on the political structure of society".[8] Yet he recognizes the limitations of the rational means–ends calculation that underpins the US approach. Of course, despite this model's shortcomings, we do need to be alert to the impact of the political situation on the shaping of social movements.

One possible way forward that has been suggested in terms of developing an adequate theoretical framework would be to combine the positive lessons of the US approach with the European approach, to which we will now turn. Whereas the resource mobilization theory focuses on the political strategy of movements, the "new social movement" approach emphasizes the formation of identities and their role in civil society. The synthesis proposed by Jean Cohen was premised on the different but related logics of collective action: the construction of identity and strategic action.[9] Thus, a social movement may, at one and the same time, struggle for inclusion in political society and for the democratization of civil society. This dual logic would apply, for example, to the Western feminist movements, which have, historically, sought inclusion in political society and the breaking down of patriarchal norms in the broader civil society. I cannot do justice here to this terrain where the incorporation of the US and European approaches is proposed. It may, indeed, find complementarities and overcome sterile counter-positions but it does not, in my view, do away with the need to develop a specifically Latin American theory of social movements grounded in the history and politics of the region.

European

Although RM ruled supreme across the Atlantic, the events in France of May 1968 unleashed a wave of innovative thinking in Europe around social movements, and the "new" social movements in particular. French scholar-activist Alain Touraine was undoubtedly a pivotal figure in theorizing this turn. Touraine argued that a transition was under way from the hitherto dominant industrial society to what he called "programmed society", not dissimilar to a whole range of theories positing the emergence of a "post-industrial" society in the 1970s.[10] For the first time, argued Touraine, "social movements are becoming the main actors of society", promoting "one project of society against another".[11] Against the regime of technocratic management, it posited a new era of self-managing determination. We see in Touraine not only a theorist of the "new" social movements but also a product of the revolutionary thinking that sprang from what the world systems theory called the "*world* revolution" of 1968: "There have only been two *world* revolutions. One took place in 1848. The second took place in 1968. Both were failures. Both transformed the world."[12] The origins of this approach are thus very different from the conservative US academic setting of the 1950s, which saw the rise of the previously discussed approaches.

One of the key shifts that was to occur after 1968 was that socialists in the advanced industrial (or post-industrial) societies shifted their attention from the organized labour movement to the "new" movements of youth, women, peace and, a bit later, ecology. The labour movement was viewed by many as a defunct nineteenth-century model that was no longer radical nor the harbinger of a new social order. The restraining influence of the dominant French trade unions, under Communist Party control, in May 1968 simply confirmed that negative verdict. It was seen as bureaucratic, integrated into bourgeois society and, basically, senile. What revolutionary potential it might once have had was long since lost to the discrete charm of the bourgeois order. Workers in the West were seen as a "labour aristocracy" living off the exploitation of the Third World, where a vigorous anti-colonial revolution was under way. These workers had been seduced and "bought off" by Western consumerism, whereas the new generation rejected consumerism and conformity alike.

The new social movements would start anew and create a new society that rejected both consumer capitalism and bureaucratic socialism. The new social movements were seen as an expression of the new capitalism that had become consolidated in the long postwar boom in the West. Advanced capitalist societies had been subject to a process of "commodification", as social life became dominated by the market, and by "bureaucratization", as the state intervened more and more at all levels of society. The "new" mass media had also led to a cultural "massification", creating conformity and repression of creativity. The new social movements thus reflected the new social antagonisms: the youth rebellion, the ecological movement and the rising of women against patriarchy. These movements were anti-institutional and anti-hierarchical and reaffirmations of individuality against collectivism. They are all based on social antagonisms other than those of social class, and the conflict between the worker and the capitalist in the factory, in particular. All forms of subordination were rejected, the imagination was in power and the future would be nothing like the past.

The new social movements rejected the "totalizing" vision of the old movements, such as the labour and nationalist movements. There was no single conflict to be resolved to reach the "promised land", in so far as there was a multiplicity of conflicts. The main thrust of these movements was the quest for autonomous identity against the "totalizing" or tutelary aspirations of the traditional social movements. Tilman Evers, in an article on Latin America, offered four main theses that account for what was specific about these new social movements:

- The transformatory potential within new social movements is not political, but socio-cultural.
- The direction of this counter-cultural remodelling of social patterns is open.
- Central to this counter-cultural distinction is the dichotomy of alienation versus identity.
- In creating an alternative cultural project, the new social movements also create the germs of a new subject.[13]

This framework is the basis for a utopian project in the true sense of the word, based on the classic Marxist libertarian and egalitarian call for "an association in which the free development of each one is the condition for the free development for all", as *The Communist Manifesto* declared boldly. It is relatively easy to show, in hindsight, that there was, in fact, no hard and fast dividing line between the "old" and the "new" social movements. The labour movement in its origins was very much like the "new" social movements today, and only gradually and unevenly becoming institutionalized. It has also had to reinvent itself periodically, and today it is rediscovering its vocation as a social movement to deal with the decline of traditional trade unionism. Labour movements were also a key component in the democratic challenge to authoritarian regimes in the "developing" world in the 1970s and 1980s. It would be quite wrong to accept the verdict of Castells, for example, that the workers' movement is no longer an agent of progressive social change.[14] Movements, by definition, can change and adapt to new circumstances through renewal and regeneration. Ultimately, Dan Clawson argues, from a perspective that is extremely open to the new social movements, that "no force in our society has more democratic potential (or radical possibility) than the labour movement".[15] This would be especially true in so far as it adopts a social movement unionism orientation that goes beyond the workplace and production issues to organize workers in their communities and around social reproduction issues.

It is also clear that the new social movement theory in Latin America was as much a cultural import as the North American RM theory approach, albeit one that was initially attractive to younger, more radical and engaged scholars. As Joe Foweraker noted early on, "The unequivocally 'new' social movements in Latin America are few and far between", and "the real overlap between new social movements in Europe and Latin America remains limited".[16] Social movements in Latin America such as the indigenous one have been seen as epitomizing the "new" category, but in fact they have long historical roots. The NSM approach also failed to grasp the historical specificity of the role of the state in Latin America and the reasons why it has been, and continues to be, at the heart of social movement politics. Even social identity in Latin America cannot be assumed to follow European patterns in so far it is often generated in response to or in relation to the state. Above all, the needs of those living under conditions of dependent capitalism cannot be equated with their European counterparts living in a "programmed" society. Poverty and not "the end of work" was the main issue underlying many social movements.

Social movements in Latin America came to prominence in the 1970s largely under military dictatorships. This created a totally different context from that set by European post-industrial or programmed society. The role of the state was central and the demands of democracy were the main driver of social mobilizations. So, for example, the women's movements of this period were concerned with survival and repression in a way that was not the case in Europe when the "new" social movements were being discovered. Fernando Calderón and colleagues have referred more generally to how there is something about the social movements of Latin America "that is impervious to the analytical categories provided by European analysts despite their richness", which "still fall prey to teleological and rationalistic biases".[17] Despite the richness of the NSM analytical categories they could still fall prey to ethnocentric biases when they were unthinkingly "applied" in Latin America. The mixed temporalities, syncretism and hybridity of Latin America, not to mention the impact of uneven development, made it a recalcitrant reality for this particular cultural import.

Our balance sheet of the NSM approach must be a mixed one. It is as specific to one global region and historical period (Western Europe after 1968) as was the RM approach. To assume its ability to "translate" into the Latin American reality was equally ethnocentric. Having said that, its impact in Latin America has been perhaps more positive, in that from it emerged the development of an indigenous tradition of critical social movement thinking around the work of Sonia Alvarez, Arturo Escobar and others.[18] In those collected volumes and their individual works, we witness a true embedding of the NSM approach in Latin American reality. The role of social movements in the democratization process, their relationship to the political parties and their internal dynamic are explored in an open and critical way. We can, in fact, see them as foundational texts in the development of Latin American social movement studies as an area of enquiry and reflection.

This new problematic – we maybe cannot call it a paradigm as such yet – has set about reinventing what power, the state and democracy meant, and could mean, in Latin America. Its truly original emphasis on the politics of culture led to a reassessment of democracy in the Gramscian tradition. It was part of – and combined with – the renewal of the left and the abandonment of Manichean or instrumentalist visions of politics. The discovery that, in politics, there was something beyond the state was a gain, despite the sometimes romantic notions of civil society that accompanied this turn. Its continued emphasis on social movements – in all their complexity and sometimes contradictory meanings – showed up the real limitations of "actually existing democracy" and the post-2000 left-of-centre political regimes that, for them, represented a retreat to state-centred politics.

Latin American

In Latin America – as elsewhere in what used to be called the Third World, now the global South – there has been a tendency towards importing social theory, with the signal exception of "dependency theory" in the 1960s, which was a genuine indigenous attempt to understand Latin America's specific form of domination. Overall, it was often the case that the latest French or US theoretical intervention was better known than any indigenous theory making in the social sciences. Inevitably, quite apart from the cultural dependence it encouraged, there was a mismatch between the theory and the national reality. This has also affected the Marxist frame that was, hitherto, perhaps hegemonic – despite different positions – within progressive thinking. Álvaro García Linera, Marxist sociologist and one-time vice-president of Bolivia, declared in this regard that, "in Bolivia, the old Marxism is neither politically or intellectually relevant, and critical Marxism, which comes from a new intellectual generation, has only limited influence ... In contrast, Indianism has little-by-little, established itself as a narrative of resistance that has recently been put forward as an authentic possibility for power."[19] We thus start with *indigenismo* as theoretical frame and resistance narrative.

The turn to an indigenous philosophy of transformation was inspired by the work and example of José Carlos Mariátegui (1894–1930), the Peruvian socialist and labour organizer who set out to "Latinamericanize" Marx and make him fit for purpose in a continent that he misunderstood so badly.[20] Mariátegui's *Siete Ensayos sobre la Realidad Peruana* (*Seven Essays on Peruvian Reality*) represents an intense engagement with Peruvian social, economic, political and cultural reality in the period leading up to 1930, when a major crisis and transition period opened up in Latin America. The 1920s saw a whole series of upheavals among the indigenous peoples of Peru that shaped – or, rather, reshaped – Mariátegui's political vision for change. This was also, of course, the period when the great Mexican Revolution was coming to the close of its most active phase. Far away, in Russia, the October Revolution of 1917 brought a new world-historical subject onto the world scene – the proletariat – and a bold ideology for social transformation: Leninism. Mariátegui, during this tumultuous period, laid the foundations for an original and critical Marxist understanding of Latin America, in his writings and his political practice.

Far removed from grandiose or general ideas, he focused his energies on social transformation as a result of popular practices and traditions. Rejecting all forms of a "class essentialism" that would reduce all life to its class origins, Mariátegui focused on the broad, emancipatory potential of social, popular and ethnic social forces. His thinking and practice were the very antithesis of the statism that came to dominate Latin American Marxism. For him, there was an overwhelming need for a "practical socialism" – springing from the daily practices of the subaltern classes – that would change society, and for a strong state that would act from above. His fascination with Peru's Inca past was not with the Inca state (and its so-called Asiatic mode of production, as labelled by orthodox Marxists) but, rather, with its communal social practices and ethos, which he saw as prefigurative of communism.

Mariátegui provides an early Marxist engagement with the situation and aspirations of the Amerindian peoples, breaking with his own early, quite orthodox socialism in a European frame. He began to focus on the land question as the main underlying factor in Amerindian subjection. Above all, he argued, against all forms of paternalism, that the liberation of the Amerindian peoples was a matter for themselves. His analysis was based on an early critique of Marxist and mainstream theories based on "dualism" between country and city, advanced and backward sectors of the economy. Rather, these were seen to be in dialectical unity, and the path of social transformation needed to be conceived in a holistic way for him. Mariátegui is extremely contemporary again today in his analysis of the "indigenous communist economy" and the "agrarian communism" of the *ayllu* (Inca community), with its principles of reciprocity and redistribution of wealth characteristic of these communists; their habits of cooperation and solidarity and their "communist spirit" were, for Mariátegui, harbingers of the socialist transformation required in Peru and Latin America more broadly. These categories were very much part of the contemporary debates in the Andean countries under left-of-centre governments after 2000.

Following Mariátegui, we could say that "we do not want [Latin] American socialism to be a copy or an imitation, it should be a heroic creation. We must give life to Indo-American socialism with our own life, in our own language."[21] This statement should not be read as a simple nativist reaction towards a foreign import, and Mariátegui's internationalism was never in doubt. It was, however, a view that was very conscious of the deeply Eurocentric nature of contemporary reformist socialism. Today we still see a tendency, both in mainstream political analysis and in radical contestation of the status quo, to mirror North Atlantic views of the world and analytical approaches. To rethink Latin America, it is necessary to develop a Latin American perspective that prioritizes the actually existing social transformation processes, on the ground, as it were. In this way, Latin American subaltern knowledge can make a genuine contribution to the current search for a social order that is sustainable and equitable, after the failure of neoliberal globalization to deliver on its promises.

Another theoretical frame that is at least partly Latin American is that of "autonomy", a concept developed not least around the experience of the Zapatistas. Autonomy also has resonance in Latin America through its relationship with the dependency theory of the 1960s, which posited the need for national and regional "autonomy" from the dominant, central or imperial powers. In the current period – and in relation to the study of social movements – autonomy can best be seen as a political philosophy and project. Autonomy highlights the centrality of indigenous political practices, which are foundational with regard to a renewed vison for social transformation. Based on concrete social practices and indigenous cosmologies, the discourse of autonomy is prefigurative of a new social order beyond the exploitation of humans and nature.

The project of autonomy has as a central driver the question of confronting power. As Gustavo Esteva puts it, "The struggle for autonomy undermines the very foundations of the juridical and political regimes that Mexico's founding fathers imported."[22] The autonomy project seeks to wrest from the state the political spaces and legitimacy they occupied through colonialism. Thus, autonomy, far from being a negative stance, is a dynamic project and a movement for social transformation. It is a rejection of all forms of domination and a call for social self-determination. Autonomy recognizes the subaltern nature of poor people's movements and seeks to give them an emancipatory vision. We might still need to question the effectiveness of this strategy, given that in practice it tends to avoid engaging with all political parties (in so far as they are seen to be part of the bourgeois state), which, inevitably, reduces the transformatory potential of this perspective for social movements.

To date the concept of autonomy has not been central in empirical social movement research in Latin America. To use the language of research methodology, it has not really been operationalized. It is often seen as a utopian political project: how can a social movement be "autonomous" in relation to the state and capital? Yet we can see in concrete social movements how they contest capital through self-management initiatives in times of crisis and negate the power of the state in creating "autonomous" territories, as the Zapatistas have. Autonomy also makes itself felt in development practice, wherein the previous "dependency" paradigm has been superseded by a range of "anti-development" initiatives more in keeping with indigenous critiques of the coloniality of power. Although, ultimately, autonomy is impossible under dependent capitalist conditions, it opens up a horizon of possibilities for social movements, providing a coherent vision of an alternative order.

Taking a longer-term view of Latin American social movements, we could argue that it is the "national-popular" frame that distinguishes it from both North Atlantic and traditional Marxist class-based theoretical frames. In Gramscian terms, what occurred in Latin America after the crisis of 1930 was the construction of a national-popular collective will based on a great "intellectual and moral reform".[23] It is this national-popular formation that overcame and surpassed the oligarchic system of hegemony, or oligarchic modernity, as we called it above. The work by Emilio de Ípola and Juan Portantiero in the 1980s around the national populisms in Latin America[24] renewed the classic debate between José Carlos Mariátegui and Raúl Haya de la Torre of the 1920s around the significance of the national question from a socialist perspective, and posed anew the relation between the national and social questions, to use the traditional Marxist terms.

Central to the development of a national-popular will was the concept of the people (*pueblo*). For Ernesto Laclau, it is only by developing and extending Gramsci's work in this area that we can overcome the exclusion/opposition between particularity and universality in the construction of the people.[25] The development of populism is probably the main difference between Latin American political development and that of other regions. Gramsci's emphasis on hegemony as anything but a systemically closed totality allows us (following Laclau) to understand populism as the Latin American manifestation and development of the national-popular will. It is a political logic that explains the deep divide between liberalism and democracy during the post-1930 period we are dealing with here. For Laclau, "populism presents itself both as subversive of the

existing state of things and as the starting point for a more or less radical reconstruction of a new world order wherever the previous one has been shaken".[26]
The old order was changed utterly by the emergence of this national-popular
ideology and worldview. It could also become radicalized at key conjunctures
when the "people–oligarchy" opposition became the dominant divide in society.
Emerging in the historical period of the 1930s, with the failure of global market
mechanisms and the limits of local laissez-faire industrialization apparent, it was
inevitable that this populist mobilization would express a strong commitment to
the development of a robust national state.

Gramsci's concept of the "national-popular" entered Latin America's political
discourse in the 1950s as theoretical backing for the then emerging populist
political movements. But, in reality, Gramsci's thinking was never even remotely
populist in intention, and nor was his practice. It is indicative, though, that
Mariátegui's orthodox Comintern critics dubbed his thinking "populist" after
his death, at least in part because he had advocated a flexible attitude towards
the American Popular Revolutionary Alliance (APRA), the national democratic
party led by Raúl Haya de la Torre. If the "national-popular" should not be
conflated with populism, what, then, was it signifying? The historic bloc united
national and popular aspirations, and in its formation the intellectuals, in the
broad Gramscian sense of the term, played an essential mediating role. It is part
of a nation-building process, but it is not, in Gramsci's usage, related at all to the
so-called "national socialism" of the European right. Rather, it is about generating new common-sense, or alternative, conceptions of the world, through the
development of existing currents within the culture of the popular classes, even
if these are deemed primitive by "high culture". Mariátegui's relationship with
the Amerindian peoples and their mobilization had a similar intent: Peruvian
socialism could never be built without them, and thus the worker's movement
needed to engage with their history, needs and aspirations.

It is in its links with contemporary notions of popular culture that Gramsci's
national-popular frame is perhaps most timely. In the peripheral or dependent
societies, the subaltern classes most often achieve awareness through a national-
popular lens. Populism is thus not simply a form of manipulation but an integral
element in the political constitution of the subaltern classes as political actors.
Certainly, the national-popular political form can create or deepen political division based on ethnicity or region. From a Northern perspective, it is very easy to
see "national socialism" as simply a form of racism and the articulator of a reactionary type of national identity. From a Southern perspective, the ever-present
struggle for national unification and against the disarticulation generated by
colonialism and imperialism puts a very different complexion on the issue.

We now see emerging a "Latin American" alternative to the "North American"
and "European" frames for understanding social movements. To surpass the

somewhat unfruitful opposition between the resource mobilization/political opportunity structure approaches and that of the new social movements, we can start with a return to political economy. Pushed to one side as a relic of the "old" Marxism and an impediment to identity politics, it is now making something of a comeback. As Timothy Wickham-Crowley and Susan Eckstein put it, we need to understand "that political and economic forces (from the global to the local) shape people's lives in structured ways".[27] These forces shape people's lives and their experience of them, but they do not determine whether collective initiatives to change these conditions ensue. An understanding of the global political economy and the nature of dependent development in Latin America is a necessary precondition for the study of social movements, but it is not a sufficient one.

I do not advocate a simple political economy approach but, rather, one based on the new "cultural political economy" perspective.[28] A lack of culture in political economy is as debilitating as a lack of politics in cultural studies. Although political economy determines the life chances of people across the globe, it is through "culture" that people ascribe meaning to social life. This cultural frame has entered the Latin American debate through the work of Arturo Escobar and Sonia Alvarez, among others,[29] which was in some ways a continuation of, or response to, the new social movements approach. Social movements find and create meaning at the cultural level, and collective action is always dependent on a process of cultural identity formation. Thus, a political economy of working women would emphasize the domains of livelihood and political engagement, but a cultural lens would direct us to more complex ways in which working women think and create new worlds for themselves and for society.

We should also take on board the call by Margaret Keck to focus on "weaving social movements back in", calling for "a more complex view of the place of social movements in politics and society than we generally get from accounts of some of the best-known Latin American social movements".[30] Inspiring stories of the Madres de Plaza de Mayo, the Zapatistas, Chilean students, Brazilian landless peasants or Argentina's *piqueteros* may provide international icons but they do not deliver a strategy for transformation in Latin America. We lose the multi-layered complexity of the real social movements and their inevitable contradictions when we opt for the heroic mode. These stories of iconic movements, as Keck argues, "may tell us very little about the state–society relationship into which they fit, their role in associational networks, and their contribution to the accumulation of social power".[31] Social movements are complex, dynamic and "*impure*" collective bodies, not amenable to understanding by linear and simplistic theoretical frames – even that of cultural political economy, which can only ever be a starting point. It is their emancipatory political grammar that we will need to focus on now as we take up the stories of some of the major Latin American social movements.

3

WORKERS

Many accounts of social movements still place the workers' movements in an important position even when they are criticizing it from a "new" social movement perspective. It was one of the original social movements, and it continues to have considerable weight even if this is now much diminished in some parts of the world. In Latin America, the workers' movement was shaped by the nature of the dependent development process, albeit not in a deterministic manner. As Charles Bergquist puts it:

> Workers, especially those engaged in production for export, have played a determining role in the modern history of Latin America. Their struggle for material well-being and control over their own lives has fundamentally altered the direction of national political evolution and the patterns of economic development in the countries of the region.[1]

The making of the working class – through immigration and industrialization – thus played a major role in the forging of contemporary Latin America. And the workers' movements have played an important role in the politics and culture of Latin America.

During the industrialization phase and the establishment of a national-popular state, workers became ever more central both in economic and political terms. With industrialization after the global depression of the 1930s, and particularly after the Second World War, labour was "nationalized", as it were. Trade unions became a key component of many nationalist movements, often with their own social agenda. When democracy was closed down in Latin America, as it was during the military dictatorships of the 1970s, the workers' movement was at the centre of resistance to its untrammelled rule. Although "new" social movements came into play then – such as the exemplary human rights movement – workers continued to resist daily, in the workplace and in the community. With democratization in the 1980s, and after the long neoliberal period of the 1990s, workers again became central under the left-of-centre governments after 2000, some-times as supporters but also as antagonists.

This chapter starts with an examination of the history of the labour movement in Argentina, originally one of the strongest in Latin America. The Peronist labour movement in Argentina is seen as emblematic of the corporatist model, which subordinated labour to a cross-class political movement. It also promoted (or allowed for) an extraordinary level of organization and social solidarity, how-ever, with an informal rank-and-file presence in the workplace and strongly com-munalist working-class neighbourhoods.

Our next case study is on Brazil, home to the path-breaking Workers' Party (Partido dos Trabalhadores: PT), which was formed by the main trade union confederation, the Unified Workers' Central (Central Única dos Trabalhadores: CUT) in 1980. This party provided Brazilian workers with a clear independent political voice for the first time. It took on an overt social movement perspective, engaging with issues beyond the workplace, such as housing and transport. Nevertheless, the impact of neoliberalism, in terms of the informalization and precarization of work, as well as its own weaknesses, has led to a much-diminished presence today.

We turn next to Mexico, long emblematic of a corporatist trade union movement and of a co-opted working class. Although the movement had considerable social weight and a political legitimacy granted by the Mexican Revolution, it was not characterized by an independent class project. In recent decades independent unions have been formed and the hegemonic role of the *charros* (corrupt union leaders) challenged, and we now have to see if the left-of-centre national government elected in 2018 will make a difference.

Finally, we turn to the transnational domain, and in particular the successful cam-paign by trade unions and others against the FTAA (Free Trade Area of the mericas) in the early 2000s. Already, in relation to MERCOSUR (Mercado Común del Sur: Common Market of the South) and the NAFTA (North American Free Trade Agreement) negotiations, Latin American trade unions had demonstrated their ability to act transnationally. This case study will seek to establish if this is a pattern for the future or not, and to reflect more generally on the future of labour as a social movement that moves beyond its corporatist modalities.

National-popular labour (Argentina)

It is undoubtedly the Peronist affiliation of the workers' movement in Argentina that is its defining characteristic. From around 1860 to 1930 the working-class movement was created mainly by overseas (European) migration, which carried with it the ideologies of syndicalism, anarchism, socialism and communism. The economy was a successful agro-export-based one, and workers such as dockers and railway workers had considerable leverage over it. From around 1930 to 1945 this model began to falter, as a result of the international recession. There was a gradual move towards industrialization, with the workforce coming largely from internal migration in this phase. Politically, the exclusionary logic of the oligarchic agro-export state began to falter as democratic demands increased. From this situation an obscure army colonel, Juán Domingo Perón, emerged first as labour secretary, and then as president from 1946 to 1955.

The interpretations of Peronism are particularly interesting from a contemporary perspective, given the current widespread disputes around the term "populism". The orthodox view is that Perón was a manipulative "populist" demagogue who misled the new internal migrants away from class politics. Stress was laid on the "irrational" element of Peronism – the mass rallies, the slogan chanting and the *bombos* (big drums). Unlike the European migrants, the internal migrants from the provinces were supposedly more susceptible to the "charisma" or authoritarian paternalism of Perón. The "revisionist" interpretation has rejected this view, however, and shown how "the participation of the working class in the national-popular movement cannot be characterised as passive, short-sighted or divided".[2] In fact, the joint participation of the old and new factions of the working class in the forging of the Peronist movement was part of a pre-existing labour movement programme and happened very much on its own terms.

The labour movement under Perón consolidated itself in a quite remarkable way, making it symbolic to an extent of the way in which labour-based national-popular movements can cohere. Trade union organization expanded exponentially, and the share of labour in national income went up from 45 per cent in 1943 to 60 per cent in 1949. Most importantly, in terms of a social movement analysis, the trade unions developed very strong internal democratic and participatory mechanisms. A sophisticated and robust system of direct democracy was developed in all workplaces, with assemblies electing delegates in open assembly. These delegates formed the *cuerpo de delegados* (shop stewards' plenary), which in turn elected a *comisión interna* (factory committee) that negotiated with management. These were able to push out the "frontiers of control" by workers in boom periods and were able to maintain cohesion even in periods of retreat, such as under military intervention.

From 1955 onwards the "Peronist question" dominated Argentina's politics. The dominant classes sought to ban Peronism but the trade unions continued to grow in strength both in the workplace and in society at large. Although its members were not necessarily motivated by a clear anti-capitalist consciousness, they understood what an authoritarian foreman was, what unfair dismissal meant and the need to combat the acceleration of the assembly line. During the

Peronist governments the trade unions built workers' homes, clinics and even holiday camps. The "dignity of labour" was established and became the new common sense for broad swathes of society. This took on a cultural aspect, as "being Peronist" denoted a divide between "us and them", the latter being the landed oligarchy, the Catholic Church – at times – and the parties of the so-called left that had portrayed Perón as a fascist and his supporters as dupes.

The peak of labour movement militancy in Argentina was reached in 1969 with the Cordobazo, Argentina's version of May 1968. This explosive semi-insurrectionary event, based on a worker–student alliance, represented a water-shed. New workers came to the forefront, symbolized by Córdoba's automobile workers. New forms of struggle merged in the workplace, with occupation now common, and in the streets. The dichotomy between Peronism and anti-Peronism began to break down, as various forms of socialism began to take root. After the Cordobazo there was a succession of national general strikes, and insurrectional situations developed. A new class struggle tendency (*clasismo*) emerged in the trade unions as the by now conservative Peronist trade union bosses came to be questioned. This wave of working-class insurgency impacted large numbers of the population, including the middle classes and small-scale provincial producers.

The dramatic labour insurgency from 1969 to 1975 (including the return of Perón to power briefly) led to the 1976 military coup, which eventually ceded power to civilians in 1983. The military dictatorship came under pressure from a series of movements, especially from a vibrant human rights movement and the emblematic Madres de Plaza de Mayo (see Chapter 6), who fought relentlessly on behalf of the "disappeared" (*desaparecidos*). International NGOs were also campaigners for human rights, and eventually the regime's international backers began to distance themselves. But what is often neglected, as it was less public, is the continuous resistance by many workers (as against the union leadership), who organized strikes, go-slows (*trabajo a desgano*: literally, "sad working"), lighting stoppages and ingenious forms of sabotage, despite intense levels of repression. It was this inchoate resistance – based on pre-existing organizational structures – that provided the backbone for an eventual society-wide rejection of the military dictatorship.

The current situation in Argentina is still dominated by the collapse of the economy in 2001 and the subsequent return of a modernized Peronism (under Néstor and then Cristina Kirchner). It was a reconstituted Peronism, with trade unions as its main social support base, that was able to overcome the chaos ensuing from the collapse of the neoliberal model of the 1990s. If the 1990s were dominated by unemployment and the "end of work discourse" – as Maurizio Atzeni and Juan Grigera put it, there was "social protest everywhere but in the workplace"[3] – trade unions would be back at the centre of social protest in the

2000s. Along with a certain turn by the Kirchner governments towards reindustrialization and the internal market, the labour movement stepped up its level of activity considerably. Whereas in the 1990s more inchoate territorially based social protests had prevailed, after 2000 we were back to organized collective bargaining as the main expression of class struggle.

From a social movement perspective, Argentina shows the enduring importance of workers as active agents of social transformation. In fact, against international trends, the study of trade unions in Argentina has regained importance. What the most recent period since 2001 has added is a much greater focus on workers, as a broad social category, including the unemployed and – beyond the factory – the community at large. A saying in radical trade union circles in Argentina today is that "the factory is the neighbourhood" (*la fábrica es el barrio*). The growth of informal and precarious work has been a challenge for the trade unions in Argentina, as elsewhere. The turn towards the community, as a form of social movement unionism, has been matched by high-level alliances between the official trade union movement and those organizations representing both the unemployed and informal sector workers. This shows workers' movements can adapt to new situations and recognize the importance of a social movement, rather than corporatist, orientation.

Populism to Workers' Party (Brazil)

In Brazil the rule of Getúlio Vargas, from 1930 to 1945, had some parallels to the first Peronist period in Argentina from 1945 to 1955, nowhere more so than in relation to its corporatist labour policy. With the declaration of the Estado Novo in 1937, the Brazilian trade union movement lost whatever autonomy it had previously had and became subordinated to the corporatist state. Labour legislation protected urban workers, and wages began to rise in the 1940s, but this was at the cost of an independent union movement. By the mid-1940s Vargas was in a position to launch his own labour party, the PTB (Partido Trabalhista Brasileiro: Brazilian Labour Party), to contest what until then had been the hegemony of the Communist Party in the organized labour movement. Although union autonomy was severely curbed by the corporatist state, there were sporadic waves of strikes, and the now expanding industrial workforce became the subject of electoral competition.

The trade union movement began to expand along with industrialization in the coastal areas of the south-east. Inland, the rural large landowners began to witness incipient unionization among the workforce, and smallholders began to organize in peasant leagues. Strike activity in the early 1960s began to steadily increase. Despite the legal ban on peak-level organizations under the corporatist legislation, the CGT (Comando Géral dos Trabalhadores: General Workers' Command) was formed in 1962. Labour autonomy was growing once again, responding to changes within the labour movement. From a ruling class perspective, the "populism" of the presidents who followed Vargas and the dangers posed by a more mobilized working class led to their support for a military intervention in 1964. One of the first measures of the military dictatorship was to order state intervention in three-quarters of the trade unions and the appointment of a military overseer over their governance.

The military dictatorship (intensified after 1969) could not prevent the gradual reconstitution of the labour movement in the 1970s. In clandestine conditions, often with support from the "base communities" of the Catholic Church, the unions in the São Paulo industrial belt began to reorganize. They rapidly displaced the old *pelego* (corrupt) union leadership, which was seen as complicit with the military and an empowered industrialist class. Paradoxically, the military dictatorship in Brazil (unlike its counterparts in Chile and Argentina) promoted state-led industrialization. In a period of strong economic growth – the "miracle" years for the regime propagandists – there was a rapidly growing workforce, though wages were stagnant. This contradiction led eventually to massive strikes in 1978 and 1979. Thus, a "new unionism" began to emerge in Brazil.

The "new unionism" had at its epicentre the metalworkers in São Paulo's booming auto industry. This was a grass-roots "bottom-up" unionization drive, committed to union freedom and autonomy. It challenged frontally the ban on strikes, the government power of oversight over unions and the compulsory "union tax" for providing welfare services. It also rejected the role of the Labour Court in industrial relations and argued instead for free collective bargaining. It also rejected in practice the vertical nature of the official unions, which were based on occupational categories and banned inter-union forms of organization. Thus, a wave of organization and the sweeping critique of the corporatist state led to the formation of the powerful Central Única dos Trabalhadores in 1983, a union federation that was to play a major role in the redemocratization process.

Some analysts have declared that this "new unionism" was in fact the product of a new "labour aristocracy", seeking to protect its privileges in relation to the mass of less organized workers. The notion of "free collective bargaining" was not particularly radical and could be seen as taking advantage of the relatively strong position of skilled autoworkers in what was a dynamic industry. In practice, however, this unionization drive acted as a spark for a much wider organizing and resistance drive by the working class, in urban and rural areas alike. As Ricardo Antunes, Marco Santana and Luci Praun note, "With the emergence of 'new unionism' strikes became widespread throughout the country reaching broad sectors of the working class. There was an extraordinary broadening of class-based unions and social movements."[4] Thus emerged one of the most powerful social movements for fundamental change in Latin America.

The trade-union-backed Workers' Party, formed in 1980, began to orientate towards national state power after a series of successful state governorships. When ex-metalworker leader Inácio Lula da Silva eventually became president, in 2002, after three attempts, expectations were high that he would deliver much-needed reform and roll back neoliberalism. A pro-poor programme was developed, particularly during Lula's second term in office (2006 to 2010) and the first term of his successor, Dilma Rousseff (2010 to 2014), before the latter succumbed to a parliamentary coup during her second term (2014 to 2016). The PT was always a minority government and had to make alliances with more conservative sectors. It also gave in to the demands of the business sector and, fatally, to that of the financial sector, which was determined to keep Brazil submitted to its logic. What this meant for workers was an increased flexibility of the labour market, resulting in greater outsourcing and a general increase in precarious work.

The social movements – and, in particular, the trade union movement – show a mixed balance sheet for this period. On the one hand, unemployment fell, formal employment rose and average worker incomes increased. The CUT – with many of its key organizers now incorporated into government – held a powerful position, in terms of both collective bargaining and the broader political arena. On the other hand, its very success brought with it the danger of incorporation and a gradual move away from its autonomist roots. Union reform measures failed to get off the ground and top-down bureaucratic unionism made a comeback once radical unionism was incorporated into the tripartite (unions, employers, government) structures responsible for managing union funds. As Antunes and co-authors put it, "By significantly shifting ... to a defence action geared towards negotiation and compromise, the CUT distanced itself from its original union and political project, which gradually disappeared from its proposals and actions."[5]

The Brazilian social movement scene has displayed an incredible richness over the last 40 years. Some of the analysis has been quite simplistic, such as putting all the blame for the current turn to the right on the PT's co-option by the parliamentary system. This is not the place to analyse this very complex situation. From the perspective of the trade union movement, however, our verdict must be a mixed one. On the one hand, the political party formed by trade union leaders around Lula, along with sympathetic academics and Catholic Church based community activists, has come to an ignominious end, at least for the time being. On the other hand, however, the trade union movement has made the most spectacular gains, short of a revolution, we have ever seen. It has created a new workers' party, encouraged the unionization of the peasants and the homeless and impacted on national development policy to support a pro-poor orientation, for the first time in Brazil for a sustained period of time.

From revolution to bureaucracy (Mexico)

In Mexico, the political history of the trade union movement goes back to the great Mexican Revolution that began in 1910. But by the 1920s the unions were in disarray and the once powerful CROM (Confederación Regional Obrera Mexicana: Mexican Regional Workers' Confederation) had more or less collapsed, a sign of the economic and political weakening of the working class. Ian Roxborough notes, however, that "[t]he early thirties was a period of sustained efforts on the part of union organizers to move towards greater unity".[6] This was reflected in the formation of new national industrial unions in the mining, metalwork, oil and rail transport sectors. When Lázaro Cárdenas became president, in 1934, the average annual strike rate increased twentyfold. Although Cárdenas came to power in very different ways from Perón and Vargas, he shared their corporatist orientation towards labour, which at one and the same time encouraged organization while seeking to co-opt the results.

By the 1950s Mexican unions had become firmly bureaucratic and under the control of the notorious *charro* (cowboy) union bosses. The radical leaders of unions who remained in office were rapidly overthrown. The government could, from then on, count on the blind subservience of the union leadership. In contrast to the cases of Argentina and Brazil, in Mexico there were many layers of trade unionism, from the large industry-wide unions to state level unions, plant and enterprise unions and small local-territory-based associations. Having said that, the Mexican union relationship with the state was more fluid than in the other two cases. The greater flexibility of the industrial relations system meant that organized labour retained significant rights, and Roxborough notes that "union leaders had a more complex relationship with their membership than has typically been the case".[7] Complex webs of clientelism meant that even the *charros* had to constantly negotiate their position.

This relative flexibility of the industrial relations system and the enduring egalitarian traditions of the Mexican Revolution led to the emergence of a new independent unionism in the 1970s. There were serious rank-and-file movements emerging in the teachers' union, in some car plants and some sectors of the oil and steel industries. One of the most important manifestations of this new non-*charro* trade unionism was the Tendencia Democrática (Democratic Tendency), which achieved considerable support among electrical workers in the 1970s. In the NAFTA negotiations of the 1990s, Mexican, US and Canadian electrical workers began to envisage a future based on a common electrical network and the same employers. The Mexican tendency towards class struggle was severely repressed by government, and it has begun to recover only in recent years. This is one example of a strong national union generating strong transnational action to the benefit of all concerned.

Overall, however, the independent union movement has not really impacted on the hegemony of the *charros*, unlike the situation in Brazil, for example. The power holders had a panoply of measures that they could deploy over and above their alliance with the ruling party and the patronage this enabled them to bestow. Union elections could easily be manipulated, and intimidation would go alongside offers of patronage. Control of the union machinery could be used to silence opposition quite easily. The judicious use of concessions was another easily deployed method, and, perhaps more insidiously, there were moves to steal the radical clothes of the opposition, even if only temporarily. When the long-term hegemony of the PRI (Partido Revolucionario Institucional: Institutional Revolutionary Party) ceased at the time of the 2000 elections, many thought that the old ways could not continue. In fact, based on a supposed respect for "union autonomy and independence", the party that came to power, the PAN (Partido de Acción Nacional: National Action Party), also willingly accepted and supported the *charros* and their control over the workers.

Migration has been a major feature for Mexican trade unions, perhaps more so than most other countries. It was internal migration within Mexico that created a "new" working class in the 1970s, which became the mainstay of the independent unions. This internal migration led to an increase in social mobility – as did, of course, the migration patterns with regard to the United States to the north. Today a significant proportion of Mexico's workers reside and work in the United States, where they make up one-third of the non-US-born population. There are also many who have been absorbed by the *maquiladoras* (finishing plants) on the Mexican border. The longer-term tendency in the Mexican labour market towards informalization and migration was reinforced by the signing of the North American Free Trade Agreement in 1994, which greatly accentuated the role of Mexico as a cheap labour supplier. Market liberalization leads inevitably to labour migration, it would seem.

With approximately 15 per cent of Mexico's population living and working outside the national boundaries, migrant social movements are bound to play an important role in the making of the working class. In the United States Mexican migrant workers have played a very visible role in unionization, from the iconic campaign to unionize grape pickers in the 1960s, associated with César Chávez, to the present. In recent years it was Mexican (and Central American) cleaning workers who led the innovative campaign for a living wage on the west coast of the United States, supported by the 2-million-strong SEIU (Service Employees International Union). There are also union-to-union contacts between Mexican and US unions in relation to mutual support for migrant workers. Given the importance of circular migration, we can also see considerable cross-fertilization between the two national locations and the development of transnational collective identities.

The landslide victory of Andrés Manuel López Obrador (AMLO) in 2018 and his assumption of the presidency late that year created a great deal of hope among Mexico's workers. The independent unions have formed a new federation (the Federation of Democratic and Independent Unions) representing some 25,000 workers in the automotive, auto parts, logistics, rubber and aerospace industries. They have pledged to work with the new AMLO government to end "protection contracts" negotiated by corrupt company unions with employers against the interests of the workers. These unions had grown rich through their corrupt practices and, basically, had sought to sell Mexico as a cheap labour location. What is not clear yet is whether the independent unions have the power to seriously challenge the entrenched labour bureaucracy. Although trade unions are a diminished social power in Mexico, the established unions do still control key sectors in the private and public economy, and are thus well-established interlocutors with economic and political power in the country.

Although we are not talking of a situation akin to that of Lula becoming president of Brazil in 2002, or even Néstor Kirchner's rise to power in Argentina the same year, a new presidency in Mexico is significant for all the social movements in Latin America. That it comes after such a long period of relative stability in terms of the power bloc is itself significant. The new government immediately doubled the minimum wage, and this created a huge expectation that more radical change was coming on the labour front. In early 2019 a number of strikes broke out in Matamoros, at the eastern end of the Mexico–US border, at first in the *maquila* sector (duty-free assembly plants) but then spreading to established firms such as Coca-Cola. The *maquiladora* owners threatened to close their factories and deemed the modest wage increase sought "impossible". Although the government stood on the sidelines and the official unions collaborated with the employers, change was on its way. Julia Quiñones, a veteran leader of women workers, commented that the workers were "tired of abuse and exploitation, and if they can see hope for change they will act".[8]

Against the FTAA (transnational)

There is a widespread assumption that the workers' movement is thoroughly national in its orientation. There is some truth to this assumption, not least in Latin America, where labour movements have been inextricably linked with nationalist movements (such as Peronism). In recent decades, however, the workers' movement in Latin America has developed a transnational orientation. With the formation of MERCOSUR in 1991, the trade union movements of Argentina and Brazil were more or less forced to cooperate to create a unified labour voice in this new regional economic integration project. Likewise, in the period leading up to the formation of NAFTA in 1994, the US unions were persuaded to join with Mexican unions in common cause, after some initial reluctance, by the Canadian (specifically Québécois) unions.

Where the Latin American trade union movement developed a fully transnational orientation was in relation to the Free Trade Area of the Americas, designed to span all of North and South America to follow on from the NAFTA, but it collapsed ignominiously in 2005. Having seen its potential impact on labour and environmental standards, many sections of civil society were mobilized in opposition. It was soon evident that this was not a treaty in the common good but an expansionist project of the United States, based on its commercial and corporate interests. By the late 1990s the disparate social forces opposed to the United States – which included labour, indigenous, women's and environmental groups – had coalesced in the HSA (Hemispheric Social Alliance). This network posed an alternative to the free trade agreement based on the principles of democracy, sovereignty equality and sustainability. It began a very effective campaign against the FTAA, challenging it at every point and offering a credible alternative with strong social backing.

In her account of the FTAA, von Bülow notes how, through its mobilizations, it "created new coalitions, launched campaigns, lobbied negotiators and legislatures, held multitudinous protests and build common critiques and demands across countries. *Never before had so many different CSOs* [civil society organizations] *from the region come together to debate and mobilize transnationally around a hemispheric agenda.*"[9] As sometimes happens with social movements, the very success of the HSA in defeating the FTAA may have led to its decline. The coalition was unable to stay united and independent in relation to the new left-of-centre governments in Latin America, which sought to co-opt it or, at least, take over its agenda. Social movements began to lose autonomy, and were hence weakened as the state took on their cause regarding trade. The trade unions involved were also reacting to distinct work-related issues compared, for example, to international environmental groupings.

In assessing the success of the campaign against the FTAA, we can take various positions. On the surface, it was the newly emerging left-of-centre national governments in Latin America that could take credit for this anti-imperialist victory. At the Fourth Summit of the Americas, held in Argentina's seaside resort of Mar del Plata in 2005, it was President Chávez of Venezuela who declared the FTAA "buried" and it was Evo Morales and Diego Maradona who were in the public eye during the associated protests. If left governments can take some credit (for closing the match), so can the INGOs (international non-governmental organizations), which put in a huge effort to sustain and inform the campaign network. But, ultimately, it was the trade union movements of the Americas putting their full social weight behind the campaign that forced the political issue to a positive resolution.

There are, of course, many more daily interactions by Latin American workers movements with their counterparts in other countries. Given the migration of workers within Latin America and to the United States, there is continual transnational union/worker engagement. Trade unions in the United States have been at the forefront in organizing migrant workers, such as in the West Coast cleaning industry. Within Latin America there are many reciprocal arrangements between national union movements to represent migrant workers. Finally, there is a long-standing movement of solidarity in US student movement circles with, particularly, Central American labour struggles.[10] In the era of globalization we find the workers' movement well able to promote transnational solidarity, for ideological as much as for practical reasons.

In conclusion, we might note that the contemporary labour movement has been written off by many progressive activists and scholars as a relic of the past, but maybe they should not be so hasty. Rather than spelling the beginning of the end for organized labour, globalization has brought new opportunities for reinvention, and a sea change in both trade unions and the wider labour movement. Most notably, globalization has forced unions to think and act outside the state to build transnational solidarity across countries and sectors. Emerging transnational unionism, if it perseveres, contains the seeds of a new global movement, a new international that extends beyond labour to embrace all forces working towards a new great transformation, to use Polanyi's term.

Through labour's struggle to establish itself, build solidarity and protect its members, various types of trade unionism have emerged historically. In labour's origins, "economic unionism" prevailed. This model, with which today's activists would be most familiar, has been oriented towards securing a better price for the commodity that Marxist economists call "labour power". Market-oriented and eschewing politics, it has posed limited challenge to the status quo. Alternatively, "political unionism", wherein trade unions turn to the state for the satisfaction of their demands, has been quite common in Latin America. Finally, "social unionism" has sought solidarity across geographic divisions and in social divisions between the workplace and the wider community.

All three approaches lost traction globally in the 1980s and 1990s. The forward march of labour appeared to halt in the face of the disruptions caused by globalization. Austerity, privatization and deflationary monetary policy wreaked havoc on unions worldwide. Margaret Thatcher's famous "TINA" dictum – "There is no alternative" – was not just a slogan of the elite but a pervasive mood in society. As trade union membership declined and the links between unions and progressive political parties frayed, many began to question whether a "labour movement" still existed. Postwar economistic militancy had not yielded concrete political gains, and the collapse of the Soviet Union ushered in capitalist triumphalism and the sense that credible threats of an alternative economic system had been defeated.

As a result, many activists fighting for global transformation now began to think that the labour movement had little to contribute to progressive politics. But this belief is misguided. Viewed from another perspective, globalization, rather than being the death knell of labour, has helped to revitalize it, challenging unions to pioneer new modes of organizing and to think beyond the state. Trade unions, rather than looking inwards, are starting to join a wider set of social forces resisting the free market ideology of neoliberalism and its policy of austerity for the masses and enrichment for the elites. The future of the labour movement depends on the development of this nascent systemic rather than corporatist orientation.

After the collapse of the Soviet Union, vast swathes of the world previously under either state socialist or state capitalist regimes came under the sway of global-scale capital. If we understand capital as a social relation between the owner of capital and the worker, then the worldwide expansion of capital must lead to a global expansion of the working classes. And so it did. The number of workers worldwide more than doubled between 1990 and 2016, from 1.5 billion to 3.2 billion.

Changes in the composition of the global workforce have accompanied this quantitative increase. The geographic distribution shifted as the so-called developing world drove much of this growth, while the workforce in more developed countries experienced a slight decline. The female labour force has grown in most countries across all income levels. The occupational composition of the workforce has also undergone dramatic change, with rapid growth in the service sector as agriculture, mining and manufacturing continue to shed jobs worldwide.

The new landscape of global labour points to at least two conclusions. First, analysts who insisted on the terminal decline of labour were wrong. In the enthusiasm for the flourishing civil society of the alter-globalization movements, organized labour was often written off as a relic of an industrial past. Since 2000, however, transnational labour organizing has been on the rise, spawning new structures and organizing techniques. Second, although a truly global labour market has not yet emerged other than in a few restricted sectors, what we might call a common global working condition has coalesced, such as the spread of precarious work – a condition once limited primarily to the so-called developing world. Prevailing conditions on the ground support the development of a transnational labour strategy to become a credible change agent contesting the new globalized capitalism.

Transnational unionism can take many forms. It can operate among union executives or at a grass-roots level, while organizing can be workplace-oriented or based on collaboration with NGOs on single-issue campaigns. Successful transnational unionism has the capacity to navigate complexity and operate on multiple levels. In particular, transnationally oriented unions have used globalization to their benefit by organizing transnational labour actions, forming new transnational structures and fostering solidarity with migrant workers at home.

Labour has also showed strength by partnering with allies at different points along the globally dispersed production chain. A campaign against sweatshops in the apparel industry showed how direct action by students in the United States can support organizing by workers in Honduras. Garment workers in global production chains are usually considered weak compared to hypermobile, high-profit companies such as Nike. But such corporations are vulnerable to boycotts. Transnational union resources focused on a particular industry or country have considerable power to deny market share and thereby bolster demands at the point of production.

The persistence of this upsurge in transnational organizing is not inevitable; maintaining growth and success requires deep rethinking of the role of trade unions. To be blunt, the popular image of the trade unions as "pale, male and stale" has an element of truth to it. Membership has fallen: no more than 7 per cent of the world's labour force belongs to a union, with many of the most unionized sectors of the economy in decline. Many trade unions still take a narrow approach to defending the interests of their existing members, rather than organizing the unorganized, not least those in the informal or precarious sector. And, when international trade unions try to create a countervailing force to transnational capital, they often do so in an outdated manner, such as the bid to institutionalize at a global level the postwar European system of tripartite social partnership between workers, employers and the state.

No iron law governs how trade unions respond to crisis, however. New visions may emerge, new alliances may form and new forward-thinking leaders may arise. If we see labour as a social movement, we will discern its constant regeneration. Although it is still weakened by the ravages of the long neoliberal night, the international labour movement has, since the mid-1990s, been regrouping and recomposing. Struggles have matured from desperate rearguard actions into concerted, proactive organizing campaigns.

The status of trade union revitalization is subject to debate in both academic and policy circles. Just as types of unions differ, so, too, have their responses to globalization, the closing down of national negotiating space and the decline in membership. There is no singular path forward. Key directions include recruiting in new areas, with migrant workers an obvious option; building coalitions with other social movements; and intensifying international solidarity actions. Trade unions everywhere (not least in Latin America) are getting back in touch with their grass roots, improving their communications and looking outwards instead of inwards. Trade unions began as part of a popular struggle for democracy, and what the slogans of the French Revolution meant in that day the principles of the global justice movement could mean today.

The international trade union movement is both a transnational social movement in the making and a representative organization of workers on the ground. Its democratic structures, focus on the world of work and membership-based nature distinguish it from the campaigning NGOs, which are focused on issues of gender equity, human rights or environmental protection. Although many advocacy groups are ephemeral, the labour movement will almost certainly be around for a long time, since the collective representation of workers is essential even as its organizational form evolves.

That said, the labour movement has learnt a lot from social movements and kindred NGOs, and to an increasing degree is joining the broad alter-globalization movement. The international trade union movement certainly has the motivation to "go global" (even if it is just to survive), and it has the capacity to do so. It can and will play a central and increasing role in achieving a degree of social regulation over the worldwide expansion of capitalism in the decades to come.

In the formative stages of the labour movement, unions engaged actively with the broader political issues of the day, in particular the call for universal suffrage. There is no reason why such larger concerns cannot again move to the centre of labour's agenda, and a very good reason – the interpenetration of a host of economic, social and environmental reasons – why they should form its backbone. In contrast to the later tradition of craft unionism, the early labour organizers did not recognize divisions based on skill or race. This tradition of labour organizing, known variously as "community unionism", "deep organizing" or "social movement unionism", has been making a comeback. Its spread could open a new chapter in labour's ongoing struggle against capitalism.

4

PEASANTS

Peasants and rural landless workers have been at the forefront of recent social movements in Latin America. In fact, we are witnessing a resurgence of rural-based social movements precisely when some analysts are predicting the "death of the peasantry" because of the advance of capitalism. After providing some conceptual and historical background on peasants, we move on in this chapter to consider first the case of Brazil, where the MST (Movimento dos trabalhadores rurais Sem Terra: Landless Workers' Movement) has become one of the most significant rural movements to date. This is followed by a case study of Colombia, where the peasant-based FARC (Fuerzas Armadas Revolucionarias de Colombia: Revolutionary Armed Forces of Colombia) once controlled a territory the size of Switzerland in "independent republics", and is thus a unique case. The next case study is of Chile, where we have seen a more "classic" pattern of capitalist modernization of agriculture and large-scale agrarian reforms. Finally, we turn to the transnational domain, where Vía Campesina, which originated in Latin America, has for the first time shown the potential of the peasantry as a transnational counter-globalization force. This cluster of cases, taken together, shows the great capacity for resistance and innovation of Latin America's rural dwellers.

In Latin America

The second major historical social movement in Latin America after the workers' movement is that of the peasants and landless rural workers. From the Mexican Revolution in 1910 through to the Cuban Revolution in 1959 and the long-running insurgency in Colombia, peasants have been at the forefront of social and political transformation in Latin America. Old and new forms of capitalist exploitation combined in rural areas and so have the forms of rural dweller resistance. Thus, in Colombia, a long-standing tradition of rural organization and revolt going back to the 1950s was combined with communist insurgency models to turn the "independent republics" into instances of dual power. In a different way, in Brazil, we saw in the early 1960s a combination of peasant leagues organizing smallholders with a national confederation of rural workers, CONTAG (Confederação dos Trabalhadores na Agricultura: Agricultural Workers' Confederation), organizing rural workers. Capitalist modernization in agriculture led to the combined resistance of sharecroppers and tenants with insecure access to land and the cause of rural workers (and small farmers) working directly under capitalist relations.

Peasant movements in Latin America have had a new lease of life in the last few decades and are often seen as paragons of the "new" social movements. Of particular note are, of course, the struggles of the Zapatistas in Mexico and the MST in Brazil, the first based on indigenous smallholders, the second mainly on landless peasants. Both movements show the continued, and even renewed, importance of the landownership question despite the capitalist modernization that has transformed agriculture since the 1950s. Peasant revolts are not necessarily revolutionary; rather, they often respond to a breach of traditional norms of community and reciprocity, and are thus, literally, "conservative". But, as Leandro Vergara-Camus argues, in a comparative study of these two movements, "[t]heir understanding of the functioning of the market and their demands, which challenge the sanctity of property right, thus contain clear anticapitalist impulses".[1] These are social movements at the forefront of an original empowerment strategy and a concerted drive for the decommodification of social relations, which are having a massive regional and international impact.

The agrarian question today is very different from that of the early twentieth century, as is the notion of "peasant revolutions", which was then current. In Latin America this debate has played out between a so-called "peasantist" tendency and a "proletarianization" tendency. The first current harks back to the Russian agrarian populist theorist Aleksandr Chayanov, who asserted the viability of peasant production in the form of shared family farming. Those stressing proletarianization argue, to the contrary, that the development of capitalism leads inevitably to the demise of the peasantry, and portray the "peasants" as backward-looking romantics. Today a third paradigm is emerging, focused around "food regime analysis",[2] which seeks to show how food production is shaped by the forces of globalization. The classical agrarian question is seen as being rendered obsolete as globalization creates a new agrarian labour question, in which class fragmentation leads to the re-emergence of agrarian populism as a response to the conversion to a capitalist agri-business on a global scale.

The classical rural revolts in Latin America – Mexico 1910, Cuba 1959 and Nicaragua 1979 – were motivated not by backward-looking ideologies but by the contradictions of modernization. In all cases these economies were integrated into the world market and penetrated by foreign capital. These were mass movements for land reform, but at the same time anti-imperialist movements. Thoroughly modernist (i.e. not backward-looking) peasant movements were also closely linked to urban workers' movements. Thus, the Cuban Revolution is incorrectly termed a "peasant revolution" only by focusing on the "sierra" and not the urban underground that made success possible. What these revolutions all achieved is the break-up of the colonial-era *haciendas* (large estates) and a land reform that redistributed land titles to smallholders. We might say it accomplished a task of capitalism, by allowing modernization to proceed apace in the rural areas of Latin America.

In the current period it has become more common to view the peasantry through a postmodernist rather than modernist lens. Rather than fighting a losing battle to retain a traditional mode of production against the advances of the capitalist juggernaut, they are seen as harbingers of the future. As James Petras and Henry Veltmeyer put it, from this angle "the peasantry appears as a postmodern category, an advance representation of a new era of localized day-to-day struggles for ethnic and social identity, a social actor seeking to reclaim its popular culture and affirm its collective identity".[3] This would be the type of discourse underlying international fascination with the Zapatistas, for example. Although this identity focus on peasants as a new social movement cannot override the continuing importance of structural factors such as the rise of agri-business, it cannot be simply replaced by the "class perspective" that Petras and Veltmeyer argue for.

Movimento dos trabalhadores rurais Sem Terra: the Landless Workers' Movement (Brazil)

Brazil's hugely unequal landownership patterns had generated land-based social movements in the past, but none quite like the MST, formed in 1984. At the turn of the twenty-first century 1 per cent of Brazil's landowners owned 45 per cent of the land and, conversely, there were approximately 4.5 million landless rural workers. The MST declared boldly that "Brazil needs a popular project" and noted: "All the changes in the history of humanity only happened when the people were mobilized." Today the MST has perhaps 1.5 million members (loosely defined) and organizes across 23 of Brazil's 26 states. The active, militant and mass mobilization land occupation tactics of the MST have created a genuine social movement. By 1990 there were 13,000 rural families living on occupied land, and by 2006 that number had risen to 150,000. This movement built on previous organizing work in the countryside prior to the 1964 military coup.

An iconic rural movement of the 1960s was the peasant leagues (Ligas Camponesas), led by the charismatic Francisco Julião. This organizing initiative had its roots in the 1940s and was supported by the Brazilian Communist Party. The ligas organized smallholders and rural workers, initially in Pernambuco but then spreading to Paraíba and Goiás. The main purpose of the ligas was to provide assistance – such as legal and medical – to its members and to provide self-defence against vengeful landowners. They waged a successful campaign against the *cambáo* system of labour service by smallholders. With the 1964 military coup, the ligas were banned and their leaders persecuted, as members of the "communist conspiracy" they denounced. Other rural organizations included CONTAG, which had an easier relation with the military regime, and continues to this day, offering a more mainstream option to rural workers than the MST.

When the MST formed, in the early 1980s, it was part of a broader social movement reactivation that led to the formation of the CUT and the PT. Its ideological influences have been described, rightly, as eclectic. As with the urban labour movement, the influence of liberation theology was critical. Indeed, the Catholic Church's Comissão Pastoral da Terra (Pastoral Land Commission), which worked with the rural poor, provided the early leadership of the MST, and still has influence today. The liberation theology of the Catholic base communities (*comunidades eclesiales de base*: CEBs), with their emphasis on equality and social justice, found an elective affinity with the other promoters, which included socialists and communists of various types. Finally, we need to mention the particular impact of Paulo Freire and the radical pedagogy he inspired, which infused the early MST activities and still colours the MST's continued emphasis on popular education.

Paulo Freire's "pedagogy of the oppressed"[4] has influenced the MST not only in terms of its impressive literacy drive but also in its commitment to non-hierarchical organization methods. It has informed its commitment to "autonomy", understood as a new type of popular power grounded in participation and democratic decision-making. The MST's unprecedented emphasis on education has thus been part of this broader Freirean philosophy of action. At the Florestan Fernandes School and in other venues, often supported by Vía Campesina, the MST offers basic pedagogy along with classes in agronomy, history and various technical subjects. These schools are themselves self-governing bodies, in which students, teachers and parents co-govern. Freire's approach links pedagogy with the struggle for land and instils the values of collectivism and solidarity.

The main organizing tactic of the MST was always land occupation, which led to fierce clashes with landowners and the state in the early period. During the first wave of land occupations (1995 to 1999) there were many casualties, and President Fernando Henrique Cardoso was able to pose as a promoter of agrarian reform while condemning this "threat to democracy". The second wave of occupations (after 2003) occurred under Lula's PT government, and the MST focused more on private landed estates rather than government-owned land. By now the MST had expanded its remit to take on GM (genetically modified) goods, and an occupation of a Monsanto facility in 2003 brought it into full-frontal conflict with the government, which supported agri-business. Although the PT government was constrained in what it could do – as in getting laws implemented at state level – the MST decided it would have to continue to rely on its own resources and could not place its confidence in the political system.

The relations with the ruling party, the PT, were always a crucial element for the MST. The MST fully supported the PT campaigns in 2002, 2006 and 2010, even when it became apparent that PT governments were not going to deliver the MST's demands on land. The PT opted to centre its national development plan on the expansion of agri-business, rather than the small family farm model promoted by the MST. For Lula, the 2005 march in Brasília represented an unnecessary radicalization of the MST positions, and he clashed bitterly with its leadership. Previously, at election times, the MST had agreed to halt land occupations, in that these could "play into the hands of the right" and alienate middle-class voters who could be won over by the PT. Eventually the landslide victory of the far right in the 2018 elections made this conundrum irrelevant, but long before then most of the MST leadership and activists had turned back to their "traditional" methods of mass organizing and direct action.

A balance sheet of the MST would simply note that the consolidation of land-ownership in Brazil has continued unabated since its formation. Whereas in 1967 (after the military dictatorship had been consolidated) the Gini coefficient of landownership stood at 0.836, by 2006 it had actually risen to 0.854. Orthodox Marxist authors such as Petras and Veltmeyer charge the MST with a failure to construct a broader anti-capitalist movement. The MST slogan – "Occupy, resist and *produce*" (emphasis added) – is, indeed, hardly revolutionary: with the funding it has generated it has financed mechanization, processing plants, livestock breeding and credit granting. These critical charges are somewhat beside the point, however, in so far as the MST has developed into a singularly effective social movement, it has held together its disparate membership and it has weathered repressive periods and achieved recognition for one of the most oppressed strata of Brazil's subaltern classes.

It is not surprising that the MST has not been able to translate its considerable social power into political power. In Brazil, as elsewhere, there is a tendency for social movements to become institutionalized. There is considerable debate as to whether this was intentional and if there could have been a more radical path chosen. In practice, the demands of the MST have not been met – land has not been redistributed, agri-business rules supreme and the neoliberal model has been deepened – but it has been able to maintain and, indeed, expand a social counter-movement in the Polanyian sense. The MST has maintained strong alliances with other social movements (both urban and rural), the PT and a wide range of broader civil society organizations, such as faith-based movements. A very significant proportion of the Brazilian population supported the MST's cause – 77 per cent in 1997 – even when they disagreed with land occupation as a tactic. In terms of building a "popular option", per the stated objective, the MST must be judged a considerable success.

Peasants, land and struggle (Colombia)

Colombia has witnessed one of the most sustained peasant movements, comparable only to that of China in its importance. This was the period of the "independent peasant republics", set up during the civil war between the two mainstream parties known as *la Violencia* ("the Violence"), which lasted approximately from 1948 to 1953. In different forms this peasant insurgency continued until 2016, when the main insurgent organization, the FARC, signed a peace treaty with the government. This case study allows us to delve into the complexity of the relationship between the landownership question, peasant politics and insurgency.

The question of agrarian reform had been on the national political agenda in Colombia since at least the 1920s. The emerging rural proletariat unionized and took strike action, and peasant self-defence communities were formed to fend off landlord incursions. In the 1930s the Liberal Party broke 50 years of Conservative Party hegemony and initiated import substitution industrialization and a successful, albeit limited, agrarian reform policy. Although this was essentially about transforming the *hacienda* system into a capitalist enterprise, many landowners still felt threatened. President López Pumarejo declared in 1936 that change would come either through "agrarian reform or violent revolution". Reelected in 1942, he rapidly began to backtrack on the reformist measures. This led to the emergence of Jorge Eliécer Gaitán – an outsider articulating what today would be called a reformist populist message that appealed to both the urban and rural masses – and it was his assassination in 1948 that sparked a nearly decade-long civil war, killing some 250,000 people and displacing over 2 million: *la Violencia*.

Our interest here in *la Violencia* is only in how it generated the conditions for a large-scale peasant uprising. What began as a civil war between the Liberals and the Conservatives (blamed for Gaitán's death) and their peasant supporters soon morphed into an open land war. On both sides *la Violencia* gave cover for landowners to evict *colonos* (settlers) from their lands. Frustrations over the failed promises to carry out an agrarian reform also added to tensions. The Communist Party, which had organized in the rural areas since the 1920s, began to form armed "self-defence" groups in the main coffee regions. Many peasants seeking to escape *la Violencia* joined these newly formed self-defence communities. These armed groups inevitably entered into conflict with local landowners, the police and then the army. Violent expulsions from their land and continuous violence by armed gangs convinced enough of the population that "armed struggle" was not just viable but the only option. The "independent republics" formed subsequently were a clear example of a counter-power, whereby the capitalist state is challenged from below. Thomas Flores describes how, in the "independent republics", this emerging counter-power "established the outlines of new governance forms, including rules for the judiciary, taxation, education and marriage".[5]

With the installation of a National Front government, embracing both Liberals and Conservatives, in 1958, there was a decline in inter-party violent conflict. The left had learnt the efficacy of territorial control supported by the poor peasants and the *colonos*, however. Thus, in 1964, the FARC was formed in the "independent republic" of Marquetalia, composed largely of peasants, in particular subsistence farmers. The guerrilla movement supported peasant land settlements and provided armed self-defence for them. As this was only a few years after the Cuban Revolution, this conflict rapidly acquired a "communist insurgency" connotation, with all that entailed in terms of counter-insurgency measures. The FARC evolved from an armed formation defending peasants into a national political military organization with a 20,000-strong army and influence in more or less half the municipalities of the country.

The Colombian government was by now well aware that capitalist modernization of the rural economy was necessary, but also that it risked sparking open class warfare. A decisive move was made in 1968 with the government's creation of ANUC (Asociación Nacional de Usuarios Campesinos de Colombia: Colombian National Peasant Movement) with support from the urban elite. This was a relatively low-cost move but it also had the advantage of creating a social base for the government. It was a form of what Gramsci called *"transformismo"* – stealing the enemy's clothes, in a sense. This move fitted in with the international move in the mid-1950s through the US Alliance for Progress programme to support agrarian reforms as a means to counter the "communist threat". ANUC peasant leaders, during this period, met with local authorities to discuss investment projects, and approve their budgets and activities. What did this "social movement from above" actually achieve in practice?

The peasant union ANUC built up its strength quite rapidly after its formation in 1968, claiming 1 million members across half the country's municipalities, with strong representation in the areas of the traditional *haciendas*, where tenants and sharecroppers demanded their own land. The government even passed legislation granting land titles to them. This favourable setting was to change in 1972, however, when the government launched an agrarian counter-reform to protect large properties and landowners. Many of the local ANUC associations lost their legal entitlement, and repression against peasants resumed. As a result, ANUC split, with one group (Línea Armenia) supporting the government and insisting on legal solutions through dialogue with the government, while another group (Línea Sincelejo) declared its independence from government and advocacy of the revolutionary overthrow of the capitalist state, with some ANUC members going over to FARC while others formed the indigenous peasant armed struggle group, Quintín Lame, in 1974.[6]

Today the agrarian question is not the same one that sparked the rise of the independent republics and of the FARC. The advent of neoliberalism as the dominant economic development ideology increased the role of market forces in rural areas. Large landowners saw little incentive to engage in serious agrarian reform and, instead, encouraged by the government and the United States, began to finance private counter-insurgency armies to defeat the FARC, as they saw it as the main problem. The presidency of Alvaro Uribe (2000 to 2016) saw this military solution prevailing, and, in fact, FARC was seriously diminished as a fighting force. Not surprisingly, Uribe also launched an agrarian counter-reform programme, legalizing the pillaging of land from displaced rural dwellers. Despite the peace treaty eventually signed with the FARC in 2016 after Uribe left office, there is little sign that the Colombian government can deliver on the agrarian reform promises made to date – and that was the root cause of agrarian insurgency going back to *la Violencia*.

Nor is the FARC of today the same type of movement as the peasant-based organization of the 1950s. There was always a contradiction – or, at least, tension – between its social base of smallholders, displaced farmers and landless workers and its national aspirations, in classic Marxist mode, to seize state power. Even if belatedly, the collapse of the Soviet order in 1990 put that ambition into question. Its programme is effectively a reformist one: the development of a mixed economy and the creation of a welfare state in Columbia. As Petras and Veltmeyer note, this creates "formidable contradictory elements confronting the FARC going into the future"[7] between a modernizing developmentalist programme, with largely subsistence-based rural support, and a call for a 1950s-style promotion of the internal market at a time of maximum integration into the global economy. Social movements are based on human agency, and Colombia's peasants have shown more of this than many, but they do not make history in conditions of their own choosing, as Marx used to say.

Agrarian reform and beyond (Chile)

In Chile, many of the classical themes of agrarian reform have been played out: peasant movements and the recent turn to a full capitalist agro-export economy. The international debate between the *campesinistas* (peasantists) and *proletarianistas* (proletarianists) has fallen most squarely on the latter end of the spectrum in Chile, having less of a traditional peasantry than Brazil and Colombia. As Cristóbal Kay puts it, "The era of radical agrarian reform is over. There has been a shift from state-led and interventionist agrarian reform programs to market-orientated land polices."[8] Simply granting land titles to the half of Latin America's peasantry that lacks them will not resolve their insecurity and create sustainable well-being for their households. Land rights, in and of themselves, do not offer protection in the market, nor do they shelter peasants from counter-reforms, as we saw in the case of Colombia.

As in the rest of Latin America, the tradition of agrarian unionism in Chile goes back to the 1920s, as elsewhere involving Communist Party organizing drives. Although the regime was repressive and landowners obdurate, there was a strong movement from below to organize and resist. A massive wave of rural unionization and labour conflicts became a central focus of Chilean national politics. Throughout this period rural mobilization was the subject of moves and countermoves involving the political parties and the president.[9] The parties of the right maintained a constant struggle to prevent unionization, and this became the point of the class struggle in Chile. The 1931 Labour Code epitomized this situation, in so far as it granted some rights to organize while at the same time withholding the *fuero* (immunity from dismissal) for rural unions in particular. Not only was collective bargaining severely restricted (for example, prohibited in the harvest period) but union organizers could be dismissed freely after a successful resolution of a dispute.

By the 1960s Chilean agriculture was facing serious demands from above as much as from below. Agrarian production was not keeping up with demand and the level of peasant rebelliousness was increasing. At a regional level, the Alliance for Progress was moving towards an agrarian reform programme to pre-empt the spread of "communism", as the Americans saw it. The Christian Democrat regimes from 1964 to 1970 thus launched one of the most comprehensive agrarian reform programmes seen outside a socialist order. This is widely regarded to have been the result of inter-elite struggles and the need to curb the power of the landowning oligarchy as Chile modernized. Certainly, this political context created an opportunity for rural organizers, but it would be wrong to underestimate the importance of ongoing rural organizing. So, whereas in 1964 there were only 18 legal peasant unions, with around 1,000 members, by 1973 there were 488 peasant unions, with 140,293 members, which amounted to one-third of all Chilean agrarian workers.[10]

With land reform from above and rural unionization from below, the situation in rural areas became explosive in the late 1960s. There was a dramatic increase in strikes but also in *tomas* (land seizures), which mirrored action in the urban domain, also around land access for building housing. The move towards the final political incorporation of the peasantry was resisted by the right and split the ruling Christian Democrats. Ironically, this allowed for the electoral victory of a socialist–communist coalition, UP (Unidad Popular: Popular Unity) (1973 to 1976), which would in turn encourage rural mobilization. As Patricio Silva notes, "The deepening of the agrarian reform and the acceleration of the expropriation process fortified the radicalisation of the peasants."[11] What was particularly noticeable was an increase in the number of land seizures compared to other forms of action. Although rural unions still depended largely on the state to satisfy their demands, they were now moving beyond economic demands around wages and conditions to enter squarely into the political arena.

The Unidad Popular period was one of unprecedented social movement activation in Chile. The *cordones industriales* (industrial belts) brought together factories under workers' self-management. The urban squatters' movement converted many shanty towns into semi-liberated territories. In the rural areas organizations and occupations proceeded apace. The number of rural union members doubled in the first two years of Unidad Popular. Direct confrontations between mobilized peasants and landlords under pressure became commonplace. For a number of reasons, this did not initiate a coherent and sustainable social movement. On the one hand, the UP government, while rhetorically going beyond the Christian Democrat agrarian reform, was, in practice, limited to an Eastern-Europe-style state-dominated order. Then, from the union side, there was a serious gap between the urban-based leadership and the rural dwellers that hindered the development of a cohesive union moment, as witnessed in the urban areas and, particularly, in the mining sector.

The Pinochet dictatorship (1973 to 1990) set about redressing the balance of forces in the countryside, as in the rest of Chile. There was a wave of repression against leftist politicians and union organizers that was particularly severe in rural areas. Union leaders and activists were simply killed with impunity in a bid to prevent the re-emergence of rural unions. For the landowners, the dangerous level of insurgency, which they saw going back to 1964, had to be thwarted by any means necessary. For the military dictatorship, the presence of rural unions was deemed a threat to national security. For the peasants themselves, and for the rural communities, widespread fear led to a demobilization across the board. Given the division of democratic forces, which paved the way for the coup, it was not surprising to see the Christian-Democrat-affiliated rural confederations (such as Libertad and Triunfo Campesino) supporting this wave of repression. But the military were not minded to accept the Christian Democrats as valid interlocutors with regard to the peasantry, and thus co-option was ruled out.

The neoliberal transformation of Chile led to a new regime of accumulation and labour control in rural areas. The privatization of the reformed rural sector happened quite rapidly in the repressive context after 1973. Decollectivization was the order of the day. Chile also led in the break-up of indigenous communities in the south and the sale of their land. A new capitalist agrarian sector began to emerge as Chile's rural economy was increasingly incorporated into the global economy as the main driver of exports. The consequent casualization of rural labour has contributed, as Cristóbal Kay notes, "to the fracturing of the peasant movement. Although seasonal labourers can be highly militant they are notoriously difficult to organise because of their diverse composition and shifting residence."[12] The decline of permanent tenant labour under the neoliberal land regime has perhaps been more effective than even the original repression in the late 1970s and early 1980s in terms of preventing rural insurgency in Chile.

What we learn from the Chilean case is that the neoliberal turn in agriculture has set serious limits on the mobilization of the peasantry in the traditional way. The territorial approach (see Chapter 5) seeks to link the declining smallholder sector to the global economy through the global value chains. At most, this is a defensive posture, and one in which regional, ethnic and wider political divisions make unity difficult to achieve. The way in which the new global value chains have impacted in Chile has been through the massive expansion of the fruit export sector, based largely on seasonal female labour.[13] Although these *temporeras* (part-time women workers) are in many ways marginalized, they play a key role at the forefront of one of Chile's key export sectors. Increasingly, the organization of labour will become transnational, we could argue, with the global value chains facilitating transnational trade union links, including involvement of the global union federations, which have been pivotal in linking workers across national boundaries.

Vía Campesina

Vía Campesina (the Peasant Way) was formed in 1993 by farmer organizations in the Americas, Africa, Asia and Europe. It is a coalition of 150 different organizations across 75 countries in these continents; in its own words, it is "an international movement which coordinates peasant organisations of small and middle-scale producers, agricultural workers, rural women, and indigenous communities" (www.viacampesina.org). It advocates family-farm-based sustainable agriculture and has promoted the idea of food sovereignty.

Vía Campesina stands for a shared peasant identity across world regions and cultures, supporting implicitly the re-peasantization thesis. It represents, in terms of our purpose here, a social movement with a uniquely Latin American inflection that is also very much part of the "new" alter-globalization movements contesting the hegemony of unregulated market neoliberal development.

Vía Campesina soon evolved its positions after the first initial "get-to-know-you" meetings. It first had to come to terms with what it meant by "agrarian reform", which, as we have seen above, can mean many different things. At a time when the 1980s debt crisis was hitting hard in the global South the simple distribution of land would not suffice to sustain peasant households. An "integral agrarian reform", as Vía Campesina dubbed it, "would have to include major changes in the overall policy environment for peasant agriculture (trade, credit, crop, insurance, education, democratic access to water and seeds, etc.)".[14] Another aspect to Vía Campesina's openness to new ways of thinking began when its members met with others who shared the land but were not classified as "peasants", such as indigenous peoples, pastoralist and fisherfolk. It became apparent that an agrarian perspective that was much wider than the traditional agrarian reform model was needed to create a unified way forward.

It was the notion of "food sovereignty" (coined by Vía Campesina around 1996) that began to articulate a new paradigm of social transformation. The notion of "food sovereignty" asserts that people have the right to health, and culturally appropriate food produced through ecologically social and sustainable methods. It should be people (be they producers or consumers) who decide on their own food, not markets or corporations. This concept was posed as an alternative to the dominant international discourse of "food security", which argues that nutrition needs can be fulfilled locally or through imports, and stresses the advantages of a "corporate food regime" based on agri-business, land concentration and further trade liberalization. The food sovereignty movement gave voice to small-scale producers and those concerned with the environment and ecology. There are academic criticisms that can be made about "food sovereignty" (such as its implicit anti-modernist ontology) but as a political discourse it has been extremely successful in mobilizing and sustaining a broad movement.

Vía Campesina has shown an ability – typical of the most dynamic social movements – to learn from its interactions, both externally and internally. It became cognizant of the "great financialization" of capitalism, including agribusiness, of course – and the way it was leading to land grabbing and the broader emphasis on extractivism with regard to natural resources. Women farmers involved in the Vía Campesina debates saw through the World Bank's advocacy of granting women individual titles to land and promoted the notion of collective titles and the recognition of communal property regimes. Not only have they have shown great strategic insights but they have also been innovative tactically – more so than many other social movements. Thus, although Vía Campesina and its affiliates still deploy land invasions as a tactic, this is framed within a broader societal interest in terms of good food and the protection of Mother Earth, countering perceptions of land grabs from below, as it were.

As Annette Desmarais puts it, Vía Campesina "is unique; it is autonomous, pluralist and independent of any political, economic or other type of affiliation".[15] It is a model of a transnational democratic network organization. It also redresses the balance in terms of focus, reminding us that peasants have not all gone away, and they play a vital role in contesting neoliberal globalization. The turn from what might have been seen as material or corporatist demands around land to the widely resonant discourse of "food sovereignty" took it to a new level of influence. The horizon of this movement has gone from the local to the national, and now the transnational. The problems it faces are the problems of success that many social movements have faced in the past. Will Vía Campesina settle into a lobbying role at gatherings of the WTO and other global elite gatherings? How will this transnational level of organizing feed back into national social movements and empower them?

In Latin America the most visible peasant movement has been the Zapatistas (see Chapter 7), but, in fact, they do not play a strong role in the new peasant internationalism. The lead there is taken by Brazil's Movimento dos trabalhadores rurais Sem Terra, committed to agrarian reform and an end to free market policies. The hallmark of the MST has been massive land occupations and an astute policy of national and international political alliances. Contemporary peasant movements in Latin America – whether in Brazil, Colombia, Ecuador or El Salvador – tend to share a common anti-imperialist identity, which may merge with anti-globalization sentiment but is not necessarily the same thing. They are, arguably, more "classical" social movements than the new ones, committed to modernity (albeit not a free market one) most often within the clear parameters of the nation state. The MST strategy has been called "modernization from below with equity", and it has been effective in national and transnational fora precisely due to such a clear orientation. Although these social movements, indeed, believe that "another world is possible", this is not conceived in utopian or futuristic terms. Their solidarity has been built around traditional forms of social cohesion, such as kinship and community, even ethnic identity. Thus, we can understand that there may often be a tension between local, national and transnational strategies. Indeed, a number of the Central American peasant organizations that pioneered the new peasant internationalism have since withdrawn and "retreated" to the national political arena as a priority.

The new peasant internationalism could be seen as completing the mission of the communist Peasant International of the 1920s, albeit under very different conditions. It has effectively unified very distinct rural populations against the effects of neoliberal globalization on agriculture. Other than an agri-business that becomes a capitalist enterprise like any other, all agriculturalists are affected by WTO policies negatively. Vía Campesina articulates well the rejection of neoliberal policies that push countries into cash crop production at the expense of domestic food production. This movement also articulates clearly what it sees as an alternative, namely the sustainable use of local resources, the production of food for local consumption to overcome the problems arising when local production systems are destroyed. Thus, we have here a very clear-cut case of the new local transnationalisms that are not captured very well by the new social movement paradigm.

5
COMMUNITY

The third major historical social movement in Latin America that we need to consider is that of community or neighbourhood associations, and place-based social movements more generally. From its origins, the labour movement always had a strong community presence, and workplace–community links were stronger than in the industrializing countries of the global North. The economic intergeneration of capitalist enterprises and various forms of self-employment and marginal enterprises in part explains this synergy. More broadly, as Joe Foweraker describes, "it is often a sense of neighbourhood that sustains urban social movements in Latin America. And that is created through intense networking and complex relations of exchange and reciprocity."[1] Solidarity in the workplace is matched by a communalism that sustains social relations, builds identity and forges a platform of common demands. In the periods of military rule, when there were interventions in labour unions and left-wing parties, the mass struggle could rely on a community base and bring in other allies, such as the churches and the human rights organizations.

In contemporary Latin America there are many examples of place-based social movements, often lauded by NSM theorists who see them as exemplars of identity-based movements. Thus, Libia Grueso, Carlos Rosero and Arturo Escobar refer to Colombia's Pacific black movements as "a complex process of construction of ethnic and cultural identity in relation to novel variables such as territory, biodiversity, and alternative development".[2] Although most acknowledge the verve and dynamism of the Afro-Colombian place-based movements, we might also query whether territory is really a "novel" feature and whether these movements are harbingers of an alternative development model. Similar conceptual inflation occurred in Argentina in relation to the 2001/2 neighbourhood councils and barter economies set up to cope with the impact of economic collapse. The slogan "*Qué se vayan todos*" ("Let them all go", referring to politicians) was itself a political refrain of the far left groups, and the neighbourhood organizing, though impressive, did not outlast elections and the return of a progressive Peronist government.

To understand these current political concerns, we need to explore what we mean by "community" and how it relates to the more prevalent term in Latin America, namely that of "territory". The notion of "community" in the social sciences has, for long, had a conservative meaning, representing cohesion, stability and shared values. It has, more recently, been subverted to describe a "third space" beyond spatiality as concrete mapped form and a purely cognitive construct: where subjectivity and objectivity, the real and the imagined, the knowable and the indefinable all come together.[3] Something along similar lines is called for in Latin America by Raúl Zibechi, who argues that we need "a new language, one that is capable of talking about relationships and movements ... We need expressions capable of capturing the ephemeral, the flows that are invisible to the masculine, legalistic and rational culture."[4] Our inherited concepts, in short, are incapable of grasping the changing spatiality of human life in the current era.

The shift towards territory – more commonly used than the term "community" in Latin America – is creating a new language for the study of social movements. These are now increasingly understood as socio-territorial and socio-spatial movements. The spatial and cultural turns in the social sciences are part of the explanation for this paradigmatic shift. But it also has been attributable to the foregrounding in practice of new movements based on indigenous (Chapter 7) and environmental (see Chapter 8) politics. The radical restructuring of society and place by the neoliberal order is leading to complex rearticulations by and through Polanyi-style social counter-movements. Escobar argues in this regard that there are now alternative ways of strengthening people's capacity to resist by stressing the importance of place "by building on people's struggle for the defence of place and culture, and by fostering people's autonomy over their territory and culture".[5] This orientation is in keeping with our own cultural political economy perspective, introduced in Chapter 1.

It is important to note that the current focus on community and territory as the sites of social movement construction and meaning subverts orthodox notions of what anti-capitalism means. As J. K. Gibson-Graham has argued, we need to "open a space for thinking about 'non-capitalism' ... and the development of a discourse ... that is not *capitalocentric*".[6] Capitalism, not least in Latin America, is a radically heterogeneous system, and its contestation is not singular (as in simply anti-capitalist) but, rather, occurs in a multitude of sites, not confined to particular locations or scales of such activity. This chapter will seek to explore this conceptual paradigm through case studies of Brazil, Colombia and Argentina, where we observe different understandings of the significance of both community and territory for the construction of social movements. We find a mixture of "old" and "new" social movements in a combined form not reducible to simple calls to action. To conclude this chapter, I turn to the question of autonomy, often posed as the preferred path for social movements in Latin America but rarely examined critically.

Neighbourhood struggles (Brazil)

In Brazil, community organizations trace their origins back to the 1930s, and then a major flourishing in the 1950s. The emergence of these movements was tied to the emergence of "populist" politics, and these associations were often started by local politicians. These residents' associations – the Amigos do Bairro (Friends of the Neighbourhood) – acted as a type of municipal congress that was a sometimes directly co-opted into local government structures and was given a say in the provision of local services. Although these bodies often served to legitimize local populist politicians, they could also, as Gianpaolo Baiocchi notes, lead to a "new participatory imaginary [that] emerged in direct contrast to this vision, often through the work of activists who worked to transform existing associations".[7] These radical, and geographically situated, social movements peaked in the mid-1950s after a large-scale strike in São Paulo organized by textile, metallurgical and print workers ("the strike of the 300,000") succeeded, largely because of the massive and structured support it obtained in the working-class neighbourhood.

The critical importance of the neighbourhood in labour struggles again became evident in the 1975–85 period, as the independent trade unions and the PT (Workers' Party) began to organize. Parallel to the clandestine reorganiza-tion of a worker's movement there were increasing demands from the squatters' settlements around housing, health care, water and sanction issues. When this phase of reorganization led to a pivotal metalworkers' strike in 1980, union action was matched by mobilization in the *bairros*, which gave great impetus to the strike movement. As Lucio Kowarick notes, union organizing and mobilizing cannot alone explain the impact of the strike: "It is also explained by the iden-tification of the population with the metallurgical workers' cause, transforming the city into a broad supportive network, in which the struggle gained multiple and varied social spaces of solidarity".[8] The demands of workers in the factories could not be separated from the urban demands placed by workers and others in the popular *bairros*.

A key element in the rise of urban social movements in Brazil was the change in political positions by the Catholic Church after the Medellín Council of 1968, at which the bishops declared their support for the "base communities" and declared their commitment to liberate the people from the "institutionalized violence" of their poverty. It is well to remember that the Church was a major force promoting civilian support for the 1964 military coup through massive demonstrations, such as the Marcha da Família com Deus pela Liberdade (March of the Family with God for Liberty) that preceded it. In the 1970s, as repression hit, many priests and even bishops of the Church as a whole began to take up a pro-democracy stance. The main drivers of this shift were the CEBs, which had begun to form in the 1960s. These were genuine communities inspired by faith, bringing people together in urban rural parishes around basic social needs. The CEBs portrayed themselves as "the people", struggling against "the rich" or "the exploiters". Frei Betto, one of the leaders of this movement, expressed the new mood of resistance as one in which "people who almost always live in a sphere of necessity now for a moment live in a sphere of liberty".[9]

Many CEB members participated in the "union opposition" movement that began to gather pace in the mid-1970s. Union meetings had even sheltered in churches at the height of the repression, from around 1968 to 1972. The churches did not see themselves creating Catholic unions, as had existed, for example, in Europe. This was, rather, part of liberation theology's "turn to the poor". Its importance in terms of creating a new social movement in Brazil cannot be overestimated. Nico Vink, for example, finds that "until 1977–78 the activities of the Church were the most important form of mobilisation and organisation of the people".[10] This was a genuine articulation between the needs of the workers and the political choice made by a sector of the Catholic Church, which was key at a certain conjuncture. The CEBs, as a social movement themselves, are, of course, a topic in their own right, and one would need to examine the internal contradictions and, in particular, the later increase in influence of the Pentecostalist Churches, which attracted many women and black *creyentes* (believers).

In the 1980s and 1990 we saw the emergence in Brazil of what was then a new social category, namely that of civil society. Although it was partly imposed by the international NGOs and, later, bodies such as the World Bank, it clearly also had local roots. What emerged was a "new citizenship", premised on "the right to have rights".[11] The limits of representative democracy were being challenged, from below, as it were, as the new political imaginary of "civil society" began to articulate a non-populist relationship with the state. This was a period in which a progressive political party (the PT) occupied government, first locally and then nationally. This set up a dynamic of synergy between state and "civil society". Its most outstanding example was the movement for "participatory budgeting", which began in Porto Alegre, went national and then went international. The people found a mechanism for participation in governance that brought together the needs and dynamics of an oppressive political party in government and the broad array of social movements seeking new avenues to advance.

Civil society in Brazil in the 1990s was shaped by its diverse constituencies, which included the faith-based self-help groups, the urban poor claiming public goods and those associations linked to the state and implementing public policies.[12] This civil society can, at one and the same time, politicize issues but depoliticize them by dragging them into a state-controlled space called "civil society". This dynamic we can see clearly at play in the urban housing movement MTST

(Movimento dos Trabalhadores Sem Teto: Homeless Workers' Movement), which relied on the state to achieve the goals for housing but also mobilized a radical grass-roots movement. Under the military dictatorship these movements had been part of the broader pro-democracy movement and were quite confrontational. There was pressure, though, in the 1990s to adapt to the new political order and "participate" in various state-sponsored consultation bodies. In practice, unlike some other urban groups (such as around health issues), the struggle for housing – just like the struggle for land – could not be easily met by the state, and militancy tended to prevail.

Recent urban mobilizations in Brazil and their role in the lead-up to the successful constitutional coup against the PT government in 2016 show, very clearly, that social movements are not always left-wing. The PT governments were constrained by international economic pressures and the national political limits inherent in being a minority government. Social tensions inevitably built up, and they erupted in mid-2013, initially around rising bus fares in São Paulo, a mega-city practically overwhelmed by the contradictions of urban expansion. The Movimento Passe Livre, calling for free buses, began on a small scale, but the repression unleashed by the police led to it spreading rapidly. The issues also broadened out from transport, health and education to encompass corruption, taxation and justice, not to mention the World Cup. What began as a fairly typical far left protest with mainly student participants expanded to include trade unionists, informal sector workers, neighbourhood associations and sections of the middle class. The politics of the protest also shifted as it expanded to become predominately a protest against the leftist PT government.

The mass media took up the various conflicting causes and amplified them. The bus fare increases – the initial cause of the protests – were cancelled but the movement continued to gain traction. Although the PT could have responded in a more creative way to this wave of social movement mobilization, it was far too involved in pragmatic governmental and policy alliances, which would only increase with the election of Dilma Rousseff to the presidency in 2013. As Pedro Loureiro and Alfredo Saad-Filho note, "[T]he PT and its mass organisations were unable to channel the demonstrations towards progressive ends."[13] Symptomatic of the growing separation between the progressive social movements and the PT, this was the beginning of the end of its hegemonic project. The campaign against "corruption" – an "empty signifier" (a signifier without a referent, a word with no agreed meaning) waiting to be captured – became directed squarely at Lula and Dilma. The so-called "pro-family" causes, namely anti-LGBT rights and lowering the legal age for criminal punishment, rose to the top of the agenda and created a discourse favouring the rise of Jair Bolsonaro to become Brazil's next president.

Black Pacific (Colombia)

Black and indigenous social movements have existed since the colonial era, but they resurfaced in the 1970s, inspired in part by the international human rights movement. We could argue that "class" is still a major factor in the rise of those social movements, in so far as land (as a material good) is central to them. We also need to take into account the intersectionality governing social positions, however, which in the black movement in Colombia includes race, gender, ethnicity, class, religion and regional identity. Afro-Colombians or African descendants make up one-fifth of the Colombian population, and they are predominantly congregated in the Pacific region. The south-western Upper Cauca region in particular has been the scene of considerable social mobilizations in recent decades. There the colonial power structures have led to an agro-industry based on a sugarcane- and a mining-focused economy. The workers on the large estates are descendants of African slaves and, despite official "multiculturalism", continue to suffer multiple forms of oppression.

The expansion of the sugarcane-based industry and, more recently, large-scale mining has generated a process of social dislocation in the region, with the displacement of traditional farming patterns. With the consolidation of free market neoliberal policies in the 1990s, Afro-descendants were particularly hard hit, through proletarianization and displacement. For Irene Vélez-Torres and Daniel Varela, this ethnically differentiated impact of neoliberalism amounted to "environmental racism", as the state "deepened the impoverishment and social, economic and environmental marginalization of Afro-descendant communities".[14] The small-scale extractive and productive activities of the black Cauca communities were marginalized by agri-business and big mining. The plundering of the region thus further deepened racial inequality in Colombia, despite all the lip service paid to multiculturalism by the state and the international agents of neoliberalism.

The Afro-descendants of the Cauca Valley have been subject to extreme levels of violence – a form of "extra-economic" coercion – which has shaped the relations of production. For a time this community escaped the worst of the conflict between the FARC and the state/paramilitaries, but that all changed in the mid-1990s. The Association of Displaced Afro-Colombians (AFRODES) has documented the terror that ensued and the price paid by this community in terms of death and mass displacements. Ulrich Oslender refers to how massacres lead to movements of people and how this "forms an integral part of the embodied experience of terror and fear".[15] Not surprisingly, these black communities sought to promote a policy of neutrality between the left and the state, which only strengthened their sense of identity and need for self-determination. The "peace communities" that were formed as a result of this strategy led to a gradual process of reterritorialization and a centralizing of the claims around biodiversity.

The politics of resistance in the Cauca Valley from the 1990s onwards had race/ethnicity as the major structuring axis. The 1991 constitution, and subsequent laws on black rights, brought into the open the invisibility of black identity and culture. Organizers in the riverine Pacific communities – which were 90 percent black – saw this as an opportunity. As Kiran Asher puts it, "They attempted to rally diverse black groups around their identity as 'Afro-Colombians', and to formulate proposals for a collective 'ethnic territory' in the Pacific region."[16] The vision was one of an autonomous region with an ecologically sustainable model of development. Mainstream black politicians from the conservative and liberal parties were forced to join this conversation. They clearly had their own interests, as did the state and the various NGOs concerned with this region. For the PCN (Proceso de Comunidades Negras: Process of Black Communities), the objective was clear: "The black communities of Colombia need their own spaces (*espacios propios*) – rights over our territory – but also spaces where we can consolidate our positions."[17]

The predominantly Afro-Colombian western Chocó region is one of the most biodiverse regions of the world, so, not surprisingly, in the 1990s it became a key issue in national and international conservation efforts. The state, to some extent, hoped to harness traditional black community knowledge of natural resource management to a classic modernization project. The Projecto Bio-Pacífico was launched in 1993, funded by the World Bank and the Inter-America Development Bank, with the objectives to "preserve, develop and modernize" the biodiverse Pacific. For the communities involved, participation in this project and some greater property rights were no longer an acceptable outcome. The dynamic of the black social movement was making itself felt, particularly after the 2001 UN World Conference against Racism, held in Durban. There the Colombian movement had been a significant participant, and began the shift from an Afro-Colombian discourse to an Afro-descendant one with distinct separatist undertones. Black struggles now opened up on a number of fronts – economic, political, social and cultural – and in a multi-scale way, from the local to the global.

The struggles of the Upper Cauca are intensely regional in character, making them an exemplar of territorial/community-based social movements. The national constitution of 1991 granted collective territorial rights to the *comunidades negras* (black communities) of the region. Not surprisingly, the black social movements sought to emphasize the element of territorial autonomy. They were in many ways emblematic of the eco-territorial shift in social struggles in Latin America during the 1990s. The territorial dimension built on, and in turn reinforced, the sense of ethnic communalism, of communities that had historically been excluded from the national development project. The impact of globalization had been to diminish the importance or the obviousness of the nation state as the "container" of social struggles, thus centring much more the regional dimension. Black identity and politics in Colombia thus have a strong regional dimension and are infused with the values of territoriality and autonomous cultural practices.

The Afro-descendant movements are also clearly related to culture, especially if we take a cultural political economy approach. For Grueso, Rosero and Escobar, "The social movement of black communities embodies a politicisation of culture – a cultural politics – that has visible effects on established political cultures."[18] Clearly, the defence of place and culture go hand in hand in creating a sense of territorial and cultural rights and identities. These are not necessarily fixed cultural attributes responding to an essentialist notion of tradition, as would seem implicit in the 1991 constitution. Rather, these shared cultural practices respond to very concrete challenges posed by late dependent capitalism and the need to offer an alternative vison for their communities. Thus, the cultural identity that drives the development of the black social movements is not given or static but constantly under construction, in dialogue with other discourses such as sustainability, democracy and post-capitalist futures.

Finally, the black social movement in Colombia – in its close relation to environmental politics – is part of the broader questioning of modernist-inspired development. Arturo Escobar has analysed the Afro-Colombian movement and also, not coincidentally, pioneered the notion of alternative development.[19] The vision of development springing from the Afro-Colombian movements is clearly distinct from the modernist, rationalist and Western model. It involves the defence of place and culture, an active respect for biodiversity and a greater stress on self-sufficiency, particularly in relation to food. What is at stake in the Colombian Black Pacific is how humanity can challenge and replace the current neoliberal "deepening of capitalist modernity's triple economic, ecological and cultural conquest and transformation, a merciless attempt at doing away with the economic, ecological and cultural difference that is embodied in the practices of the ethnic communities",[20] as Escobar puts it. This is one area in which Latin American social movements are very much in the vanguard internationally.

Territorial struggles (Argentina)

The making of the labour and popular movements in Argentina was always based on place. The formation of the labour movement in the early twentieth century depended on forging a new national identity superseding that of a migrant's community of origin. Class consciousness was forged in the immigrant quarters and the notorious *conventillos* (cheap rental buildings) as much as in the workplace. When general strikes occurred in 1905, 1910 and 1919, resistance was built across the community. A slogan of 2001, after the crisis, declared: "*La nueva fábrica es el barrio*" ("The new factory is the neighbourhood"). But, in a sense, the *barrio* was always the locus of consciousness formation. Seemingly "new" social movements, such as the famous *piqueteros* of the early 2000s, mobilized precisely in those communities/territories where there was a dense social network and an experience of common struggle. Collective bonds of solidarity and habits of self-organization are the basis on which social movements form.

In the making of Peronism as a labour-based national movement, place was critical. Students of Peronism have struggled with the complexity of an ideology that was, at one and the same time, emancipatory and limiting in its authoritarianism. The way it impacted on workers was mediated in complex social and spatial ways, which included the neighbourhood, where much political organizing occurred. It was there that Peronism built up a dense network of what can only imperfectly be called clientelism. It created not just a nationalist ideology but a sense of citizenship and a vision of dignity and respect with deep roots. When Peronism was overthrown in 1955, the resistance that ensued was driven by clandestine union units and mobilized communities. With Perón – but also more broadly across Latin America – we see clearly the pattern whereby the popular class consciousness was built in the mass rallies of the public plaza as much as in the workplace.

The neighbourhood associations formed during this period continue as an urban social movement today and are known as the *sociedades de fomento* (development, as in community development, associations). These neighbourhood associations would today be known as NGOs, CSOs (civil society organizations) or part of the third sector. They were created in the *barrios* – sometimes spontaneously but also with local political backing at times – and brought neighbours together around urban security issues but also to claim better public works from the municipality. Daniel García Delgado and Juan Silva find that the migrants who moved out of the *conventillos* to the outskirts of the city, where they could build their own houses, "developed communitarian links, mechanism of solidarity and promoted a recomposition of the social networks and new strands of horizontal solidarity".[21] The participation of neighbours in the *sociedades de fomento* promoted the values of community autonomy, and their utopia was a country where the communitarian citizen was central.

Throughout its recent history Argentina's social movements have been marked by sharp, geographically localized eruptions, from the Cordobazo of 1969 onwards. The unions in Córdoba had issued a clear anti-imperialist and anti-capitalist programme in the 1950s and they were very much a political vanguard. But Córdoba was also a radicalized student city, and a general strike in May 1969 soon turned into a semi-insurrectional episode, driven by workers and students but also with the full participation of the community. Later, in the early 1970s, as the country moved towards the return of the ageing Perón in 1973, there were a series of local town seizures, known as *puebladas*, protesting against electricity price rises in many cases: the Rocazo, Mendozazo, etc. The example set by the working class in Córdoba (mainly well-organized auto and metalworkers) in resisting the regime and employers had loosened the grip of fear over the population, and these new geographically based revolts of wider social layers in popular uprisings emerged with a clear anti-dictatorial purpose. The return of Perón (1973 to 1976) was followed by another military dictatorship (1976 to 1983), which was extremely repressive, and such expressions of popular anger were not possible.

With the return of democracy in 1983 there was an upsurge in popular mobilizations that initially, and to a considerable degree, took the form of geo-graphically specific uprisings. These events, known as *vecinazos* (*vecino*: neigh-bour), began in 1982 around increased taxation issues. The defeat of the military in the Falklands/Malvinas War in 1982 led to a certain decompression of the terror regime. Local community associations came out openly against the military-imposed system of mayors and the associated patronage. The *sociedades de fomento* were core organizers of these uprisings but they were joined by new, more participatory layers of the *vecinos*. One of the most salient of this wave of citizen mobilization was the Lanusazo of 1982. This citizens' revolt brought together the *sociedades de fomento*, housewives' organizations, pensioners asso-ciations, small traders, regional trade unions and popular libraries. The path of democratization would be marked by renewed labour struggles but also a new, geographically based citizens' social movement (even if it did not call itself such).

The collapse of the neoliberal economic model in 2001 led to the most acute epi-sode of community-based revolt, known by some as the Argentinazo: a national version of the Cordobazo. Events began in mid-December 2001 in Buenos Aires, with a series of *cacerolazos* (banging of pots and pans), as a spontaneous reaction in mainly middle-class suburbs to the freezing of bank accounts. Participation in these protests spread to the impoverished, unemployed, precarious professionals and small business owners. From those events derived the *asambleas vecinales* (neighbourhood assemblies), which rapidly gained considerable territorial con-trol: a genuine form of dual power. Mass assemblies were held in the plazas or in neighbourhood clubs, in an intense, practically feverish, atmosphere as the political crisis deepened. With the collapse of the currency towards the end of 2001, an alternative economy began to emerge centred on the *clubes de trueque* (barter clubs); they were born out of necessity, but they soon became the new normal. Eventually elections were called, and a renewed Peronist figure (Néstor Kirchner) emerged, representing the new mood of insurgency but tasked with normalization.

The collapse of the economy led, inevitably, to a whole series of factory closures. Resistance here passed through the pre-existing trade union organizations and traditions of struggle. Thus began the movement of the *fábricas recuperadas* (recovered factories), which by 2018 embraced 315 factories employing over 10,000 people. Some of these are linked to local social or political organizations, others are independent. One factory that achieved international exposure was Zanon (rebaptized Fasinpat), which is one of the largest ceramics factories in Latin America. What began as a demand for the factory to reopen was soon converted into a classic worker self-management (*autogestión*) experience. Having control of the factory and keeping jobs does not mean that this is necessarily a viable economic alternative. When seen in conjunction with the mass uprising of citizens, however, who refused to be passive victims of the economic crisis and thus of workplace-based struggle, it had an exemplary effect both nationally and internationally.

The third strand of the 2001/2 social explosion centred on the mobilization of the unemployed or *piqueteros* (pickets), who used road blockages as their main forms of direct action. Already, in the 1990s, massive route blockages had been used successfully by demonstrators. The new unemployed often worked in large factories and had trade union experience. Many on the left joined this campaign, which may have been divisive in the long term but initially gave it an organizational lift and resources. The *piquetero* rapidly became a symbol of working-class resistance and garnered sympathy, and even support, across society: from small merchants threatened with bankruptcy, a middle class recently impoverished because of the loss of their savings, and "ordinary citizens" who simply admired their tenacity and fightback spirit. Eventually the *piquetero* movement was weakened by fierce internal fighting between the far left groups and political co-option by the Kirchner government, which channelled considerable social welfare payments to the unemployed.

Autonomy

The concept of autonomy came to the fore in the Latin American social movement problematic with the publication and reception of John Holloway's *How to Change the World without Taking Power*,[22] based on the Zapatista experience, which it sought to codify, in a sense. Where "autonomy" gained greatest political purchase in practice, however, was in Argentina after the 2001 revolt analysed above. A series of movements were run together – the events of 20–21 December 2001, the occupied factories and the *piqueteros* – and seen as exemplars of a new "autonomous" political practice. That those events were both time-limited and discrete did not seem to matter – nor that the *piqueteros* were very largely organized by left groups and hardly autonomous in any real sense. Nevertheless, a distinct "autonomist" political current emerged in Argentina, and was also projected internationally. So, what is the meaning of "autonomy" and how does it impact on the study of social movements?

"Autonomy" can refer to independence from capital, from the state and/or from the hegemonic relations of dependent capitalism, but in our case we are referring to autonomy with regard to political parties. In the broader sense, workers as creators of value are, or should be, autonomous from capital, and their associations (trade unions) likewise. Independence from the state is the second major assumption, with a strong view that attempts to capture state power are doomed, reminiscent of classic anarchist philosophy. In addition, "autonomy" can refer to an indigenous resistance to colonial domination. Gustavo Esteva articulates this position: "The indigenous people' proposal for autonomy seeks to recover faculties and competences that the state has taken away from them. Above all they view to organize their own political and judicial spaces so that they can practice their own way of life and government."[23] It is in this last variant that we can see the very real purchase of the autonomist perspective in relation to the community/territorial struggles covered in this chapter and the variety of indigenous struggles discussed in Chapter 6.

Ana Dinerstein has written, from a critical autonomist perspective, that "autonomy of social movements via-á-vis the state and capital is both possible and impossible",[24] meaning, essentially, that capital, the state and the development process will always seek to capture/co-opt autonomy. Capitalism in fact thrives on the creativity and autonomy of the workers, and the state is revived and reformed through autonomous struggle; likewise, the development process is energized by counter- or alter-development practices. Even so, autonomy allows for self-definition and a refusal of imposed categories, such as of "unemployed" by Argentina's *piqueteros*. Autonomy can perhaps best be understood as the intersection between power and the construction of the subject. As Massimo Modonesi puts it, "In this intersection, autonomy appears as part of the process of construction of the socio-political subject that is as the condition of the subject that by emancipating, dictates its own norms of conduct."[25] Autonomy is thus about self-determination and the conditions for the possibility of emancipation.

There have been, not surprisingly, many criticisms of the autonomy perspective, particularly from an orthodox Marxist perspective but also from further afield. For Judith Hellman, what she calls the "fetishism of autonomy" responds to Northern researchers' own commitment, as "children of 1968", to the affirmation of solidarity and the struggle against hierarchy and alienation.[26] Hellman also argues against the "anti organizational bias of the work of those who are pleased and excited by the spontaneity of isolated grass-roots movements".[27] There is, for sure, a danger that researchers will choose to see what they find attractive politically.[28] Since this critique by Hellman and others, a Southern epistemology of affirmation and autonomy that is not subject to these same concerns has become more firmly established. There is, of course, more than a whiff of the old anarchist tropes in the autonomist discourse, however, even though they are not always recognized and explicit.

The major weakness of the autonomy perspective is thus perhaps its tendency towards apoliticism. In the refusal to engage with the state, it runs the risk of not being able to intervene in politics. Electoral abstention (as has been the case with the Zapatistas) can become a principle from a strict autonomist perspective, thus disabling political advancement. For example, the autonomist current in Argentina took the conjunctural slogan of 2001, "*Qué se vayan todos*", as an autonomist banner not to be surrendered. What we need to do, perhaps, is to distinguish between the autonomy of the indigenous movements in terms of their social base and the essential task of forming political alliances with other social forces in pursuit of common goals. The construction of a popular subject (*el pueblo*) necessarily passes through the construction of alliances and the articulation of a multitude of autonomous social subjects.

6

WOMEN

One of the social movements in Latin America that most clearly shows both "old" and "new" facets is the women's movement. Most Latin American countries experienced the emergence of classical liberal feminist movements in the early twentieth century. Oriented towards suffrage issues, these movements were the start of a bid to "engender" citizenship – clearly a precondition if it is to be a universal good. This early feminism could probably be classified as an "old" social movement, in so far as it made demands on the state and was clearly political in its orientation. Contemporary feminisms emerged in the late 1960s, at least in part in response to the military regimes and their suppression of social and individual rights. Feminists saw clearly how the military state was inextricably linked to patriarchy, in a terrible symmetry impacting on all domains, from consumption to repression. Male violence and state violence were, arguably, one and the same, and women's reproductive rights were dramatically curtailed. Later, in the 1980s, we saw a flourishing of women's participation in communal and other social movements. These *mujeres populares* (working-class women) brought a different dynamic to the struggle, with their emphasis on what became known as practical gender needs, rather than the strategic gender needs prioritized by the feminists.

This second-wave mobilization of women coincided with neoliberalism's cultural, political and economic restructuring of society. Free trade policies, the reduction of state services and the weakening of social policy all impinged directly and disproportionately on women. Although many women participating in these actions were not, or did not see themselves as, feminists, their public participation in social movements inevitably impinged on their "private" lives. As they moved from passivity to a new combativeness they began to also take on the patriarchal attitudes of the political or trade union bosses, as well as that ever-present feature in their daily life. In the wider feminist movement there was a growing divide from the 1990s onwards between the *autónomas* and the *institucionalistas*, the latter being more committed to working within the new democratic institutions and, to some extent, leaving behind the militant social movement orientation characteristic of the anti-dictatorial struggle period.

It is important to note at the outset that the women's movements in Latin American cannot be interpreted through Northern theories. Thus, for example, the context in which second-wave feminism emerged in the North Atlantic in the 1970s was a very particular situation that cannot be generalized. In Latin America, in contrast, this was the period of the military dictatorships, so feminism here was much more tied to the revolutionary struggle. The social context was also quite different in Latin America, as, for example, in regard to the "family wage" and the whole notion of "housewife", which does not really apply in the same way. Verónica Schild argues that "the feminist movements that emerged in [Latin America] were not merely imitative of US experiences, often they involved reconfigurations of pre-existing currents – socialist, anarchist, Catholic, liberal – with traditions of activism, research and cultural interventions stretching back to the nineteenth century".[1] We will, of course, complicate the matter further by showing that there is no unified "Latin American feminism" either.

One of the most important general concepts to come out of research on/with Latin American women is the distinction between "practical" and "strategic" gender needs. The whole notion of "women's interests", or that of a unified category of "Latin American women", needs to be questioned. Having said that, we can usefully deploy Maxine Molyneux's distinction between "practical" and "strategic" gender interests as a preliminary step in an overview of feminism(s) in Latin America. Following Molyneux's formulation, "strategic interests are derived from the analysis of women's subordination and from the formulation of an alternative set of arrangements", while "practical gender interests arise from the concrete conditions of women's positioning by virtue of their gender within the division of labour".[2] This basic distinction may help us distinguish not just the various types of women's movements from feminist movements as such but also the grey area in between.

This chapter starts with an overview of two very different women's movements in Latin America: the Madres de Plaza de Mayo association, which emerged in the late 1970s, and the more recent Ni una menos campaign in Argentina. These were both quite particular movements, in distinct periods and with very different politics, so the comparison between them provides interesting insights. We turn next to Brazil, which had seen the rise of a "classic" feminist movement in the 1970s and then a more complex array of women's movements subsequently, wherein many of the key feminist political debates were played out. In Venezuela under the Chávez government (1999 to 2013) we saw the emergence of a "popular" women's movement tied closely to the governing party. It was dynamic and new but not without its contradictions. Finally, we turn to the transnational domain and the way Latin American feminists "went global" in the 1990s. I also refer to what has been called the NGOization of the feminist movement (or part of it), and what that might tell us about the category of civil society and its relation to social movements.[3]

Madres de Plaza de Mayo to #ni una menos (Argentina)

Feminism in Argentina has a long history, one of the earliest in Latin America. The first feminist newspaper in Argentina was launched in 1896, *La Voz de la Mujer* (*The Voice of the Woman*), an anarcho-communist-feminist outlet whose slogan was "No god, no master, no husband". The Socialist Party's women's wing, for its part, launched a struggle for equal rights, better educational opportunities for women and reform of the penal code. In the early twentieth century one of the most active women's organizations was the Club de Madres de Buenos Aires (Buenos Aires Mothers' Club), which shared the widespread notion of a morally superior maternal nature. These examples show the widely different politics of the early women's movements, which cannot be reduced to a generic feminism. Women's participation in politics is also closely related to the rise of Peronism as a national-popular movement. Women gained the right to vote under Perón's government in 1949, and Peronism has also generated the only female presidents in Argentina: Isabel Perón (1974 to 1976) and Cristina Fernández de Kirchner (2007 to 2015). Women also played a strong role in the Montoneros, the Peronist armed struggle organization of the 1970s.

After a cycle of social movement mobilization that began with the Cordobazo of 1969 and included the disastrous return of Peronism to office (1973 to 1976), a brutal military coup in 1976 initiated a counter-revolutionary wave. Trade unionists and other activists were hounded down alongside the guerrilla fighters who were the ostensible enemies. This was a very "masculine" regime, and one of its claimed aims was to "defend the family" from communism, feminism and all other alien ideologies. One of the first social movements, formed in 1977, that created some resistance was the Madres de Plaza de Mayo (Mothers of Plaza de Mayo), so-called because they began their campaign to make the regime accountable for the "disappearance" of their sons and daughters by walking around the central square in downtown Buenos Aires with white handkerchiefs covering their heads. Their claim to be "just" mothers was both real and a tactic to avoid repression, which they did for a while, but not for long. Eventually they became more "political" and acted as the conscience of a society that had tolerated the most brutal forms of repression.

The Madres have been much studied, and there is considerable debate around their "maternal" version of resistance politics. The subsequent political evolution of the Madres after the return of democracy in 1983 and the resurgence of

Peronism in 1989 would point against any essentialist maternalism as a characterization. Nevertheless, as a women's movement, composed of mothers, it did develop a unique and potent identity. It was, of course, closely linked to the nascent human rights movement, which it both empowered and depended on for wider support. The Madres introduced a new absolute into the politics of Argentina: the return of their sons and daughters alive. With the return of democratization, they continued their campaign very effectively, both to recover their grandchildren from the repressors families they had been given to after their mothers were killed and for the unconditional punishment of all those responsible for the repression. They played a major role in shifting the discourse away from the notion that both left and right were responsible for the "dirty war".

Much later, after democracy was consolidated, another women's movement emerged in Argentina in 2015, Ni una menos (Not one more woman killed). It is well to remember the patriarchal nature of society in Argentina, where divorce was introduced only in 1987 and abortion was illegal until 2020. The immediate cause of Ni una menos was a series of brutal femicides in the final days of Cristina's government. Its promoters included a number of prominent feminist journalists, lawyers and artists. The first demonstration brought over 300,000 people out onto the streets of Buenos Aires. The organizers made the most of their cultural capital, and the campaign spread like wildfire. It also expanded its definition of gender-based violence beyond femicide to take up free and safe abortion, sexual harassment and, in association with some trade unions, the gendered nature of the violence caused by economic adjustment.

Ni una menos is, arguably, a precursor of a new international "digital" feminist wave: a single-issue campaign, partly social-media driven, partly the result of old-fashioned cross-sector organizing. It is democratic in its way of operating and inherently transnational, having had an exemplary impact in Latin America but also in Southern Europe. It has led to sentencing reform in Argentina and hotline services being set up for women at risk of domestic violence. Above all – as the Madres did for another era – Ni una menos has shifted the terms of the debate around gender in Argentina. That the right-wing government of Mauricio Macri (who replaced Cristina as president in 2015) lent enthusiastic support to the movement might be worrying at one level, but it also shows the considerable political and discursive impact this recent women's movement has had in Argentina. Through Ni una menos, Latin American feminism joined the global women's movement with a distinctive approach.

In taking a longer-term historical view of women's social movements in Argentina since 2001, we would need to factor in women organizing in the community, as unemployed organizers (*piqueteros*) and in the occupied factory movement. It could be seen as a "womanist" approach to assume that women everywhere would promote "women's interests" when they engaged in social movements. This approach has focused on the articulation between different social milieus and movements, however, which does allow us to develop a distinctive politics of gender and citizenship in Latin America. Arguing along these lines, Graciela Di Marco proposes we should "foreground ... the process of building the 'feminist people', a notion that refers to the chain of equivalence that allowed for the emergence of a people, exceeding the category woman, while also acknowledging that women's movements were a nodal point for its constitution".[4] This *pueblo feminista* (feminist people) would thus stand counterposed to a masculinist Catholic/integralist people, opposed to women's rights and democracy. A clear discursive divide was thus established.

In the popular assemblies following the 2001 crises, as in the struggle by the unemployed to secure decent benefits, women predominated, sometimes massively. These women based their practical politics on the principles of self-determination and autonomy. They demanded labour rights but also at the same time gender rights, as in their support of Ni una menos against all forms of gender-based violence. These demands can lead, following Di Marco, "to the formation of 'popular feminism' and laid the ground work for its articulation with women from other movements as well as some men in the constitution of the 'feminist people'".[5] In taking these movements to the streets, the new "popular feminism" has been truly transgressive of both the state order and liberal politics, representing a social movement of a new kind.

It is clear that there is not one women's movement in Argentina but, rather, a mosaic of various formations, ranging from left factions, feminist strands, liberal feminisms, women in popular movements and gender-based violence activists. This should warn us against any forms of essentialism – that is, the idea that there are single, unified, women's interests. It also alerts us, though, to the power and creativity of the women's and feminist social movements and the disruptive but also constructive power they may have. The question of Peronism – and the broader national-popular discourse mentioned above – alerts us also against facile transpositions of Northern feminist paradigms to the very different reality of Latin America.

Feminism and the state (Brazil)

The feminist movement in Brazil traces its roots back to the middle of the nineteenth century. It petitioned for female suffrage to be included in the 1894 republican constitution, but was unsuccessful. In the 1920s the Brazilian Federation for the Advancement of Women (affiliated to the International Women Suffrage Alliance) began a campaign, which was successful in 1932 under Vargas. The 1934 constitution (strongly influenced by this campaign) declared equal rights and equal pay/working conditions for men and women. The citizens' constitution of 1988 – developed during a wave of democratization – extended these rights, with women having equal rights with regard to agrarian reform. Access to abortion is still severely restricted, however, and the levels of violence against women are high. This is the context in which the contemporary feminist movement emerged after the long military dictatorship that came to power in 1964, as part of a decade or so of popular mobilization.

The military coup of 1964 intensified its repressive nature in 1969 with a "coup within a coup", which severely impacted feminism's ability to pursue practical and strategic gender needs. There were certainly mobilizations as part of the wider community-based struggles around the cost of living. It was around 1975, however – not coincidentally International Women's Year – that an explicitly feminist movement began to emerge. Its early activists included women who had been part of the armed struggle organizations, active between 1969 and 1973, who returned from exile with experience of Northern feminist movements. The dominant political discourse was an orthodox Marxist one that prioritized women's integration into the workforce and into the broader anti-capitalist struggle. Around issues such as day-care, however, it found common cause with women's earlier mobilizations in the community.

An autonomous women's movement began to emerge in the 1980s, and it rapidly forged links with other social movements such as the trade unions and various groups in the community. By now, as Alvarez recounts, there was "a significant degree of ideological consensus on the fact that women's movements needed to focus on how gender power relations, as well as class relations ... affected women's lives in all social groups and classes".[6] There had previously been a divide between the feminism of the professional groups and the assumed maternalism of popular women. Now the latter were seen to be perfectly able to articulate strategic as well as practical gender needs. As was common elsewhere, poor, indigenous and working-class women were also motivated by issues such as contraception and gender-based violence as much as by the "practical" issues of housing and the cost of living.

With the re-emergence of political parties as moves towards democratization accelerated, the divisions within the feminist and women's movements came to the fore. Party politics was still seen as a male domain, even with the PT, which was beginning to shape up as a left pole of attraction. Autonomous or even independent feminism did not find this a conducive milieu to advance the cause of women. This began to change gradually, mainly as a result of active feminist lobbying. The economism of the left and its political vanguardism were gradually muted as the feminist message sunk in, though political calculation was also in operation. The shift in the PT's position and its endorsement of reproductive rights, as Alvarez puts it, "reflected the significant impact that woman's movements organisations had on political society's gender discourses".[7] Even so, the role of the Catholic Church in the formation of the PT prevented it from immediately endorsing the decriminalization of abortion. We see here how there can be clear contradictions within the broad umbrella of progressive social movements.

At its first party congress, in 1991, the PT, under pressure from an active feminist lobby, decided on a 30 per cent women's quota for all internal decision-making bodies. The PT rapidly advanced towards a clear progressive understanding of the gendered nature of citizenship. Class essentialism – and the centring of the proletariat as revolutionary subject – was gradually set aside. This strategic shift equipped the PT well for its role in local government, which included several state capitals by the early 1990s. Women's practical and strategic gender needs were addressed in a number of novel ways, not least through the famous "participatory budgets". As Fiona Macaulay puts it, "The centrality of the politics of everyday life, of neighbourhood/consumption as well as workplace/production issues of citizenship, of 'popular empowerment' in the PT, demasculinises politics."[8]

In parallel with these positive experiences on the ground, this period also witnessed a shift in the priorities and *modus operandi* of the dominant women's movements. Organizing for the Fourth World Conference on Women, held in Beijing in 1995, and its aftermath led to a reconfiguration of feminism that Alvarez has referred to as "NGOization", which, under cover of improving effectiveness, steadily deradicalized the movement. The social movement aspect declined as "professionalization", foreign funding and an external orientation were now prioritized. In the emerging, still basically neoliberal democracies of Latin America, the notion of liberal citizenship was clearly dominant. The NGOs (most often linked to what was becoming known as "global civil society") became central agents of the gender agenda and squeezed out more radical, but less well-funded, alternative modalities. The gap between this professionalized/transnationalized layer and the grass roots became more pronounced, and working-class women were again placed in the role of "clients" or supplicants.

The turn towards the state to answer the demands of the women's movement produced mixed results. The CNDM (Conselho Nacional dos Direitos da Mulher: National Council for Women's Rights) was established after the fall of the military regime in 1985, and was a high-level recognition of the feminist agenda. It was able to incorporate the vast majority of its demands into the 1988 constitution. The government of Fernando Henrique Cardoso (1995 to 2002) was less committed to the gender agenda, however, and the CNDM was downgraded to a secretariat, regaining ministerial status (along with racial inequality and human rights) only in 2015. The PT governments from 2003 to 2016 did see, however, the much more ambitious National Plan of Policies for

Women coming into effect. This positioning of gender to the centre ground was reversed by the de facto government of Michel Temer in 2016 and, even more, by the election of the far-right candidate Jair Bolsonaro in 2019 on a Christian "pro-family" ticket.

In Brazil we have seen a clear distinction between a feminist movement (*movimento feminista*) and a women's movement (*movimento de mulheres*). The latter was sometimes viewed by the first as too diffuse and open to manipulation by the Churches and the sectarian left. Feminist movements, for their part, would still be accused of being "middle class" and representing a politics divorced from an abstract class struggle. Thus, for example, Mara García Castro argues that the "autonomous" or "radical" feminists have been co-opted by the powers of the state and basically, "institutionalized".[9] By focusing on "fixed identities and immediate rights", they have dissipated the potential of a unified women's movement under socialist feminist leadership. We do not need to accept the critique in full to realize it does capture something of the trajectory of Brazilian feminism since 1970. In that sense, these debates, which had an impact across Latin America, can still be usefully revisited.

Mujeres populares (Venezuela)

Prior to the Chavista "revolution" of 1999, Venezuela had a small feminist movement, as was the case in most countries of the region. But, with Chávez declaring "I am a feminist" and the Chavista government claiming that feminism was integral to its project, feminism entered another domain. What we need to assess here is the significance of the massive entry of *mujeres populares* (working-class women) into the political process. Was this simply a political co-option project? Was it just a form of institutionalized and bureaucratic feminism created from above? As with the overall Chavista political process, there are no simple answers; most attempts at simple answers have been found to be contradicted by the facts. The unprecedented engagement of and by women in the Chavista process, I would argue, is one of the most important women's movements, in the broad sense, that we have seen in recent decades, and it certainly repays close attention.

Women were, arguably, incorporated into the Chavista process through a squarely "maternalist" discourse. This maternalist ideology promoted gender policies that aimed to maintain women in the home. It was an essentialist view of women as homemakers and childbearers and, in relation to the proclaimed Chavista revolution, builders of the nation and of place. This view is well expressed by the head of the Soy Mujer (I Am a Woman) programme, for whom "when one says I am a woman it is saying I am home, I am family, so that the woman can, form her home and with her family, develop".[10] Promoting public policies to keep women in the home and defining their development in terms of their family role can hardly be called feminist. Nevertheless, it was a powerful reformist programme, combined with other measures to address practical gender needs.

The Chávez government, essentially, saw itself addressing practical gender needs. Thus, for example, the mothers from the Misión Barrio Adentro provided financial support, job training and sex education for several hundred thousand female slum dwellers. The Children of Venezuela mission provided stipends to low-income pregnant women and to families of disabled children. Yanahir Reyes, who was a community educator in this milieu and a supporter of Chávez, provides an insight into the politics of this drive to advance practical gender needs.[11] Reyes argues that, "although we haven't had 50 per cent representation in politics, women are participating in different political spaces. Chávez left us a wide, ready-made path, to continue constructing and consolidating equal relations. Clearly Chávez benefited women more than anyone else."[12] This issue, and the argument posed, take us back to the notion of empowerment: can an outside agency substitute for the self-organization of and consciousness building by someone else?

Chávez, it is well to remember, had committed to building "twenty-first-century socialism" in Venezuela. This meant increasing social ownership, creating workplace democracy and directing production to satisfying social needs. It was under that last rubric that some of the country's oil wealth was directed towards the *misiones sociales* (social missions) designed to expand access to education and health care. Women were the main beneficiaries of the *misiones* and their main drivers on the ground. Women mobilized and entered the public political sphere as never before. Reyes argues that "during Chavismo, each day, women are creating a very important transformative process. In the area of nutrition ... which has to do with people assuming political responsibility for their diet, women take leadership. The issues of nutrition, education and grassroots work all had a woman's face, the transformation and revolution have a woman's face."[13]

The question, though, is whether a "woman's face" means it is a women's movement or addresses strategic gender needs. Except in relation to gender-based violence, there were no significant moves forward in this domain, and, even in terms of gender-based violence, Venezuela only kept pace with the rest of Latin America. The mobilization of women at grass-roots level and in the local political structures of Chavismo did not translate into national political gains. We could argue that having women participate in government-sponsored soup kitchens was no different from what had occurred under neoliberal regimes and can hardly be seen as a gain for women. The issue, then, is whether these women were actually building spaces of gendered democratic community participation. The sustainability of Chavismo was perhaps always in question – because of its reliance on oil wealth and the charismatic leader not least – but there is no reason to write off the political experience of the *mujeres populares* in Venezuela because they did not follow a recognizably socialist or radical feminist development path. There is clearly a mixed and contradictory experience here to be studied in more detail at local level and in different periods.

The critique of Chavista "feminism" was developed by various feminist currents in Venezuela, not all part of the political opposition, who would have had obvious reasons to be sceptical. Thus, the feminist collective Comadres Purpuras (Purple Comrades) argues that, "during the Chavista period, a significant number of young women ended up being co-opted ... Instead of an organized struggles for woman's rights, what happened was an organization of young women in different posts that worked only for the mobilizations called by Chávez."[14] From this perspective, all the advances for women achieved under Chávez – laws against gender-based violence, the creation of the Woman's Development Bank and the Ministry for Women's Affairs, and social advances – were negated by their instrumental purpose. Chavismo from this perspective (a Chavista feminist one) in practice consolidated patriarchy and entrenched the dominance of men in Venezuelan society. Political developments since the death of Chávez in 2013 seem to corroborate this assessment, with the authoritarian turn of the government and the openly instrumental approach to mobilization.

Notwithstanding the criticisms by "Chavista feminism", the massive incorporation of woman into the *consejos comunales* (communal councils) had a transformative effect. Just as there was a "feminization of poverty" under the previous neoliberal order, so, under Chavismo, as Sara Motta puts it, there was a "feminization of resistance".[15] The poverty alleviation programmes under Chávez, the missions, combined the provision of public goods with an education programme influenced by liberation theology, all adding up to a transformative moment in Venezuela's history. Women were the drivers of the *misiones* and of the *barrio* resistance against the attempted coup against Chávez in 2002. This empowerment of women – and the addressing of strategic as well as practical gender needs – was in contradiction with the official government feminine discourse of nurturing and self-sacrifice.

To be clear, many women who participated in the Chavista *proceso* did not necessarily identify as Chavistas. They may have just been involved in soup kitchens. They may have even engaged on the basis of a maternalist understanding of women's nurturing and family responsibility roles. But Sujatha Fernandes notes that "they have stories of identity that come from the barrios or parish and which form the basis of alternative social and community networks".[16] These dense community-based and territorial networks go back at least to the citywide insurrection of the Caracazo in 1989, which represented an early massive rebellion against neoliberalism. This set of events was a founding myth for

Chavismo but it is also part of a broader history of community organizing and the creation of semi-liberated territories in the Venezuelan capital. The story of women organizing in Venezuela cannot be reduced, then, to that of the small feminist groups linked to the parties of the left.

Global sisterhood (transnational)

Since the 1980s Latin American feminisms have gone regional, and then "gone global". How does this transnational engagement impact on the politics of the domestic feminist/women's movement? I trace briefly here the turn beyond the national domain and explore some of its consequences for current transnational social movement debates and practice.

In the mid-1970s there was a gradual realization in parts of Latin American feminism that the nation state could not be the limit of its engagement with society. A series of regional *encuentros* (encounters, gatherings) were organized on a biannual basis in various Latin American cities from 1981 onwards. Experiences were shared, different tendencies vied for hegemony, and some common ground was found. Overall, the transnational turn at the regional level empowered the participants and added a degree of cross-fertilization across the various national experiences. The ground was being set for a transnational turn in Latin American feminism.

For the first *encuentro*, held in Bogotá in 1981, Alvarez notes how "word spread through established international feminist networks, primarily reaching white, middle-class, university-educated women".[17] The wider women's movements were not reached, so transnationalism began as an elite domain of politics. Indigenous and rural women were particularly noticeable by their absence. This had changed towards the end of the decade, and Alvarez recounts how, at the 1986 *encuentro* in Taxco (Mexico), there was "a massive presence of poor and working class women".[18] This was not without tensions, as some of the original feminist organizers now themselves felt marginalized. Transnationalism can create synergies, advance positions and create common ground but it can also exacerbate tensions when women from very different backgrounds – such as Southern Cone academics and Central American ex-combatants – come together.

These tensions were to take on a different character in the 1990s, as both democratization and neoliberalism deepened their grip across Latin America. The new development regime promoted the classic feminist demand of "autonomy" – or empowerment – which fitted in with the neoliberal emphasis on the individual. The downside, as Schild puts it, is that "the language of contention has … been transformed into a tool of regulation: 'autonomy' and 'equality' are now redefined through a liberal discourse of individual rights that is focused on empowerment thought the market".[19] At the political level, this turn translated into a form of global liberal feminism that assumed common purpose across regions. This culminated in the 1995 Beijing conference, at which much of the diversity of Latin American feminism was subsumed under the discourse of "global sisterhood".

The Beijing process in Latin America – that is to say, the regional preparation for this global event – created, or deepened, divisions in Latin American feminisms. There was a growing strand moving towards a privileged relationship with international agencies. They began to act as "consultants" and became mediators between global civil society and the women's movements on the ground. The new democratic regimes in Latin America also acted in a way that tended towards the co-option of key activists, even as key feminist themes were mainstreamed in political discourse. Alvarez has referred to "the absorption of some of the more culturally acceptable items of the feminist agenda".[20] After Beijing – driven by the new feminist NGOs – the informal *encuentros* of the 1980s were replaced by more formal and professional (in terms of participants and *modus operandi*) *redes* (networks), which would prioritize the transnational domain for political and funding reasons.

The transnational orientation of Latin American feminisms was inseparable from the rise of what became known as "global civil society", and the international aid regime oriented towards it, as a "soft" form of neoliberalism, to counter the harsh image of the structural adjustment policies. The construction of civil society was part of the support for democratization in Latin America, but it was also an objective for the newly emergent neoliberalism in the 1980s. What was defined as "civil society" – a vague catch-all term referring to all that stood between the economy and the state – was also part of the drive to reduce the effectiveness of the developmental state and enhance the role of the market. Its impact on Latin American feminisms was a certain level of co-option and depoliticization as professionalization drove out or marginalized working-class women. There is a lesson here for all transnational social movements, in so far as success in one sense can spell a setback in other terms, in this case shifting a radical social movement into a more ambiguous international NGO domain.

7

INDIGENOUS

If there is one movement that symbolizes the "new" social movement ethos in Latin America it is probably the indigenous people's movement or movements. Arguably, in Bolivia and Ecuador they are the most important social movements active today, but we must be wary of generalizing, in so far as Peru – with a higher Amerindian proportion of the population – has not experienced similar movements. One argument accounting for the rise of the indigenous movements is that the shift from the corporatist state to the neoliberal model in the 1990s encouraged "ethnic" or identity demands. Nevertheless, Carmen Martínez Novo, based on her research and that of others, concludes that, in Ecuador anyway, "the desire for inclusion and social mobility are stronger motivations in indigenous cultural politics than the search for difference, which might only be a means of achieving the first objective".[1] In other words, the "new" indigenous movements, seen even as postmodern by some commentators, may have objectives akin to that of the very "old" labour movement and are not "new" purely identity-based movements with a cultural rather than socio-economic perspective. Their liminal position thus makes them a particularly illuminating case study.

For neoliberalism, formal political equality meant recognizing the individual and cultural rights of indigenous peoples, especially when promoted by NGOs, so long as it did not impinge on economic policy-making. Thus, decentralization (as the state retreated) and the encouragement of a depoliticized civil society enabled indigenous mobilizations, but then, in practice, their demands could not be met. This led to the emergence of powerful indigenous movements in Ecuador and Bolivia. In the first country some dubious political alliances that led them to support a military coup detracted from their democratic credentials and set them back considerably. In Bolivia, by contrast, the indigenous movement was able to craft a solid set of social and political alliances with non-indigenous sectors, the trade unions, the Church and some NGOs to create a sustainable social movement and the landslide victory of Evo Morales in 2005. The relationship between the indigenous movements and the left governments of Morales and that of Correa in Ecuador have not always been smooth, but that is not surprising from a political rather than essentialist perspective. But the determinant is always politics and not some form of new "identity politics" that trumps all.

The new indigenous movements in Latin America have placed the state under interrogation. They question whether the nation state as currently constructed, and with its colonialist origins, can properly represent all the citizens. The neoliberal state's acceptance of multiculturalism is but a thin form of democracy and not necessarily an advance on the previous corporatist state prior to 1980. This version of multiculturalism celebrates a folkloric "other" while denouncing the actual indigenous activists as fundamentalists. We cannot, on the other hand, conflate all indigenous movements with a benign pluralist civil society that is always democratic. Indigenous movements always engage in politics, internally, with the various actors of the national polity and, increasingly, transnationally. Their politics will be, necessarily, complex and often contradictory.

The indigenous movements in Latin America have sparked some of the most interesting debates on the nature of social movements and how best to study them. It is well to remember that it is as recently as in 1982 that the United Nations began discussions around the draft Universal Declaration of the Rights of Indigenous Peoples, and completed deliberations only in 1990. So, to what extent do developments in Latin America reflect these transnational debates and vice versa? Deborah Yashar also asks, pointedly, "What are the conditions under which strong ethnic identities are compatible with, and support, democracy?"[2] We might ask in addition not only if this is a single indigenous movement but, also, whether there is a clear-cut demarcation between indigenous and *mestizo* ("mixed-race") communities, as is sometimes assumed.

We start this chapter with an outline of the influential indigenous movements in Bolivia and their links with the broader social struggles and with the leftist governments of Evo Morales (2006 to 2019). I pay particular attention to what Bolivia's sociologist and one-time vice-president Alvaro García Linera has called the "creative tensions" therein between the social movements and the political system. The next section is centred on the rise of the influential Pachakutik indigenous movement/political party in Ecuador, its alliances and its even more fraught relations with the progressive government of Rafael Correa (2007 to 2017). We then turn to the indigenous movements of Mexico, which have a long history and are quite diverse. Inevitably, however, attention is centred on the indigenous social/political movement of Chiapas, the EZLN (Ejército Zapatista de Liberación Nacional: Zapatista Army of National Liberation): the Zapatistas, who created a liberated territory they control to this day. Behind the overinflated rhetoric of Zapatista studies we examine the conditions from which the movement emerged as well as its successes and limitations as an indigenous movement. Finally, we turn to the Zapatistas in terms of their international reception: a unique confluence between a Latin American indigenous movement and the global justice movement that was emerging in the mid- to late 1990s.

Indigenous hegemony (Bolivia)

Bolivia is the country in Latin America with one of the highest indigenous proportions in the population, at over 60 per cent. There is a long history of indigenous social movements in the country, particularly since the national revolution of 1952. Historically, there have been two main strands of indigenous discourse: *indianismo*, based on ethnic identification and opposed to the once dominant trade union mode of struggle; and *Katarismo* (after the Aymara leader Tupac Katari, who was executed in 1781), which combines ethnic and class consciousness and is open to alliances with the trade unions and others, in pursuit of state reform. Given the social composition of Bolivia, the indigenous and peasant social movements have often in practice been fused. This movement has been particularly important since the mid-1980s, when the once powerful miners' union – the proletarian backbone of the 1952 revolution – went into decline as mining was run down and many ex-miners turned to cultivation, including the coca leaf.

From the mid-1980s onwards the neoliberal programme of government dismantled the state sector and led the informal work sector to grow to 70 per cent of total employment. Popular discontent began to grow from the mid-1990s and renewed the combative traditions of the 1952 revolution, as well as expressing a new wave of *indigenismo*. New social movements were beginning to emerge, not least in terms of organizing the coca growers, which included many of the redundant miners. There was a rapid crescendo of struggles from 2000 onwards. The privatization of water in the city of Cochabamba led to the famous "water wars" in 2000, led by indigenous social movements, which put together a true mass anti-neoliberal coalition. At the same time there was a semi-insurrectionary movement by the Aymara peasantry of the highlands, which, through mass mobilization and road blockages, placed these indigenous peasants firmly on the political map again.

The social demands of the mass movement led to the emergence of a "political instrument", as it was called, namely the MAS (Movimiento al Socialismo: Movement towards Socialism), in the 1990s; it was formally launched in 1999. It began as a rural-based party, reliant largely on the coca growers on the fringes of legality, but it broadened its support base later. In the 2002 elections its leader, Evo Morales (an indigenous small farmer), came in a surprising second, but in 2005 he actually won, with nearly 55 per cent of the vote, and became president early the next year. His government's main planks were set by the social movements and included the nationalization of gas, the calling of a national assembly and the end to impunity for all state repressors. Morales held a pivotal role as mediator between a by now professionalized party and its urban wing and the indigenous peasant movements, which had created the party and catapulted it to victory.

Morales' government launched an ambitious reformist programme. It reasserted Bolivian sovereignty over the country's natural resources and addressed the highly unequal distribution of wealth. The neoliberal economic model was replaced by one that said it was "social, communitarian and productive". The rent and profits generated by the mining and hydrocarbon sectors began to be diverted to small-scale manufacturing and social spending. By 2010 extreme poverty levels had fallen from 38 to 25 per cent and the gap between the richest 10 per cent of the population and the poorest 10 per cent had fallen from 130 times to 60 times.[3] Compared to Ecuador there was a much stronger rapport between the government and the social movements, particularly the indigenous movement, which was the foundation and base of a new indigenous-popular hegemonic order.

Not surprisingly, the relationship between the Evo Morales government and the social movements did not always go smoothly. Alvaro García Linera, vice-president of Bolivia for the whole Morales period but also a Marxist sociologist, referred to these relationships as ones characterized by "creative tensions". There were fierce clashes with the miners' union and with indigenous communities around environmental issues. And, certainly, many viewed the MAS and participation in the state/government as a path towards upwards social mobility. In the early period of the Morales government (2006 to 2009) the main conflicts were with the right wing and separatism in the eastern provinces. Since then, particularly since the 2010 *gasolinazo* (successful protests against the removal of state subsidies on gas), some social movements have, quite naturally, clashed with the government around specific issues and demands.

The importance of the Morales period is that it inevitably invited engagement and critique, not least from the transnational solidarity movement. The list of criticisms was quite extensive: the middle class had expanded, unionization had declined, unnecessary concessions had been made to the Eastern elites, business interests had been favoured, the role of social movements had diminished, traditional clientelism has been reinforced and there had been "a pragmatic emphasis on outcomes and immediate needs".[4] The basic argument was that, although it was conceded that there had been improvements, the social movements had been demobilized. This view was contradicted, however, by the flourishing of oppositional social mobilizations that the critics pointed to. The underlying critique was that Morales was not building socialism and his government was, essentially, another form of neoliberalism.

A forthright critic, Jeffrey Webber, has argued that, "since Morales came to office in January 2006, the government has implemented a political economy rooted in a reconstructed neoliberalism".[5] Far from a situation characterized by "creative tensions", Webber argues that the government was marked by "patterns of political and ideological containment, co-option and pacification".[6] It would be naïve to deny that any progressive political movement would seek to contain social mobilization outside its control or to co-opt the leaders of contestatory social movements. We cannot escape the sense that this criticism lacks realism, however, in not recognizing the national and international context, and simply imposes a purist socialism from the outside on a very complex and, of course, conflictual political process.

It is not a question of "defending" the Morales government but of understanding it. We can note, for example, that, although the MAS and Morales were not the main protagonists of the "water wars" in Cochabamba and the "gas war" in El Alto, "they were the only ones capable of constructing a political project and an electoral programme where all the unsatisfied demands of the popular sectors and the subaltern classes could find space", as Paula Klachko and Katu Arkonada put it.[7] Morales had proved to be adept at balancing the reforming drive of the social movements and the *realpolitik* of the international order. To fault him for being financially prudent seems somewhat beside the point. A realist interpretation of the Morales period would probably show considerably more successes than failures. The acid test, of course, will be the fate of the social movements after Morales and whether they will emerge stronger or weaker, as the critics fear. The dramatic events of 2019, with Evo Morales being driven out by a right-wing civil/military coup, have changed the parameters of this debate, of course, but it will still be possible to determine whether the left turn reflected the priorities of the social movements or falsely misled them, as the anti-statists of left and right alike argue.

Indigenous movements and the state (Ecuador)

Ecuador witnessed in the 1990s the most significant indigenous social movement in Latin America to date. In a country where between 25 per cent and 45 per cent of the total population of 16.6 million are classified as indigenous, the umbrella organization CONAIE (Confederación de Nacionalidades Indígenas del Ecuador: Confederation of Indigenous Nationalities of Ecuador) was able to organize nearly 80 per cent of the indigenous population. The largest ethnic grouping in Ecuador is the Quichua, who are related to the Quechua peoples of Bolivia and Peru. The highland Quichua population is predominant but there is also a significant Quichua presence in the Amazon, along with other smaller distinct, often isolated, groupings. CONAIE has offered a balanced overall umbrella to all the indigenous groups in Ecuador, and successfully overcame an earlier period in which left-wing groupings tended to manipulate their internal politics for party political advantage.

The history of indigenous peoples organizing in Ecuador can be traced back at least to the 1940s, when the Communist Party launched an organizing drive with the highland indigenous rural workers. This led to the creation of the Federación Ecuatoriana Indígena (Indigenous Ecuadorian Federation) in 1944, which was not led by indigenous workers but was committed to agrarian reform. The 1964 agrarian reform law ended the semi-feudal *huasipungo* (hacienda land leased for labour obligations) system and led to a wave of indigenous organizing for communal lands.[8] The Catholic Church was very active during the 1970s, with an emphasis on cultural identity rather than class issues. There was also the emergence of a new indigenous leadership, benefiting from improvements in the education system, that was better able to resist the patronage and attempts at co-option by conservative and left-wing parties alike.

A turning point in the emergence of an indigenous social movement came in 1990, with a national indigenous uprising directed at land and education issues but within a clear indigenous form of identity. The 1990s saw a steady increase in the level of CONAIE's organizational remit and strength. Militant actions included roadblocks, boycotts, government office occupations and even the kidnapping of government officials. By 1995, as Donna Cott recounts, "the movement had a long list of substantive achievements: control over a state-supported bilingual education program, the collective tilling of millions of hectares of land, and the repeal and rewriting of the agrarian reform law".[9] Following a classic dual strategy of social movement/political party activation, CONAIE launched a new political party in 1996, Pachakutik (literally, Quechua for "a change in the Sun"; thus a movement of the Earth that will bring a new era), for which hopes were initially very high.

In the political struggles since the mid-1990s Pachakutik has not, however, matched the spectacular rise of CONAIE as an indigenous social movement. At its first electoral outing, in 1996, it did make quite considerable gains, especially in areas with a large indigenous population. It thus translated CONAIE's considerable political capital and grass-roots organization onto the parliamentary arena. A right-wing populist, Abdalá Bucaram, became president, however, with some indigenous leaders in support. Bucaram's openly neoliberal economic policies led to a mass uprising, and he was removed in 1997. In the 1998 elections Pachakutik increased its electoral strength, with indigenous leader Nina Pzcasí becoming vice-president of the National Congress of Ecuador. This period closed with an attempted military-indigenous coup in 2000 against the government of President Jamil Mahuad. Its failure led to a reorientation towards local and regional politics, from which Pachakutik became one of the largest political parties.

Pachakutik was finding that electoral success and the principled formation of political alliance were harder to achieve than short-term mass mobilizations. When Lucio Gutiérrez became president, in 2003, he offered the indigenous party four Cabinet posts as a reward for its support. The problems of this alliance were soon to outweigh the benefits, and the president proved adept at exploiting divisions in the indigenous political movement. When in 2005 another popular uprising brought down the president, the indigenous movement played only a minor role in the mobilization. When Pachakutik put up its leader, Luis Macas, for the presidential list in 2006 this was publicly disavowed by the Amazonian indigenous group. In the end, outsider Rafael Correa, leader of the PAIS Alliance party, won easily and set about building the Citizens' Revolution, joining the turn to the left then sweeping Latin America, and steadily outflanked the indigenous social and political movements.

This phase (2000 to 2006) shows how the indigenous movement could gain power but also rapidly lose it. As Mark Becker puts it, "Through these gains and reversals, it became clear that indigenous movements were strong enough to bring governments down but not united enough to rule on their own – or even in alliance with others."[10] During his two terms in office, Correa made significant social and political gains. Inequality was reduced dramatically (particularly in urban areas) and health care and education increased. There was an independent foreign policy and the Citizen's Revolution promoted democratization in many areas of life. Correa did not achieve this social transformation in alliance with the indigenous social movement, however, which played an ambiguous role in the 2010 attempted coup against him, allowing Correa to accuse it of being a pawn of the right-wing parties and of US imperialism.

This is not the place to offer a full and nuanced appraisal of CONAIE as a once powerful indigenous social movement, but I can offer some points. The main question might revolve around the issue of multiculturalism and the indigenous movement's commitment to identity politics. In this regard, Emma Cervone has argued: "The Correa government offered a favourable conjuncture that apparently offered a possibility for social transformation, however we have not seen an indigenous political project that went beyond a rejection of neoliberal political economy."[11] The very ambiguity of the multicultural discourse – and its enthusiastic adoption by global neoliberalism – was also a weakness. Since then we have seen a turn in indigenous community politics away from ethnicity and towards concrete calls around social and economic reforms.

The events of October 2019 in Ecuador should caution us against hasty judgements on social movements, which are always developing in ways that are not always obvious to the observer. What began as a transport stoppage against an IMF-imposed fuel price rise soon became an indigenous uprising such as had not been seen for over 20 years. CONAIE had found new, younger leadership and a capacity to mobilize that was unstoppable. After ten days of occupying the national capital, Quito, the movement's demands were met and the fuel increase was annulled. The indigenous columns had come down from the highlands in a demonstration of strength and determination. They received support from students and workers, even from the middle classes, who were incensed by the curfew and the disproportionate repression being meted out, which included invasions of the universities, where the indigenous protestors took shelter at night. CONAIE emerged from this trial of strength greatly fortified, to become the single most important social actor in the country.

Comparing Ecuador to the Bolivian case can be instructive. It explains why an extremely powerful and effective indigenous social movement became disorientated and far from effective under Correa's progressive political regimen. Veronica Silva explains this in terms of the mistaken political alliances developed by CONAIE, which meant that, whereas "in Bolivia social moments and parties had equal bargaining power during negotiations … this is far from the case in Ecuador".[12] A strong political position held by a social movement can, in other words, be dissipated and the movement can become weakened and fragmented. The building of indigenous national-popular hegemony, as happened in Bolivia, is not automatic. In its absence, of course, politicians such as Correa will emerge who will successfully appeal directly to the urban poor and the impoverished middle class to offer a vision of national renaissance capable of mobilizing large sections of this population.

Revolt in Chiapas (Mexico)

There is no doubt that, as Neil Harvey puts in, "the key innovation of the EZLN has been to make recognition of the rights and cultures of the indigenous peoples an integral part of democratization in Mexico".[13] This movement needs to be seen in its context, however, and not mythologized, as has happened, to some extent, in the international literature. The Zapatista rebellion of 1994 created an opening for a national debate on indigenous self-determination, and the First Indigenous Congress was held in San Cristóbal de las Casas in 1996, with some 1,200 delegates representing over 300 distinct indigenous communities. Among the people of Oaxaca, community autonomy, based on ethnic and linguistic commonality, goes back to 1938. Currently there are also ongoing indigenous social movements active, particularly in Oaxaca, and in Guerrero, where important experiences of indigenous autonomy have had considerable impact.

The causes of the 1994 Zapatista rebellion are complex and not restricted to the actions of a small post-1968 "armed struggle" group, the EZLN. Harvey's survey of the literature concludes that the causes included "a combination of eco-logical crisis, lack of available productive land, the drying up of non-agricultural sources of income", on the one hand, and "the political and religious reorganiza-tion of religious communities since the 1960s and the rearticulation of ethnic identities with emancipatory political discourses",[14] on the other hand. All the contradictions of capitalist rural development were present in Lacandón forest areas but also a particularly active indigenous community, in which religious-driven organization in particular was very strong. These two forces came together precisely at the time when Mexico was on the eve of forming a single market with North America that would accentuate the contradiction.

The eruption on the national and international scene of the Zapatistas on 1 January 1994 was preceded by nearly 20 years of organizing. During this period the diocese of San Cristóbal de las Casas engaged in a dynamic organizing drive with the indigenous peasantry. Internal displacements from the area led to Chiapas becoming a centre of alternative thinking, manifest, for example, in the Coordinadora Nacional Plan de Ayala (Coordinator of the National Plan of Ayala). There was a steady build-up of mobilization against dams, vigils in the urban plazas and demonstrations. It was in this silent but determined move towards insurrection that the small EZLN appeared on the scene in the late 1980s, after a failed *foco* experience in the classic 1960s rural guerrilla model.

When the Zapatista revolt took place, after elaborate planning, it created an immediate material and discursive impression. The seizure of the public plazas in four cities and three towns in the state of Chiapas, including San Cristóbal, the once royal colonial capital, had an instant impact – as did the basic demand by the Zapatistas, which could have been written by Emiliano Zapata in 1910: "Work, land, housing, food, heath, education, independence, freedom, democracy, justice and peace." Even the right to bear arms had historical resonance and widespread legitimacy, which prevented full-scale war by the state against the risen people. The symbolism of several thousand armed indigenous peasants entering the public plaza was not missed, as Adolfo Gilly recounts how "the image transmitted to the entire country, prior to any proclamation, was that this was an Indian rebellion. It was not a traditional guerrilla movement, it wasn't a *foco*, it wasn't even a mutiny or a disorderly agitation."[15]

The achievements of the Zapatistas have been considerable, not least in demonstrating in practice that "another world is possible", as the World Social Forum articulated. Once the initial realization that a march on Mexico City, like that realized by Emiliano Zapata and Pancho Villa in 1914, was not going to be possible, the Zapatistas set about building "autonomous municipalities" in Chiapas. The rebel municipalities were based on Juntas de Buen Gobierno (Good Governance Communities), known colloquially as *caracoles* (snails) – a Zapatista mascot. The *caracoles* meet in assembly and elect (and deselect) their representatives, who are tasked with managing education, health and community safety/justice. All families contribute time to the collective endeavour and food is shared. Emigration out of Chiapas is still an important feature of this indigenous community, however. And it is still encircled militarily and isolated politically.

In a comparative study of the MST and the Zapatistas, Vergara-Camus concludes that "the MST's more pragmatic politics of alliance has probably yielded more short-term results than the Zapatista maximalist one".[16] In a sense, the EZLN refuses the definition of politics as the "art of the possible". What the utopian separatism of the Zapatistas has demonstrated is an extraordinary resilience and capacity to survive. In terms of its composition, we need to distinguish the EZLN (still subject to a Leninist military discipline) and the indigenous social movement it coexists uneasily with. The politicization and experience of direct democracy achieved in the Zapatista communities has had a long-lasting effect over the last 25 years, locally, nationally and globally (see "Zapatismo" section below).

There are considerable limitations to the Zapatista experience, however. The sheer time that has elapsed since the uprising – a quarter of a century – in some ways "normalizes" Zapatismo. It did not achieve its national objectives and its remit geographically is quite restricted. Indigenous autonomy cannot be achieved in a small, isolated community. At a minimum, a regional-level influence would be required for that to be viable. Nor has poverty been seriously reduced in the Zapatista-controlled areas, even if health and education levels have improved considerably. The experience of Cuba – and the restrictions on, if not impossibility of, building "socialism in one island" – needs to make us sceptical of Zapatismo as a way forward for Mexico's indigenous peoples.

The Zapatistas have managed to create an exemplary struggle that has united indigenous, agrarian and gender struggles. The articulation of land and democracy with indigenous rights is a signal achievement. The weakness has lain in the implementation of this discursive success. Basically, the Zapatistas – under cover of their vison of "autonomy" – have shown a quite sectarian attitude towards other progressive political forces in Mexico. Thus, in the political mobilization Otra Campaña (Other Campaign), Zapatismo mobilized a vast layer of young people against the candidacy of Andrés Manuel López Obrador in 2006, who lost by a narrow margin. The Zapatistas in doing so also turned their back on the other major indigenous movement, APPO (Asamblea Popular de los Pueblos de Oaxaca: Popular Assembly of the Peoples of Oaxaca), and the democratic opposition within the trade union movement (Diálogo Nacional: National Dialogue), which had thrown their weight behind López Obrador's democratic movement, which eventually succeeded in gaining the presidency in 2018.

Zapatismo

Zapatismo as a transnational cultural political movement is, arguably, distinct from the indigenous movement that emerged on the territory of Chiapas
in Mexico. The Zapatistas were variously called the "first post-communist
rebellion", the "first informational guerrilla movement"[17] or, more prosaically,
"armed democrats". They were, in a sense, all of these and none of these. The
Zapatista rebellion, for a start, is simply incomprehensible outside the context
of the history of the Mexican Revolution. When an indigenous army marched
in to take over San Cristóbal de las Casas in 1994, it immediately and automatically triggered a historical folk memory of Villa and Zapata's peasant armies
marching into Mexico City in 1914. This points to the crucial role of discourse in
constructing and understanding Zapatismo. As Adolfo Gilly puts it: "The EZLN
has inaugurated a debate about discourse, within discourse and through discourse."[18] The mobilization of the Zapatistas and their construction as an international pole of attraction is, fundamentally, a discursive construction. Gilly
refers to the Zapatistas as a "singular combination of ancient myths, mobilized
communities, clandestine army, *golpes de escena*, literary resources, and political
initiatives".[19] It is a unique and complex concatenation of social force, ideas and
political circumstances that produced Zapatismo. It is not, realistically, a new
transnational model for revolution in the era of globalization. The international
communication of the Zapatista revolt is, however, the most significant single
episode of global solidarity since the Spanish Civil War in the 1930s. For this to
have occurred, Zapatismo must have touched certain chords, in particular creating a general "democratic equivalent" that served to create common ground
for various diverse struggles against globalization. In this sense, Zapatismo
is seeking neither to reconstruct a mythical past nor to pursue a totally utopian future. Rather, Zapatismo has clearly articulated "*Ya basta!*" ("Enough is
enough!") to neoliberal globalization and its failure to create a modernization
process characterized by social inclusion and basic human dignity.

In the mid-1990s – as neoliberal globalization was getting into its stride –
the Zapatista revolt achieved a certain "re-enchanting of the world". Another
world seemed possible; history had not come to an end. What this led to was
a remarkable flourishing of a transnational Zapatista solidarity network, which
is our main interest in this section. What was most remarkable – and most
interesting to the theme of globalization and contestation – was the speed at
which this solidarity movement spread and consolidated its activities. Harry
Cleaver, a radical US economist at the heart of this movement, describes how "it
took six years to build the anti-war in the 60s, it took 6 months to build the anti-
war movement in the Gulf War, and it took six days to build an anti-Mexican
government movement in 1994".[20] The transnational Zapatista support network

went through various phases. During 1994 the transnational Zapatista solidarity network began to take shape around the activity of international activists who arrived in Mexico to protest against the state repression of the Zapatista revolt. In 1995, according to Thomas Olesen's meticulous history, "the transnational Zapatista solidarity network starts to develop an infrastructure of its own. The very intense activities in this phase are mainly aimed at monitoring the human rights situation in Chiapas following the Mexican army's invasion of EZLN territory in February 1995."[21] In subsequent years the network became intensely politicized as Zapatismo became, to some extent, a transnational (albeit mainly virtual) social movement. There were also intense phases of more traditional "solidarity" work, as, for example, subsequent to the Acteal massacre in December 1997. There have also been fairly quiescent periods, and, more recently, a move by the Zapatistas to regain some control over their rather disparate international support networks.

This remarkable internet movement or network of transnational solidarity has not been without its critics on the left. Judith Hellman advances a coherent critique in the *Socialist Register 2000*, where she argues that "virtual Chiapas holds a seductive attraction for disenchanted and discouraged people on the left that is fundamentally different than the appeal of the struggles underway in the real Chiapas".[22] There, on the ground, not everyone is a "Zapatista", there are divisions and weaknesses, and *realpolitik* did not always reflect the seductive political rhetoric of Subcomandante Marcos (an EZLN spokesman) online. Nor is "civil society" such a homogeneous and progressive milieu as the international supporters of Zapatismo might believe. There are romanticized, essentialized views of indigenous peoples permeating the virtual Zapatismo, and vicarious participation through transnational solidarity may well act as a roadblock to grass-roots activism, according to this critical perspective.

In the *Socialist Register 2001*, Justin Paulson, an active member of the Zapatista solidarity movement, responds to Hellman. Although he accepted that the second-hand and third-hand transmission of events on the ground through the internet can lead to a certain "flattening" and loss of complexity, overall it was positive: "It may well be that the ability of Zapatismo to stir up support around the world has less to do with oversimplification of the message, and much more to do with the vitality and resonance of the message itself."[23] To take up Zapatismo outside Chiapas is not to avoid struggle but to internationalize it. The struggle for *dignidad* (much more than "dignity") by the Zapatistas is a universal one, and its generalizing across the world is thus positive. Although some may well be seeking to "revolt vicariously" by taking up Zapatismo, many more visit Chiapas or learn about it in detail and become informed participants in "World War IV" (a Zapatista term), between neoliberalism and a dignified existence. This exchange was extremely interesting – over and beyond the specifics raised – because it problematized the new global solidarity modalities.

Not just the left but also the international counter-insurgency think tanks saw in Zapatismo a new mode of social "netwars", whereby both sides vie for access to the media and for public opinion. There is a popular image lying behind these interpretations – from a left and a conservative position alike – that Subcomandante Marcos sat with a laptop in the middle of the jungle, consciously reaching out through the internet to construct international solidarity. In practice, the Zapatista online presence was mediated through support structures, as we saw above. In reality, very little of what became the international phenomenon of Zapatismo, especially after the 1999 "Battle of Seattle", was part and parcel of how the revolt occurred in practice. Marcos and his colleagues went into the revolt expecting either that the masses would hear their call to war or ignore them. In the event, civil society, across Mexico and then further afield, did not support armed revolt but did support the Zapatistas' aims and sought to shelter them from repression. The new way of "making revolution without seizing power" was forced on them, and was not a far-sighted aim there from the very start. Nor was the motivation of the indigenous *campesinos* that new and, rather, resounded with the fervour of "primitive rebels" across time. Thus, Comandante David, when asked in 1996 about the motives for the uprising, said that "Indians have never lived like human beings ... but the moment came when those very same indigenous *pueblos* started to make themselves aware of their reality by means of reflection and analysis, and also by studying the Word of God, thus they began to wake up".[24]

Taking a broad overview of the Zapatista transnational solidarity network, Olesen is undoubtedly correct to conclude that "the interest and attraction generated by the EZLN beyond its national borders is matched by no other movement in the post-Cold War period".[25] It certainly appears to vindicate, in many ways, the more positive reading of globalization as a process that has made the world more interconnected physically, socially, politically and culturally. The very "local" indigenous world of Chiapas became a "global" issue and had an impact, directly and through its "demonstration effect", across many other places. There was no "centre" to this transnational solidarity network, as there had been with the "old" internationalism, and the network mode of capitalist development was truly reflected in the mode its contestation took. Its impact in creating and providing a beacon of hope for the anti-globalization movement has been considerable.

My own view is that "international Zapatismo" is no more homogeneous than civil society "on the ground" in Chiapas. There are undoubtedly analysts supporting tendencies imbued with Eurocentrism who see the revolt in Chiapas in terms of the "noble savage" (Jean-Jacques Rousseau), who will redeem comfortable corrupt Westerners. There is more than a whiff in this milieu of Jean-Paul Sartre's foreword to Frantz Fanon's classic *The Wretched of the Earth*, in which he argues that "to shoot down a European is to kill two birds with one stone, to destroy an oppressor and the man he oppresses at the same time: there remains a dead man and a free man".[26] Nevertheless, the Zapatista revolt has had an overwhelmingly positive resonance across the world, teaching and energizing a whole generation of young activists that another world is, indeed, possible. The dangers of "armchair activism" seemed more than outweighed by the exemplary courage and originality of the Zapatistas. Thus, we see how the study of social movements in Latin America needs to reach beyond the national to embrace the transnational and global wherever possible

8

ENVIRONMENTAL

A globally recognized facet of the "new" social movement wave is, of course, the environmental movement(s). Against the resource extractivism that prevails across Latin America, the ecological social movements call for a new environmentally aware development strategy. Brazil's plans to build a series of hydroelectric dams across the Amazon by 2020, flooding conservation zones and displacing indigenous peoples, is symbolic of what they are struggling against. The environment transcends politics, certainly class politics, and it is beyond left and right, at least in theory. Environmentalism in Brazil has taken a more explicitly socialist flavour, however, ever since the killing of Chico Mendes, environmentalist and rubber tapper, in 1988, which received global attention and became iconic for the global environmental movement. The articulation of ecology and socialism has meant that the trade unions are heavily involved, as are many indigenous and peasant movements. Thus, this particular articulation of what is perhaps best seen as an "empty signifier" – the environment – has become a paradigm for other social movements across the global South.

International NGOs have been particularly important in the creation and sustaining of environmental social movements. During the neoliberal era they were encouraged to bypass the state to deliver services. They also sought to encourage what they saw as "civil society", although local understandings might have differed. They played a central role in promoting indigenous rights and sustainable development. They advocated for environmental legislation and promoted ecologically friendly small-scale community economies. Thus, environmental social movements inflected by international NGOs have a very distinct politics, which has often brought them into conflict with the progressive governments of Ecuador and Bolivia, for example, especially when ecological concerns and oil or gas exploration have clashed.[1] A very different ecological politics was practised by the progressive governments with their far-reaching political philosophy of Buen Vivir (Living Well), which promoted an ecologically sustainable approach to development based on the cosmology of the Amerindian peoples.

Extractivism is widely seen as the principal mode of economic domination in Latin America. It is rooted in the colonial logic of the Americas as a source of gold and silver. Colonialism – and, after colonialism, dependent capitalist development – placed Latin American economies as providers of raw material. The extraction of minerals, oil, gas, wood, agrarian produce and other natural resources led to an outward-export-oriented development model. Traditionally it has been based on "enclave" economies – foreign-owned outposts, such as mines – but nowadays it can have a much wider reference point. For Eduardo Gudynas, extractivism retains dominance despite the fact that "multiple social impacts, such as displacement of local communities, ruptures in community relations, erosion of indigenous worldviews, prostitution, networks or corruption, smuggling, have been identified".[2] Extractivism has led to negative spill-over effects socially but also in terms of the economy – which becomes unbalanced – and politics, which becomes open to capture by narrow interest groups.

Since the advent of the left-of-centre governments across Latin America after the year 2000 the issue of extractivism, or neo-extractivism, has come to the fore as a critical lens. Neo-extractivism was seen as positive by some commentators and the progressive governments, as it generated the rent to finance increased social spending. The negative environmental impact of, for example, open-cast mining was set to one side when set against the short-term social (and, it must be noted, political) benefit the rents of extractivism generate. The progressive governments sought to justify the neo-extractivist policy by saying it was no longer foreign plunder and served to uplift the popular masses. Even by that logic, the benefits can only be temporary, and there was an increasing understanding that natural and social sustainability go hand in hand; any other position is difficult to sustain from any progressive standpoint.

This chapter offers three case studies of quite distinct but also paradigmatic environmental struggles in Latin America. I examine first the water wars (actually, water and gas wars) in Bolivia, a remarkable global event whereby a community mobilized successfully against a multinational corporation's grab of a natural resource, which opened up a cycle of indigenous/environmental struggles. In relation to Ecuador I examine a pivotal struggle between a progressive government and the indigenous movement over its failure to protect a natural heritage area. This event was a political turning point in Ecuador. The third case study is of political ecology in Brazil, a movement that perhaps pioneered the alliance between the ecological and trade union movements. The challenges in Brazil are huge in the face of corporate and state opposition, despite support from international civil society. Finally, I turn to a new emerging environmental politics, namely Buen Vivir/Sumak Kawsay, an indigenous ecological philosophy in the Andean countries. Buen Vivir, in all its various facets and contradictions, is examined with a view to proposing it as a major Latin American contribution to global social movement theory.

Water wars (Bolivia)

Social movements played a pivotal role in the success of the Movimiento al Socialismo and Evo Morales in Bolivia, none more so than the "wars" around natural resources, specifically water and natural gas, between 1999 and 2005. These movements around natural resources were part of a broader struggle for recognition and empowerment on a scale not seen since the 1952 national revolution.

Water, in Bolivia's rural areas, has always been scarce and poorly managed. In keeping with the neoliberal turn in water management (codified in the Dublin Principles of 1992, which decided on the commodification and de-statization of water), the Bolivian government in 1999 decided to award major contacts with multinational corporations to privatize water services. Not surprisingly, these companies, as they had done elsewhere, raised water rates exorbitantly,[3] to an extent that was simply not affordable for local communities, and a major struggle over natural resources began. This was backed by the international counter-discourse that water was a human right and not just a commodity.

The first Cochabamba water war erupted as a subsidiary of the US Bechtel corporation privatized the city's water system in 1999 and imposed a rise in water rates of an average 300 per cent. Neighbourhood communities and large segments of the broader civil society began to organize and mobilize this machine. As Waltraud Morales notes, "The Cochabamba Water War generated global sympathy and support, to such a degree that a localized Bolivian social movement quickly mushroomed into an international anti-privatization and anti-globalization movement."[4] Although the protest globalized, it was also intensely localized, with an effective appeal by indigenous leaders to customary water rights that were now being obliterated. It seems water warfare broke out in El Alto in 2005, which saw the predominantly Aymara residents placing roadblocks that effectively prevented access to the capital city, La Paz. By 2006, after ineffective moves by the state to mediate a solution, the private water company Aguas del Illimani was forced to close down.

The question of natural gas had a long history in Bolivia, being part of the history of extractivism. In the past, tin and nitrates were key products to be looted; now it was oil and gas. Protests over natural gas privatization plans led to the overthrow of a few Bolivian presidents from 1999 onwards. These "gas wars" would come to be viewed as both symptom and cause of a deep crisis of legitimacy in Bolivia. The gas war began in 2003 over a commercialization scheme through a pipeline that ended in a Chilean port, which resulted in widespread popular protest. The background was Bolivia's loss, in the nineteenth century, of its nitrate-rich Pacific coastline, which gave rise to nationalist resentment. Faced with fierce repression by the state, the popular forces found a great degree of resilience and coherence, which gave them a form of solidarity. The government of President Gonzalo Sánchez de Lozada fell, as did the hydrocarbons law that had led to the popular revolt.

The struggle to nationalize the natural gas reserves resulted in an even more militant outburst in 2005, centred around the La Paz/El Alto area. Neighbourhood councils became the organizers of a virtual insurrection, and solidarity spread through local blockades, hunger strikes and fierce clashes with the forces of the state. The indigenous protestors of the Aymara communities of El Alto were to the fore, among them Evo Morales, president of the coca grower's federation, and Felipe Quispe, head of the peasants' union and Pachakutik, the newly formed indigenous party. The die was cast for fundamental regime change.

Taken as an integrated phase of environmental activism, the water and gas wars in Bolivia were of an unprecedented intensity and effectiveness. They were central to the formation of a hegemonic peasant-indigenous block and became the solid social base of the Evo Morales/Alvaro García Linera governments that first came to power in 2006 and were re-elected in 2009 and 2014. These were not only struggles over natural resources; they were about democracy and popular sovereignty. Taken together, they were a constitutive phase of the turn to the left in Bolivia and Latin America as a whole.

Struggles over water and natural gas both engage with the current turn of neoliberalism to "accumulation by dispossession", which mirrors the early stages of capitalist development and the land enclosures. The first Cochabamba water war, in 2000, created a strong impression that the unregulated market of neoliberalism was being checked by popular resistance. Susan Spronk and Jeffery Webber argue, however, that, "given the negligible role that water plays in the regional political economy, the social movements that emerged during the water wars involved a more micro frame and politics than the gas wars".[5] They locate the true "revolutionary potential" of the Bolivian social movements in the gas struggles and their demand for nationalization. Although a comparative perspective on social movements is, indeed, very interesting, as it may draw out strengths and weaknesses, it seems somewhat forced to do this according to an externally imposed logic, such as the movements' respective "revolutionary potential" rather than their own self-defined aims and objectives.

It is not in the nature of social movements, however, to simply switch off when a progressive – even social-movement-friendly – government is in office.

Towards the end of 2010 there was a revolt, involving strikes and demonstrations, over an increase in the price of gas (the *gasolinazo*). Raúl Zibechi notes that "the first popular uprising in the region against a government of the left took place in Bolivia. It was caused by an excessive increase in the price of fuels".[6] There were other conflicts in the mining zones, along with various strikes and popular resistances. Jeffery Webber argued in 2013 that "taken together … these do appear to represent signs of growing discontent to the left of the MAS in the tradition of left-indigenous insurrection from below",[7] although he went on to admit that "the contentious moments thus far have remained fragmented and dispersed with no socio-political articulation of a left alternative to the MAS". Perhaps, though, it is unrealistic to expect social movements to be permanently mobilized and assume they might not just lend critical support to what was widely seen as a government of the people.

Water sector reform continued to be an issue under the left-of-centre governments in Latin America, not least in Bolivia. Water poses very directly the demand for "decommodification and universalisation of basic needs through the creation of public, non-profit, community-based models of water management, the service of the community and the common good" (Red VIDA: Vigilancia Interamericana para la Defensa y Derecho al Agua: Inter-American Network for the Defense of the Right to Water).[8] This approach poses wider protests, as part of a Polanyian counter-movement whereby society reacts against the deprecation, both social and environmental, caused by an unregulated market. We must note that, although the Morales government has taken a very progressive stance at the United Nations and other international fora, in Bolivia it has been quite repressive of some popular mobilizations. Water activists, such as those protesting against the Madera River dam project, and the protests regarding exploitation of the Isiboro Sécure Indigenous Territory and National Park (TIPNIS: Territorio Indígena Parque Nacional Isiboro Sécure), which is considered the most biodiverse region in Bolivia, have, for example, been denounced by the government as a threat to the revolution.

This is not the place for a general assessment of the role of social movements during this period but, in relation to water movements, we have a case study that is quite delimited and therefore may be amenable to clear-cut conclusions. Philipp Terhorst and colleagues conclude a close study of water reform by stating that

> the politics being pursued [in Bolivia and Ecuador] are not what the water movements hoped for. The changes that are taking place in the water sector are limited and contradictory. Water movements have achieved recognition as political actors, architects of new agendas … [but] left governments have blocked the participation of social movements and the development of non-hierarchical forms of power.[9]

Without ongoing mass mobilizations, this is not a surprising outcome of real politics, perhaps, and it does explain why many water activists have said "One won but one lost", even if that is perhaps too pessimistic an appraisal.

Extractivism and politics (Ecuador)

Rafael Correa came to office as president of Ecuador in 2007 on a wave of popular insurgency and with high hopes for his progressive agenda. The "Citizens Revolution" would shift resources to poor and marginalized groups, and it would also be ecologically sustainable. In practice, though, his agrarian policies favoured large-scale agro-industry and his environmental policies went against the precepts of Buen Vivir (Living Well) enshrined in the constitution. Correa argued, as Becker puts it, "that extractive economic activities would boost the economy, provide more employment, contribute to spending for social programs, and that all this could be accomplished without negative environmental implications".[10] The notion of "socially responsible" large-scale mining became popular, with the idea that state control could protect the environment better than small-scale local mining on an informal basis.

Inevitably, Correa's environmental policies led to clashes, with local social movements in particular. The constitution granted local communities the right to consultation over the siting of mega-mining projects on their land, but they did not have a veto. The environmental rights group Acción Ecológica accused the government of breaching the constitution and breaking its promises to the poor and marginalized, who were never the beneficiaries of mega-mining. Alberto Acosta, who had been minister for mines and president of the 2008 Constituent Assembly, broke with his close ally Correa and called for a reaffirmation of the principles of Buen Vivir.[11] Not all on the left criticized Correa's policies quite so categorically, as they were mindful of the development and modernization imperatives. Thus, Sara Caria and Rafael Domínguez argue that "the country has undergone a much needed transformation that compensates for the eclipse of environmental sustainability".[12]

President Correa was a bold proponent of "twenty-first-century socialism" on the international scene, sometimes sounding even more radical than Hugo Chávez (Venezuela) and Evo Morales (Bolivia). His popularity was undoubted and his majorities at the polls were unprecedented. But his environmental policy inevitably caused some of the social movements to react, not only the small environmental movement but also the much more powerful indigenous movement. Thus, in 2009 there was a massive protest as part of a "Day of Mobilization for Life" against the new mining laws, which led to many injuries and set in train a dynamic of confrontation. This conflict in the Amazon region was accentuated by Correa's accusations of "terrorism" and "destabilization" against what he called "infantile environmentalists" and "infantile indigenists". From below, it seemed more like a case of the state being the traditional agent of control it always had been, with its policies set on development for the few and not the many.

A major plank in President Correa's environmental policy was the Yasuní– ITT (Ishpingo-Tambococha-Tiputini oil fields) Initiative, launched in 2007 as a bold new path towards a sustainable biological-knowledge-based society. The Yasuní National Park is nearly 1 million acres on the north of the Ecuadorian Amazon, with a high degree of biodiversity, and home to several indigenous peoples. The Ecuadorian government made a novel proposal to the United Nations in keeping with the principle of shared responsibility for sustainability and environmental protection. In 2010 the government signed an agreement with the UNDP (United Nations Development Programme) to create a trust that would receive donations to, essentially, take Yasuní out of potential oil production in exchange for international compensation. Thus, international compensation would be dedicated to the development of renewable energy sources in Ecuador as part of a national energy transition plan.

The origins of the Yasuní plan came from various elements within civil society, especially from those who had suffered from the devastation caused by the oil industry in the Amazon region. For Alberto Acosta, minister for mines at the time, there were several underlying objectives to the Yasuní plan: to preserve biodiversity, to protect the lands and lives of the indigenous peoples who live there, to protect the climate in everybody's interests and, finally, "to take a first step towards a post-fossil-fuel era in Ecuador".[13] Essentially, the Yasuní buyout would prevent some 410 million tons of CO_2 emissions. Germany's initial support augured well but a series of events led to its collapse. There was a perception that President Correa was "holding a gun at the head of world leaders: give me the funding or I will exploit the oil (which he eventually did)", and his withdrawal from the initiative and the resignation of the foreign minister led Acosta to hint that "there were suspicions that oil interests had played a very important role [in the negative outcome]".[14]

Given that some of the main facts are still shrouded in secrecy, it is hard to draw definitive conclusion on the environmental politics involved. We can say, however, that an initiative such as this one depends on the involvement of civil society, which was not obviously apparent. Although this idea regarding Yasuní pre-dated Correa's election in 2006, it rapidly became his project. We can also say that the basically utopian nature of the initiative was inevitably going to clash with the realities of international relations, not to mention the self-interest of the oil companies and sectors of the state. Le Quang articulates a quite positive overall evaluation, arguing

The Yasuní–ITT initiative was a public policy that respected the rights of nature by encouraging humans to live in harmony with it. However, it was not simply on environmental policy, it also took into account economic and social elements and questioned the extractivism of our current development model. The initiative was the first in the world to articulate social justice and environmental urgency.[15]

Set against the failure of the 2009 Copenhagen climate summit, it does, indeed, take on an exemplary role.

The Yasuní–ITT saga seemingly came to an end early in 2019, as I was writing this book. This beacon of hope for good environmental governance in one of the most biodiverse regions of the world was finally laid to rest. Correa's successor as president, Lenín Moreno, approved a plan that would allow oil drilling in a buffer zone of a protected area along the border with Peru that had hitherto been off limits for drilling. The UN and indigenous communities warned of the immediate and real danger posed to isolated indigenous communities. Barely a decade after the path-breaking Ecuadorian 2008 constitution, widely regarded as a new paradigm for indigenous rights and the rights of nature, this was a massive blow. The Amazon had seemed safe under President Moreno after a successful 2018 referendum, not to mention his promises to the UN that he would step up protection of the environment.

In terms of an overview of environmental politics and social transformation, there has been a tendency by the orthodox left to counterpoise "Pachamamismo vs extractivismo".[16] This implies that the Buen Vivir discourse (see "Buen Vivir" section below), and its reference to the Quechua deity Pachamama, is somehow just a smokescreen for what is, basically, an extractivist development strategy. From a modernization and mechanical Marxist perspective, extractivism is simply the way in which development takes place in countries with natural resources like Ecuador's. The perspectives of the environmental movements reflected in this chapter would point towards the unsustainability of such a view. This is not to deny that there are compromises that are needed between development – even sustainable development – and environmentalism. Nevertheless, environmentalism cannot be reduced to a mystical worshiping of a pre-Colombian deity, the Pachamama.

Amazon and dams (Brazil)

In Brazil, as elsewhere, engagement with the environment began from a conservationist perspective. Thus, in 1950 the FBCN (Fundação Brasileira para a Conservação da Natureza: Brazilian Foundation for the Conservation of Nature) was formed, composed mainly of professionals with backgrounds in agronomy and the natural sciences. Their strategy was not one of mass mobilizations but, rather, one of lobbying. They were quite successful at that, and in influencing law-making in the area of environmental policy. In the 1970s various other groups were formed that were slightly less cautious in terms of a mobilizing strategy, and these became loosely connected with the redemocratization movement. There were the ecological crusades mounted by a group of artists. Another group in Porto Alegre mounted a successful campaign against agro-toxins, which included symbolic demonstrations. A campaign against the siting of an international airport in the south-west of São Paulo attracted considerable attention, as the University of São Paulo, where many PT founders worked, was sited in that area.

In the mid-1970s, coinciding with a degree of political opening by the military regime, there was a gradual shift in ecologist movement from environmentalism to ecopolitics. Environmentalism – in its urban and rural incarnations – was presented as being apolitical. The compromising, dishonesty and impurity of party politics was rejected in favour of purity of purpose and refusal to engage in politics. Middle-class youths in particular were attracted to this movement and its ostensible post-materialist values. At the end of the decade the defence of the Amazon against ongoing depredation became a popular issue in Brazil, as it was internationally. In the early 1980s, as the transition to democracy gathered pace, this ecological movement began to engage in the political arena. In 1986 the Partido Verde (Green Party) was formed, providing an explicit ecological political voice alongside the other social forces engaged with the Amazon and other ecological issues, which included the new trade unionism, neighbourhood associations and the Christian base communities.

Through engagement with the Constituent Assembly in 1986 the environmental movement began to sharpen its political focus. This took the shape of a shift from environmentalism to a form of ecopolitics. This was defined, according to Eduardo Viola, as "ecodevelopment, pacifism, decentralization of energy sources (in a opposition to nuclear power stations and large-scale hydroelectric schemes), quality of life, … social justice … ecological agrarian reform … and general environmental education".[17] The environmental movement in Brazil took a big leap forward with the holding of the World Conference on the Environment and Development in Rio de Janeiro in 1992. The Rio agenda helped broaden the support for environmentalism in Brazil across civil society. National coalitions with other social movements emerged and the concept of "sustainable development" became a unifying discourse. It also legitimized a turn towards a more restrictive "conservationism", however, opposed to the focus on socioeconomic development issues.

As Angela Alonso and co-authors explain, "A new frame came about: neoconservationism. Incorporating local social issues, characteristic of the socio-environmental agenda, and global matters, of the green agenda, neo-conservationism became the common language between environmental groups, ranging from the pioneers of the 1970s to those newcomers in the 1990s".[18] An epistemological shift also occurred from the notion of ecosystem to that of biodiversity, focused on the protection of the habitat of animal and vegetable species (as well as indigenous groups deemed of low environmental impact). The internationalization of the Brazilian environmental agenda symbolized by the focus on the Amazon led, for example, to a new focus on genetically modi-fied organisms. Not only did this represent an externally imposed restructuring of a Brazilian social movement but it also led to a reworking of history, with, for example Chico Mendes, the rubber tappers' union organizer killed by land-owners in 1988, being declared an "environmental martyr".

It was around the issue of the Amazon that many of the tensions in Brazilian environmentalism emerged, not least in terms of its relations with the inter-national environmental NGOs. The Amazon was/is a region of intense defor-estation and general depredation, as well as ongoing murderous attacks against its inhabitants. It has also seen a vast expansion of environmental NGOs; from around 40 in 1980 to over 2,000 by the end of the 1990s.[19] Western governments, the World Bank, charities and the big international NGOs (such as Greenpeace and WWF) all fund activity around environmental issues in Brazil. This was to put huge pressure on the Brazilian environmental movements, which now found themselves very much in a partnership rather than a contestatory mode. Working in cooperation with government and de facto subordination to international funders and NGOs led to a series of tension and splits internally. As elsewhere, the "fundamentalists" in the eco-logical movement found themselves at odds with the "realists", who adapted well to the new dispensation.

The news in 2019 that the Brumadinho dam had burst, causing over 250 fatalities, brought home to an international audience how vital the campaigns against the big hydroelectric projects in Brazil had been. Dams were once widely regarded across the global South as symbols of modernization. They created energy for industrialization and for people's homes. Dams have played a very large role in Brazil, going back to the huge Furnas dam on the Rio Grande, built in 1958, and now Brazil has the third largest capacity in the world. The current plans to extend dams to the Amazon region has given rise to widespread opposition, not least internationally. The anti-dam movement in Brazil, which gathered steam in the 1980s, has had considerable impact in terms of creating new planning frameworks and involving local communities in the debate, and it has scored some significant victories. This has helped create an international network of anti-dam campaigns and forced the World Bank to introduce more stringent environmental impact assessments into its loans.

The anti-dam movement had its origins in alliance between the rural unions, Catholic groups and local communities. In the 1990s the various regional campaigns coalesced into the MAB (Movimento dos Atingidos por Barragens: Movement of Dam-Affected People), which is an effective national-level organization. MAB has successfully mobilized local communities and mounted non-violent occupations to defend the rights of river dwellers and, in particular, indigenous communities. Other protest against dams have been much more inchoate and forceful. These are sometimes supported by the MST, which is far and away the best-organized rural social movement (see Chapter 4). Sabrina McCormick, in a study of the Brazilian anti-dam movement, draws particular attention to the role of experts (in planning hearings, for example) and whether or not a particular campaign has attracted international attention.[20] We could perhaps think of the anti-dam mobilizations as a campaign rather than a social movement, but that would be a moot point.

The Brazilian environmental movement was seen in the early 1980s as one that epitomized the "new social movements" in Latin America. For many, it was symptomatic of the post-1968 movements that they were not class-based, had "non-material" objectives and were not open to bargaining and co-option. There has, more recently, been an argument, put by Kathryn Hochstetler, for example, that "there are many definitions of popular movements ... [but] by virtually all of them, Brazilian environmentalists do not comprise a popular movement".[21] This is because its members are predominantly middle-class professionals: scientists, teachers, civil servants, and so on. Although I accept that its class composition distinguishes it from the trade union or peasant movements, I am not clear why this should disqualify it as a social movement. We have seen that this movement has clear social goals, it organizes collectively and it pursues its objectives through mobilization in conjunction with other social movements.

Buen Vivir

Since around 2000, coinciding with the rise of the left-of-centre governments, a new development and social movement discourse has emerged in Latin America. The Buen Vivir discourse (Sumak Kawsay, in the Kichwa language, or Suma Qumaña, in the Aymara language) translates poorly into English as "living well".

There are, at least, three main ways in which we can approach Buen Vivir: as an indigenous philosophical orientation opposed to the Western developmentalism paradigm; as a contributor to the alter-globalization project of the commons; and as an environmentalist project articulating a new relationship between nature and humanity. From a social movement perspective, it is from all three angles that we need to engage. Social movements in Latin America necessarily need to define themselves with regard to the national development project, they also engage transnationally with the wide family of other globalization movements and, finally, they increasingly see the importance of engaging with environmental sustainability.

Latin America, from 2000 to around 2015, lived through a political spring that was quite unprecedented in the depth and breadth of progressive social transformation. New paradigms of social change and political experimentation arose that are, arguably, contributions to a new global sociology. What the dependency approach meant to the 1960s, in terms of an overarching development paradigm, so today the concept of Buen Vivir/Sumak Kawsay captures well the radical edge of current alternativist thinking. It breaks decisively with the economism of dependence and foregrounds culture. Essentially, it speaks to the extended reproduction of life rather than of capital. It advocates a different civilizational model from that of individualistic capitalism in which community values and respect for nature take priority. It is a development paradigm now enshrined in the constitutions of Ecuador and Bolivia and causing ripples across the region. Sumak Kawsay works on the premise that there are two transitions under way in Latin America: a relatively recent transition towards socialism, barely 100 years old, and a longer-term transition out of colonialism that goes back to the fifteenth century. An end to all forms of racism, and greater self-determination, form part of this longer-term struggle. It does not deny at all the relevance of Western forms of representative democracy, but adds the need for participative and communal forms of democracy. Although this new cosmovision does not simply rearticulate ancient indigenous practices, and is characterized by a profound hybridity, it does represent a challenge to Eurocentrism. It articulates new principles of production and property, identity and subjectivity and, not least, a new way of understanding the world and producing knowledge about it. The philosophy of Buen Vivir expresses a critical approach to the ideology of progress and the search for alternatives to contemporary society. It poses a rupture with former ideologies and practises of development, offering "an opportunity to construct collectively a new development regime".[22] Buen Vivir recognizes the values inherent in nature and the expression of oppressed or subordinated indigenous knowledge and cultures. In Ecuador, it is seen as a set of rights including those to health, shelter, education, food and environment; while, in Bolivia, it is an ethical-cultural principle alongside others such as dignity, freedom, solidarity and reciprocity. Buen Vivir seeks to articulate development needs with ecological criteria and promotes an ethics of development that subordinates economic objectives to ecological criteria. It acknowledges culture and gender differences and argues for new strategies to secure food sovereignty, control of natural resources and water as a human right. It brings to the fore the importance of bio-politics, and its biocentric conception of socialism represents a critique of Marxism as much as modernization theory. We can also, of course, think of Buen Vivir in terms of a utopia, always a necessary part of social transformation processes, as, indeed, is argued by a former Ecuadorian minister for planning, René Ramírez.[23]

We can, in evaluating Buen Vivir, point to the contradictions between its postulates and the ecological actions of the governments that have adopted it as state ideology, such as Ecuador. As development theory it has also been rejected as simply romantic and backward-looking, with little purchase on the contemporary needs of the people. A more nuanced critique comes from Radcliffe, for whom (in Ecuador) "contentious politics between the state, governments and social movements shaped Sumak Kawsay's institutionalisation combining grassroots elements with neoliberal forms of governmentality and postcolonial statecraft".[24] So the grass roots, contentiously – in brief, a social movement element – confront a state that is still essentially colonial. As with the autonomist current (see Chapter 5), it remains to be seen whether the proponents of Buen Vivir can carry out the political alliances and discursive articulations necessary for it to become a hegemonic vision for a post-neoliberal and postcolonial future for Latin America.

My view of Buen Vivir is that it is the most significant Latin American contribution to global social theory since the dependency theory of the 1960s. Dependency pointed towards a gap in Marxist theories of imperialism: they were all views from the global North, never the South. For all its various inconsistencies – a downplaying of class conflict, for example – dependency was an epistemological breakthrough at the time. Buen Vivir is also quite diverse, and is in some aspects inconsistent. It is also, arguably, utopian, in so far as it is hard to envisage it acting as government strategy. Nevertheless, it breaks the Northern grip on development theory and the dominant approach to ecology, which, for all its ostensible globalism, is mainly North-centric. Buen Vivir, above all, reunites present-day Latin American social movements with their pre-conquest past. An indigenous ecology that already makes inroads into peasant movement concerns could yet relate to the concerns of urban workers and become a powerful social movement in the years to come.

9

WAYS FORWARD

In order to start thinking about the future and charting the way(s) forward, we need to conduct a mapping of social movements in Latin America today, building on what we have found out in the case studies above. The notion of cognitive mapping is integral to our cultural political economy approach, which seeks to depict social space, and in our case social movements, in the current epoch. We need a method for "cognitive mapping" to understand the current state of play of social movements in the new political era now opening up in Latin America "after" the progressive turn. On this basis, we can move to the second section of this conclusion to examine the lessons we can draw from our six case studies in relation to the theoretical framework we laid out in the opening chapters. What was presented as a mosaic of distinct social movements for the sake of analysis is now shown as a holistic and integrated social counter-movement. I examine their relation to state politics, NGOs and civil society as well as their international projection. Finally, I seek to move "beyond the fragments" in terms of the dispersed, even divided, map of social movements in Latin America today. What is the common social or political denominator that might make the whole greater than the sum of its parts? We explore, in particular, the notion of "democratic equivalents" and the way in which social movements might become harbingers of a new social order.

Mapping

The categories of analysis that informed our case studies in the pages above are the obvious ones. We have focused on the complex and contradictory relationships between social movements with the state, political parties and civil society. It moved us beyond the old belief that social groups have "interests" that they pursued automatically. We must examine instead the complex process of grievance articulation, protests around them and the construction of social movements with a clear objective. We need to examine their articulation with other social movements and mediations with the political process. Finally, we need to examine the national and transnational alliances they form. We need to bear in mind the conclusion of a study of Latin American social movements, namely that these constantly overflow our theoretical agendas, and, as Millie Thayer and Jeffrey Rubin argue, we must "reach for open-ended conceptions that go beyond the limits offered by the term 'social movement' to describe what [we] see".[1]

The notion of cognitive mapping with which I now propose to take this analysis further is linked to the idea of dialectical criticism and the Sartrean concept of totalization. Put plainly, it is a way of establishing whether the whole is greater than the sum of the parts. Can we map the state of play of social movements in Latin America today building on our six case studies above? It was literary critic Frederic Jameson who brought the aesthetic of "cognitive mapping" to a wider audience, based on his understanding that, "without a conception of the social totality (and the possibility of transforming a whole social system), no properly socialist politics is possible".[2] Currently there seems to be an inability to grasp the system as a whole, in part because of an emphasis on the local and the particular. Although a refusal of Jean-François Lyotard's "metanarratives" and totalizing perspectives has good reasons, it should not bar us from seeking an understanding of particular social movements as part of a broader counter-movement.

The idea of cognitive mapping first came to light in urban studies.[3] It suggested that urban alienation was directly related to the mental incapability of the cityscapes. The imaginary sense of a city is often an absent totality for its inhabitants, or, conversely, a myth. The same could be said of social movements. This exercise is not about homogenizing difference but, rather, a way to enhance alternative imaginaries. Alberto Toscano and Jeff Kinkle build on Jameson's original idea "to think a system so vast that it cannot be encompassed by the natural ... categories of perception", which is an impossible task, but argue that, in the intent to map, "lies the beginning of wisdom".[4] Our normal categories of perception are, perhaps, inadequate to grasp the role of individual, or even collective, agency in an era of ever more complex postmodern globalized capitalism. To orient ourselves, we need better cognitive maps of the social movements in Latin America to understand both their complexity and potential for transformation.

To be clear, I am not proposing the type of map that Jorge Luis Borges wrote about in his short story on "the rigour of science", in which he imagines an empire in which cartography is so advanced that the experts set out to draw a map that will be a perfect rendering of the kingdom. Of course, such a map would be an absurdity, for obvious reasons. Ours is thus not a Borgesian map but a practical guide that simplifies to make intelligible, to aid a cognitive mapping of the terrain of the social movements and to assist in drawing out connections and synergies.

We can start our mapping exercise of social movements in Latin America by developing Maristella Svampa's four politico-ideological matrixes for understanding social movements today: the communitarian indigenous-peasant matrix; the populist-movementist one; the traditional left class matrix; and the new autonomist one.[5] Each matrix has its particular political dynamic with its own internal tensions and, of course, national particularities, but considering these together can take us some way towards the elaboration of a new paradigm for the study of Latin American social movements.

The peasant-indigenous cluster of movement is inscribed in the *longue durée* of Amerindian history. It centres communal rights, the legitimacy of indigenous knowledge and the ever-present reality of resistance, truly exemplifying Foucault's original insight into the power–resistance integration. There are tensions within this cluster of movements, between a bid to recreate autonomous indigenous communities and the tasks of engaging through alliances in the struggle for democratization.

The second broad cluster of social movements, responding to the medium-term historical memory, is that of the national-popular movements. These go back to the period from 1930 to 1950, with the construction of a national industrializing state and the emergence of populist leaders. This national project has to some extent been sidelined by globalization but it retains purchase and animates broad sectors of the masses.

The third set of social movements would be those created around a class-centred left, which acts within a 1970s mind-set. Its class essentialism isolates it from the emerging "new" social movements, not least the indigenous movement in its new incarnation. Nevertheless, it continues to have purchase, especially among the trade union and unemployed workers' movement.

Finally, responding to the more recent, post-2000 past, we find a cluster of movements responding to the "autonomist" orientation. The theme of horizontal democracy prevails, as does the rejection of party politics as it exists today. It responds to the failure of the traditional left and finds its emblematic form in the *piqueteros*.

These distinctions are congruent with what we found in our case studies in the chapters above. As the role of social movements across much of Latin America continues to manifest itself, we need to bear in mind this multi-layered complexity and its differential historical time frames. The long frame from the pre-colonial period, through the national-popular and class phases of the twentieth century and on to the autonomist currents of this century are always intertwined and not discrete periods. The process of uneven and combined development applies to the broad phases of dependent development in Latin America, but also to its social movements. The indigenous uprising in Ecuador in 2019 had its roots in the very early stirrings of the original peoples resisting colonialism;

the new rise of Peronism in Argentina harks back very directly to the 1940s and the emergence of a national-popular movement; the massive contestation of the Chilean "model" is overdetermined by the symbols and memories of the Popular Unity period in the 1970s. And the remarkable flourishing of a new autonomist radical feminist movement in many countries over the last decade is part of transnational currents of thought/action and the culmination of a long period of organizing. All these currents can exist in the same place even if the temporalities are distinct; their development is always uneven but combined.

A general lesson we can learn from this mapping of our diverse case studies is that simple oppositions – binary opposites – do not assist us in obtaining an overview of social movements in Latin America. For too long we have seen stark counter-positions in the analysis and practice of Latin American social movements: are they exemplars of old or new movements? Does their stress on the social element preclude engagement with the political domain? Do they just protest but prove unable to offer an alternative to the status quo? Are they autonomous or subordinated to the state or a party? Is their activity contentious or simply routine? Are they formal or informal social movements? I will develop an analysis here that accepts fluidity and no firm boundaries between these categories. Above all, I will avoid premature closure of our developing Latin American paradigm.

Another, possibly complementary, approach to the "mapping" of social movements would be Antonio Gramsci's proposed methodology for a history of subaltern social groups. The subaltern classes are not just the working class for Gramsci, despite his orthodox communist affiliation. The category of the subaltern is more akin to the contemporary notion of the "multitude", as developed by Hardt and Negri.[6] Gramsci at various points included the proletariat, peasants, women, religious groups and colonial peoples. In the methodology he painstakingly developed in his prison notebooks, Gramsci points to the need to examine

1. the objective formation of the subaltern class through the developments and changes that took place in the economic sphere; the extent of their diffusion; and their descent from other classes that preceded them;
2. their passive or active adherence to the dominant political formations; that is, their efforts to influence the programs of these formations with demands of their own;
3. the birth of new parties of the ruling class to maintain control of the subaltern classes;
4. the formations of the subaltern classes themselves, formations of a limited and partial character;
5. the political formations that assert the *autonomy of the subaltern classes*, but within the old framework;
6. the political formations that assert *complete autonomy*, etc.[7]

This rough methodology should not be taken as a ready-made positivist model that can be applied mechanically. There would need to be intermediate phases, and the historian of the subaltern was being urged by Gramsci to discover the origins and development of each phase. So long as we do not take the phases of subaltern development as static or universal, Gramsci provides many hints for the mapping of the complex development of the subaltern groups in Latin America. Economic development – the national-popular and the free market neoliberal phases, for example – provides one set of parameters. The relation of the subaltern to the political domain is another phase of our ongoing mapping exercise, and, in particular, the formation of political regimes designed to co-opt them, as with Latin American populisms. Finally, with Gramsci we need to understand that the subaltern develop internally (for example, from the early "friendly societies" to contemporary trade unions); they assert some level of authority within the dominant order (such as national-popular movements); and, finally, they seek to "assert complete autonomy". The ability to promote autonomy could be taken as a measure of a movement's success, rather than the unrealistic measure of whether it has achieved its objectives. In this way, autonomy is a stepping stone or element in the long struggle to achieve the objectives of a movement, some of which might well be utopian.

Lessons

In critical social movement theorizing, the pioneering work of Alan Touraine stands out, but it does not really help us understand the mosaic of social movements in Latin America that we have studied in this book. For Touraine, "a social movement is the action, both culturally oriented and socially conflictual, of a class defined by its position of domination or dependency in the mode of appropriation of historicity, of the cultural models of investment, knowledge and morality towards which the social movement itself is oriented".[8] By definition, only societies that have reached what Touraine considers the highest levels of historicity, namely post-industrial ones, can fulfil these criteria. In Latin America, by contrast, for Touraine, what we see are different forms of collective mobilization that do not constitute "social movements" in this strong sense. Social actors in Latin America, from this perspective, seek not historicity and the offering of a global political alternative but simply to be allowed to participate in the political system. This attempt to rule out, by definition, Latin American social movements from the global family of movements is not, in my view, particularly helpful. It also confirms our need to develop a specifically Latin American paradigm for the study of social movements.

As for the orthodox Marxist reading of social movements, I find it just does not have the language to deal with their complexity. For classical Marxism, a social movement is generally taken to be the one heading towards socialism – that is, the labour movement and the broader socialist/communist movement. Other social movements tend to be read through a grid and conceptual language rather restricted to unions, parties, vanguards and a narrow conception of the class struggle. Michel Foucault, who really was not the anti-Marxist he has been portrayed as, was very aware of these limitations – but from the inside, as someone who was once part of the communist movement, having been recruited by Louis Althusser. For Foucault, there was a pressing need to develop a new vocabulary to deal with the post-1968 social movements in particular: "I wanted to react against a certain hagiographic glorification of Marxist political economy due to the historical good fortune of Marxism as a political ideology, born in the nineteenth century and having its effects in the twentieth".[9] Of course, since that interview in 1978 various Marxisms and post-Marxisms have emerged that have engaged in more fruitful, less necessitarian, more libertarian theories of social movements, but that dogmatic tendency still lingers.

In establishing a balance sheet of the social movements in Latin America over the last 25 years, we could return to Foucault's notion of resistance introduced at the start of this book as a sensitizing concept. The essential understanding we need to grasp is that power and resistance have an integrated, simultaneous existence; it is not first one, resulting then in the other. They are not cause and effect but co-produced. As Joseph Rouse puts it, for Foucault, "[p]ower is not something possessed or wielded by powerful agents, because it is co-constituted by those who support and resist it".[10] Even the rules of domination are constantly renegotiated by the subaltern classes. In all our case studies we have seen the well-spring of resistance in every sphere of life. We have seen how agrarian reforms are designed to answer the resistance of the rural populations. Suffrage laws are approved in response to the organizing and agitating of feminist movements. It is those who resist and those who refuse what is who are the future for Foucault, not the "party of the proletariat" he once joined.

In terms of analysing/understanding the phases or sequences of social movements, our starting point needs to be, I would argue, Karl Polanyi's notion of social counter-movement, the second of our original sensitizing concepts. There have been other attempts to carry out a periodization of Latin American social movements according to Nikolai Kondratiev's long economic waves,[11] but they have not been convincing. There is always a degree of economism in any vison that postulates, for example, trade unions being more active in an economic downturn – or an upturn, for that matter. Polanyi's broad-sweep historical movements of market expansion (and social disembedding of the economy), followed by social counter-movements (and the re-embedding of the economy within social relations), are reflected in Latin America's social movement trajectory. Thus, the intense neoliberal unregulated market phase of the 1990s was, as per Polanyi's intuition, followed by a wave of social counter-movements in the early 2000s, the water wars of Bolivia in 2000, the "Argentinazo" in Argentina 2001/2, and so on, as we have seen in the previous chapters.

The first lesson from the post-2000 upsurge of social movements in Latin America is probably the increasing importance of "place" in the making of these movements. Maristella Svampa has argued that "one of the constituent dimensions of the Latin-American social movements is *territoriality* ... Both in urban and in rural movements, territory appears as a space of resistance and, also, progressively as a site of resignification and the creation of new social relations."[12] We could argue that social movements have always been based on/in specific territories, but the role of "place" has increased dramatically in the era of globalization. As the Polanyian expansion of market relations over pre-existing social relations accelerated, so did the defensive role of place-based social movements. Place can no longer be seen as a simple physical context for social mobilizations but, rather, needs to be understood as an integral constitutive element of social movement agency.

This point is made in its strongest form by the indigenous movements and those of the Colombian Black Pacific, in which the social-territorial dimension became a major feature, as we saw above. They have not created "liberated territories" in the classic national liberation model – with the partial exception of the independent republics of Colombia in the 1950s – but they have led to a new relationship between society, politics and place/space. Contesting the hegemony of the state has inevitably led to a struggle for the decentralization of state power. The spatial location of a given community of resistance – be it an urban ghetto or a remote rural region – has also created new identities as part of social movement creation. The struggle for social change can be translated, in the era of neoliberal globalization, into a territorial form of indigenous national identities. As Sarah Radcliffe notes, "Social movements highlight the spatial nature of [state] power through their transgression of the spatial rules organizing Latin American geographies"[13] – thus breaking the hegemony of the postcolonial state, in parallel to globalization's undermining of the national state.

The second major lesson we can take from this period in Latin American social movement history is the importance of "autonomy" in the theory and practice of social movements. Based on a reading of Zapatismo that mirrors an earlier (mis)reading of the Cuban Revolution by Régis Debray,[14] John Holloway argues for autonomy (in the sense of self-determination) as both project and movement.[15] This is autonomy as negation of what is: the world of capital and political domination. Autonomy thus becomes a movement of permanent negation; a "scream", as Holloway puts it. Although this view achieved some resonance in Argentina through the events of 2001/2, it has been rebutted by most organic intellectuals of the social movements. So, for example, Guillermo Almeyra, though sympathetic to the notion of autonomy as a means to construct counter hegemony, notes how the Zapatista vision "took refuge in a not very well defined apoliticism – reflected in Holloway's *Change the World without Taking Power* – characterized by a silence and almost total lack of discussion around the big national and international issues of the day".[16] Autonomy, other than in a hegemony frame, rapidly descends into an apolitical "scream".

An underlying problem with a liberal reading of "autonomy" is that it is often equated with a liberal reading of civil society's autonomous social sphere. Civil society was a vehicle for democratization in the 1980s, largely as a constructed category. In the 1990s, encouraged by the international discourse around civil society, much of the left in Latin America endorsed it as the new path towards democracy and an acceptable form of socialism. This left, as Sonia Alvarez and co-authors note, "turned away from Leninist practices and developed new relationships with the progressive church, emerging social movements, and middle class 'fellow travellers' linked to NGOs".[17] By the 2000s the fellow travellers had become hegemonic at the level of discourse, and many turned openly to the right in discerning a "good" (moderate) and "bad" (populist) left.[18] The language of civil society – which included autonomy, hegemony and empowerment – sought to capture the upsurge of social movements described in this book, sometimes with success and often creating divisions. We might also consider whether "autonomy" is not more often a sign of isolation and weakness rather than a marker of what is most progressive.

Finally, the third lesson we might take from the case studies above is the need to stress the critical importance of boundary crossing as a marker of social innovation in social movement thinking and action since 2000. Although, for the sake of presentation, I have discussed six case studies as discrete phenomena, they are clearly interlinked in practice. For one, our classification of movements is to some extent arbitrary: for example, Zapatismo can be presented as a peasant movement and as an indigenous movement, but also even as part of the new family of alter-globalization movements. This is not at all surprising, given that identities are multi-layered and complex. It does mean, however, that the presentation of the mosaic of social movements in Latin America needs to be dynamic and historicized. They can only ever be understood within the totality of the social relations they exist within. Their strategic choices, too, are relational, and taken in relation to other parts of the broad mosaic of social movements.

What is most noticeable, when we stand back from the particular case studies, is how the real dynamism and creativity are occurring in the interface between social movements. Thus, women's movements and community-based movements not only interact but are often coterminous. The same can be said about peasant and indigenous movements, as we saw above in relation to the Zapatistas. Peasant movements also intersect with environmental movements, and the "environmentalism of the poor" creates a distinctive political discourse. Place-based or community-based movements are also, of course, populated by various social categories striving for better conditions. The labour movement, too, has always interacted with other movements, from the traditional worker–peasant alliances to more recent engagements with feminism and environmentalism. In the dynamic articulation between social movements we find examples of social innovation as the crossing of boundaries creates new social subjects (such as *mujeres populares* or ecofeminists) and emancipatory discourses and practices. This may be the most interesting area for social movement researchers to now explore, breaking away from the national case study, and thinking transnationally (which is already happening to some extent) but also cross-sectorally, in so far as social movements are not compartmentalized, not least in the hybrid societies and social movements of Latin America.

Beyond the fragments

Having advanced the concept of "cognitive mapping" to better understand the Latin American social movements and drawn out some of the lessons of these case studies, we need to examine, finally, how they might move "beyond the fragments" to constitute a powerful counter-movement in the years to come.

The need to move "beyond the fragments" of the social movement mosaic today is urgent, given the turn to the right in many countries once deemed part of the progressive turn. The left in office was not able to successfully administer its political and economic successes. It fell in many cases into charismatic personalist rule rather than building solid and sustainable political institutions. A tragic example was the Morales/Linera government in Bolivia, which ignored a plebiscite to allow a fourth term in office in 2019, ran anyway, won by a narrow margin but then, amid widespread accusations of electoral fraud, was forced to resign. Some progressive governments, such as that of the Partido dos Trabalhadores in Brazil, allowed corruption to flourish and pollute the political domain, even if their leaders did not directly indulge in these practices themselves. They quite often had a solid economic situation to start with, but this was frequently squandered by economic mismanagement that was not forgiven by the electorate. They did achieve an advance in the living standards of the popular classes but often unnecessarily alienated the middle classes – again, something for which payback at election time was inevitable. It could be argued that both the social democratic and Bolivarian options are now closed or limited and that the time to build a new progressive strategy is now upon us. The construction of a new counter-hegemony to renew the progressive mission will, inevitably, have the social movements we have been framing here at its very core.

A basic principle for any new progressive optic for understanding and empowering social movements would be the overarching importance of agency in the analysis of social movements. From a Latin American social movement perspective, E. P. Thompson's *The Making of the English Working Class* is still a key reference point, given the continued importance of community, customs and non-capitalist relations (such as the informal sector). Thompson's "history from below" famously states that the working class "was present at its own making".[19] For Thompson, we have first "a multitude of individuals with a multitude of experiences", and it is only in periods of social change that "we observe patterns in their relationships, their ideas, and their institutions". The making of social class[20] – and social movements – must thus be seen as a relational process, one based on experience and with agency to the fore. Against all structural approaches we need to see participants in social movements as active and conscious actors in the making of these movements. In making collective claims, these movements – like the original formation of the working class – create their own discursive narrative to political power.

There has been much debate internationally, including in Latin America, on the merits and limitations of Thompson's *The Making of the English Working Class*. His emphasis on the historicity of class and social movements is well taken, as is the notion that class is an outcome of experience. The structural determinants of the formation of the working class are, perhaps, less well developed in Thompson's account but he was responding to the then dominant quite mechanistic and economistic vision of working class formation. What is most valuable to retain, and what has had most impact in Latin America, is Thompson's reconstruction of how ordinary people reacted to key historical events through a patient trawl through surviving documents, poems and songs. We can thus read events through the mental and emotional maps of those who lived them rather than through their reconstruction by professional historians and politicians. The discourse about the working class thus created allowed for the building of solidarity across trades and empowered the social movements to press collective claims and a moral argument for redress of their situation.

We also need to foreground politics in any study of social movements from a social transformation perspective. The classic epistemological breakthrough in labour and social history came with Gareth Stedman Jones's study of Chartism, which was the bedrock of Ernesto Laclau's later rereading of labour history in Latin America. Against all the vast historiography on the rise and fall of Chartism as one of the most significant movements in early labour history, Stedman Jones demonstrates that, "given the existence of good material grounds for discontent, it was not consciousness (or ideology) that produced politics, but politics that produced consciousness".[21] In the past it was simply assumed that poor conditions led to some form of "class" consciousness. The rise and fall of Chartism – and social movements in Latin America, I would argue – cannot be attributed to economic trends, divisions in the movement or lack of consciousness but, rather, "to the changing character and policies of the state – the principal enemy upon whose actions radicals had always found that their credibility depended".[22]

In Latin America it is Ernesto Laclau, as we saw above, who has most clearly articulated and developed this insight in a way that is quite central to the study of contemporary social movements. For him, "the construction of the 'people' is a political act par excellence ... The *sine qua non* requirements of the political are the constitution of antagonistic frontiers within the social and the appeal to new subjects of social change."[23] The development of populism is probably the main difference between Latin American political development and that of other regions. To this day, in international commentary on the "left populism" of Hugo Chávez, for example, we find a quite ethnocentric emphasis on the irrationality of populism and a constant tendency to see it as the enemy of "normal" political development, towards class patterns and progressive social transformation. It is also deemed the enemy of development, of course, which can come about only through the unrestricted operation of the market without political interference. The old order was changed utterly by the emergence of this national-popular ideology and worldview. It could also become radicalized at key conjunctures when the "people–oligarchy" opposition became the dominant divide in society.

Two further concepts from Laclau and Chantal Mouffe help us centre the notion of articulation, which builds on the contingent, undetermined links between social movements. One is the concept of "empty signifiers", through which Laclau considered the nature of populism in political discourse, the creation of a popular hegemonic bloc such as "the people" and the importance of affect in politics. He argues that the basis of populism lies in the creation of "empty signifiers": words and ideas that express a universal idea of justice, and symbolically structure the political environment. Against those who see populism as a threat to democracy, Laclau argues that it is an essential component of it. The other key concept is that of "democratic equivalents", defined by Mouffe as

a chain of equivalence between the different democratic struggles to recognise the specificity of the demand ... not unite all demands into one single and homogeneous movement ... [but] establish ways in which, for instance, the feminist or the anti-racist movement could work together ... [O]ur struggles are not exactly the same, but are going to be linked in such a way that, for instance, the demands of women will not be met at the expense of blacks or immigrants.[24]

Today's social movements in Latin America do in practice articulate their alliances in terms of democratic equivalents, and we are very aware of how concepts such as "freedom" or "democracy" are empty signifiers until they are articulated by particular political forces.

It is this articulation that creates hegemony and also counter-hegemonic movements. In Latin America the struggle to constitute ruling class hegemony has always been incomplete and inconsistent, with nothing like a *bourgeoisie conquerante*.[25] The counter-hegemonic movements that were successful were invariably constructed around democratic demands. The "articulating instance", in Laclau's terms, cannot be preordained (as in "the working class") but can "result only from the hegemonic overdetermination of a particular democratic demand".[26] Thus, we can see how demands for human rights, land or employment can trigger equivalential logics across society and thus begin to articulate a counter hegemonic movement. The notion of overdetermination allows us to capture the multiple (often opposed) forces active in any political situation, which is always a complex whole.

Social movements such as, for example, the trade union movement can evolve from a sectional role to a popular one through such a process. Latin America has always been characterized by the popular – or, more precisely, plebeian (*plebeyo*) – nature of subaltern eruption into the public space.[27] This process, with a strong cultural component only partially captured by the appellation of nationalism, leads to the critical importance of the "people" (*pueblo*) in the construction of counter-hegemony. As Laclau puts it, "A plurality of demands which, through their equivalential articulation, constitute a broader social subjectivity we will call popular demands – they start, at a very incipient level, to constitute the 'people' as a potential historical actor."[28] We thus see, as part of this process, a cross-fertilization across the various social movements – for example, ecology and feminism impacting on labour and the indigenous movement, creating a new contestatory philosophy.

It is this philosophy of Buen Vivir as utopia we turn to finally in our bid to move "beyond the fragments". The Buen Vivir cluster of philosophies is, arguably, the most salient Latin American contribution to global social movement theory. As Jameson puts it, in another context, "What these utopian oppositions allow us to do is, by way of negation, to grasp the moment of truth."[29] Thus, the Buen Vivir political philosophies are constructed as an ideological critique of their opposite: a dependent, wasteful and unequal development regime. The imaginary futures envisaged allow us to diagnose the present situation and offer critical alternatives. Along with other current global concerns around the "Anthropocene", the Buen Vivir philosophy offers a utopian horizon that breaks with binary oppositions (such as humanity versus nature) and offers a new development paradigm that other social movements in Latin America are increasingly engaging with.

Knowledge in Latin America has hitherto been marked by the coloniality of power. This has not only privileged scientific over "non-scientific" forms of knowledge, but has coloured the way the rest (which are not the West) have been able to conceive of nation building, revolution and, last but not least, utopia. There are few revolutionary or utopian projects in the majority world that did not have to centre a decolonization or "race" as part of its undoing of the old order and the construction of a new utopian – and thus necessarily postcolonial – order. What we need to carry out to construct a utopia fit for purpose in the majority world is a shift from the centre to the margins of the world system. We should talk not just about alternatives and other worlds but also about alternative ways of thinking about alternatives. The dominant epistemologies remain marked (if not trapped) by their European origins, and this includes arguably all the various "post" epistemologies. Not to put too fine a point on it, the non-European subaltern is missing from rational universalism, from Western non-nationalist forms of emancipation and, by and large, from dominant utopian thinking. The Buen Vivir discourses may help us explore the various ways in which the economy has become decentred and the dominance of capitalism deconstructed, thus opening up livelihood strategies that go beyond calculative rationality. We now need to seek out the waypoints to make the utopian destination of Buen Vivir a viable project, with a transitional programme to bridge the gap between the here and the now, and the better place we want to be in, that will bring people with us.

10

METHODOLOGICAL APPENDIX

Research on Latin American social movements has, on the whole, not been transparent in terms of its methods or the craft of gathering or constructing data and then analysing it inductively or deductively. As Benedicte Carlsen and Claire Glenton put it, "Transparency and accountability are key elements in any research report not least in qualitative studies. Thorough reporting of methods allows readers to assess the quality and relevance of research findings".[1] We cannot simply take on trust the robustness and relevance of the research methods deployed. Whereas in the past – at least in sociology and anthropology – the question of methods, be it participant observation or ethnographic methods, practically dominated, today there is more focus on the politics of epistemology than on the "how I did it" angle. Being methodologically reflexive and self-critical is essential, I would argue, to be a good researcher (and, yes, that does need to be defined, of course). Our starting point is the rather startling discovery, based on a systematic trawl through Latin American social movement studies, that even with a fairly minimal definition of transparency only a miniscule proportion were transparent or structured, or "provided the information that a serious reader would require for even minimal interpretation".[2]

To address this problem, I have consulted with a number of active researchers on Latin American social movements (see Acknowledgements), who are reflexive in their methodologies and are conscious of the need for transparency whatever the particular method they prefer to deploy, as well as drawing on my own experience as researcher and teacher. This chapter will advance in a few distinct moments, as it were. First, I approach the broad question of knowledge: what is a social fact? Is it given or constructed? What does critical realism tell us about doing research on social movements? What do we mean by "constructivism" and can we think in terms of a "grounded" social theory? How do we avoid the twin pitfalls of empiricism and theoreticism?

We then move on to a more applied domain, as it were, namely the question of engagement. In critical, and even mainstream, social research today there is an emphasis on "engaged research".[3] This takes us into a family of research methodologies, including community-based research (CBR), participant observation (PO) and participant action research (PAR) in particular. I ask how these methods might be deployed in Latin America social movement research. Next, we turn to the question of identities, how political identities are formed and the basics of discourse analysis. Other related methodologies to be considered include life histories, oral histories and focus groups, all centred on the making of subjectivities. Finally, we turn to politics, by which I mean really the politics and ethics of social movement research. What does "critical engaged" research mean and what is a scholar/activist in practice? This is a uniquely conflicted aspect of methodology, but one in which we also see unique practices and philosophes emerging from Latin American social movement research.

Knowledge

Social movement research is different from most other social research in terms of its engagement, given the broad sympathy of most researchers with the aims and the aspirations of their "object of analysis". We can take as two examples to introduce the question of knowledge the methodologies of two key social movement researchers, Alain Touraine and Alberto Melucci. They show us how far away social movement research is from the positivist vision that sees social research mirroring natural science research. For Touraine, the main method to be deployed is the "sociological intervention", defined as "the action of the sociologist, whose aim is to reveal social relations and make them the main object of analysis".[4] Researchers are more than witnesses to the activities of the social movement; they confront, they engage and they promote self-analysis. They push the participants of the social movement from giving testimony to questioning the basic principles of the movement. The researcher, for Touraine, in not someone who just asks questions, but who also proposes and engages in the self-analysis.

Melucci is critical of Touraine's methodology while sharing much of his "1968" motivation. He argues that "the missionary-teacher role assigned to the researcher (evident in the concepts of 'emancipation' or 'conversion') is a respectable ethical option, but as such is not a valid procedure or a guarantee for methodological rigour".[5] In terms of the sociology of knowledge, this approach tends to confuse or conflate the role of researcher with that of political actor. Although this critique might have resonance in relation to contemporary approaches to engaged research (see below), it also finds a parallel with 1950s US action research, motivated by social integration objectives. What this points us towards is the need to make the role of the researcher more central in our analysis of the knowledge creation process. We need to problematize the researcher–social actor relationship, which cannot now be seen as somehow external to the research process.

In terms of knowledge production, Melucci points us towards a complex and realist ontology, which is the nature of reality. Innovative research techniques or methods do not suffice on their own. What is called for, argues Melucci, is "a situational epistemology, which social research increasingly needs if it is to break out of the illusion that it stands outside or above the circular observer actor game".[6] Melucci is critical of both structuralist-functionalist approaches to social movements, which see them as symptoms of social disorder, and of traditional Marxism, which sees them as expressions of objective social conditions and contradictions. The "situational epistemology" advocated by Melucci is congruent with the critical realist approach to knowledge. We cannot, in brief, see social movements as either determined by structural preconditions or, simply the expression of values and beliefs. Our methodology thus necessarily needs to be reflexive and sensitive hermeneutically – that is, in terms of the theory and methodology of interpretation.

The critical realism approach to the study of social movements has, in turn, been criticized for not going far enough in recognizing the role of social movements in creating knowledge. For Sara Motta, the critical realist approach to social movements reproduces the separation between abstract knowledge and concrete experience, an epistemological dualism that is debilitating.[7] Motta advocates, instead, a "prefigurative epistemology" based on new relations between researcher and movements and an understanding of how "the universal and systemic are immanent to the concrete".[8] A radical democratic methodology of social movement research needs to destabilize the researcher, as it were, and understand the knowledge implicit in the making of social movements. In Latin America such an approach has considerable resonance given the widespread understanding of Paulo Freire's "pedagogy of the oppressed" and the faith-based prefigurative epistemologies of liberation theology.

We can start our epistemological exploration by understanding that all knowledge of social movements is grounded. We also need to understand that the methods we may deploy in studying them are not a mere toolbox we can choose from at random. Our methods are governed by theories or epistemologies. So, data collected by one method/theory cannot readily be reinterpreted by another conceptual framework. Our theory of knowledge of the social needs to constantly counteract any naïve sociology of the social with its illusion of immediate knowledge. The main principles we need to bear in mind are enunciated clearly by Pierre Bourdieu, Jean-Claude Chamboredon and Jean-Claude Passeron: social facts are constructed, not given; theory dominates the research process, from its planning to its completion; and, without theory, it is impossible to interpret a single event.[9] Against all forms of empiricism, or the positivism that treats social facts as data, we need to foreground theory in the research process and in the development of appropriate methodologies.

We can go further, with Bourdieu and colleagues, and argue that "the less conscious the theory engaged in a practice – the theory of knowledge of the object and the theory of the object – the less controlled it will be, and the less well adapted to the specific object".[10] A questionnaire, a coding instrument or a form of statistical analysis are, in fact, theories in action in so far as they are procedures for the construction of facts and relations between facts. Thus, every methodological choice we make – and this applies as well, of course, to partici- pant observation and the whole ethnographic tradition – needs to be interrogated closely from an epistemological standpoint. This understanding may also guide us later in our discussion of "ethical neutrality", which governs the whole edifice of research ethics (politics) in so far as it is often conflated with the "methodo- logical neutrality" dear to the heart of the positivist school, for which facts are simply data to be gathered as empirical evidence, to be interpreted later, through logic, as the exclusive means to certain knowledge.

The approach to methodology and research I have been outlining can be related to the social constructivist (or constructivist) philosophy of science, for which knowledge is constructed as opposed to created. Put somewhat simply, it is often seen as relativist (and related to postmodernism) in contrast to realism. Peter Berger and Thomas Luckmann articulated an early version of construct- ivism based on the premise of the social construction of reality.[11] Society is thus seen as both an objective and subjective reality. Much the same could be said for social movements; hence the intuitive appeal of this approach. Language is seen not as an uncomplicated means of transmitting thoughts; rather, it makes thought possible by constructing concepts. This approach thus also feeds into the "language turn" that lies behind the rise of discourse analysis, discussed below. The accusation of relativism and the rejection of an objective social reality is not really persuasive, in so far as constructivism does not make ontological claims, simply positing an epistemological model for the social construction of knowledge.

Having established the problems associated with a positivist approach, which believes that facts can simply be "gathered" (not constructed), and a naïve empiricism, we must also consider the danger of theoreticism. This is not just about valuing theory over practice or abstract knowledge over concrete action. Theoreticism is seen sometimes in social movement research when a strong the- oretical framework unduly shapes the actual research process so that findings are shaped to fit the pre-established framework. To guard against this danger, I am proposing a form of "grounded theory light", which takes on board the spirit of grounded theory if not its full methodological set of precepts. Grounded theory emerged in the 1970s as a research strategy that saw concepts emerging from empirical research data. Thus, it is empirical reality that provides the raw material for theoretical constructions, which can never be abstract; rather, they must always be grounded in social reality.

Nowadays grounded theory is taken to be a "family of methods"[12] that can assist researchers in developing concepts of theories based on their empirical findings. The obvious criticism is that social facts are constructed and not given, but grounded theories advocates that we may start off with "sensitizing concepts" and then move towards a constructivist grounded theory. In relation to social movements, Alice Mattoni has argued that, hitherto, grounded theory had been deployed in "a scattered and implicit way" but that it "can work as a flexible source of guidelines in developing research on grassroots political participation and mobilization".[13] Early "grounded theory" aversion to social theory was part of its positivist heritage but there is now a move towards a "constructivist grounded theory"[14] that still focuses on the rich data immersion/analysis phase but also stresses the need for "theoretical sensitivity" during the research process.

What I have tried to show in this preliminary section is that the term "methodology" is not just a box of research tools. Every choice of method we make needs to be evaluated in terms of its epistemological significance. Research techniques are not epistemologically innocent, in other words. To set out to "measure" something (such as attitudes) through questionnaires and statistical analysis is to assume a theoretical frame of how society works, for example, as an aggregate of individuals. As Bourdieu and colleagues put it, "All scientific practice, even and especially when it blindly claims allegiance to the blindest empiricism, involves theoretical presuppositions."[15] And, on the other hand, we also need to steer clear of all forms of theoreticism, whether they be the highly developed frameworks of the US rational choice models of social movements or certain types of Marxism that still trace their heritage back to the "theoretical practice" of 1970s Althusserianism, which elevated theory into a self-contained domain.

Comparison

The comparative method is, in one way, an obvious one; a single case study can never yield generalizable results. This text has always compared and contrasted various cases of a given social movement rather than just go with the iconic cases known internationally. The comparative method seeks to develop explanatory hypotheses about social or political events or movements. We thus find the major studies of Barrington Moore and Theda Skocpol on the genesis of revolutions placing their main emphasis on the causal hypotheses they pose rather than on the day-to-day events, which are more like evidence for their case.[16] There is a more modest version of the comparative method, which Daniel Ritter describes thus: "Rather than strive for universal generalizability, comparative historical researchers delineate their studies thematically, temporally, and/or geographically to only include cases that can reasonably be grouped together".[17] This would, indeed, be the rationale behind the choice of case studies in the chapters above.

This raises the first question that the comparative researcher needs to answer, namely whether to go for the "most similar" or "most different cases". In the first instance, we compare similar cases that differ only in terms of the dependent variable, so that we can identify the independent variable; in the latter approach, we take very different cases that have in common a dependent variable, so that any other circumstances can be regarded as independent variables. Thus, for example, in Skocpol's study mentioned above, we see a comparison of fairly similar revolutionary events set in different national contexts. The purpose was to find similarities that might explain the causes of revolution, thus making it a most different example. A most similar method example would be to compare the labour movements in Argentina and Brazil, which are broadly similar, to identify what the cause might be for a different outcome, which could be, for example, the different internal structures of their trade union movements.

Another distinction to make within the broad family of comparative methods is that between variable-oriented research (discussed above) and a case-oriented approach. The variables approach has tended towards statistical measures and a claim to "scientificity". The case-oriented approach (as used in this text, for example) seeks a "thick" description of the context in which a given phenomenon – for example, a social movement – emerges. As Donatella della Porta puts it, "In a case-oriented approach … an in-depth knowledge of a small number of cases provides the basis for generalizations … while wider relevance should be controlled through further research."[18] That approach sets up with modest gains in terms of understanding a given social phenomenon without making possibly unsustainable claims of more universal validity. This is an approach with possibly great potential in the study of given social movements in Latin America, and is, indeed, adopted by scholars of the women's or indigenous movements, even if they do not name the method as such.

Another variant of the comparative method that needs to be considered is the "incorporated comparison" proposed by Philip McMichael.[19] Rather than seeking "scientific" rigour through statistical or variable-based enquiry, this approach focuses our attention on a non-experimental comparative-historical approach. An ahistorical social science will inevitably reify the social phenomena we study. The incorporated comparison, by contrast seeks to conceptualize variation across time and space, and thus comparison is "incorporated" into the very process of defining the object of analysis, as we did with the variety of social movements considered in this text. It would probably be a limitation of many "conjunctural" studies that they do not incorporate the historical dimension, without which a social movement is decontextualized and left in a timeless limbo.

A pioneering comparative study of Latin America was Fernando Cardoso and Enzo Faletto's *Dependency and Development in Latin America*, first published in 1969 though not appearing in English until 1979.[20] Adopting what they call a historical-structural methodology, the authors design a complex picture of dependence (on the world market) as a conditioning situation, not a defining factor, of political and social development in Latin America. The study focuses on the inequality and exploitation of the development process and how these mechanisms of domination are maintained by the political process. This structural frame allows for agency, and the authors show how the class struggle has produced different political regimes. Social movements enter the picture not just as being produced by these wider processes but also as active agents of collective projects for agrarian reform workers' political representation and community development.

There are major comparative studies in Latin America that have focused on the labour movement. One such study was that by Ruth and David Collier on the interaction between critical junctures, the labour movement and regime dynamics.[21] Over the course of almost 900 pages these authors develop a complex comparative method based on a horizontal study of the labour movement in eight countries. The comparisons are paired on the basis of similarities of certain factors deemed relevant by their theoretical frame, such as the role of the state in labour relations. The book moves back and forth between the historical case studies and the comparison deemed theoretically and empirically relevant. Another example is Charles Bergquist's *Labor in Latin America*,[22] which examines four countries based on their similar export-oriented economies, which he posits as a major factor in the development of a labour movement. Bergquist is aware of how this type of structural historical analysis can easily become economistic, and he applies a strong corrective by emphasizing the agency of workers and trade union.

Two more recent comparative method approaches to the study of Latin American social movements are Leandro Vergara-Camus's comparison of the Brazilian MST and the Zapatistas as peasant alternatives to neoliberalism and Chris Hesketh's comparison of popular mobilization in Chiapas and Oaxaca.[23] Although there have been comparisons of the MST and the Zapatistas as social movements and their shared radical orientation there had not been hitherto a systematic comparison, presumably because of their considerable differences. By stressing the way in which they are embedded in very different rural contexts and cultural settings, Vergara-Camus shows how there were both differences and similarities in the outcome in ways that might not be captured by individual case studies. Hesketh, in contrast, studies two social movements in Mexico within a broadly political economy frame. Interestingly, it deploys both the "incorporated comparison" method mentioned above and also the "extended case study" approach, which rejects the positivist tendency to separate the subjects and objects of research as well as fact and value. In both texts the comparative element and the theory of capitalism deployed does not obscure the importance of social agency in explaining the rise and development of social movements.

Engagement

There has been a strong move in recent years towards what is known as "engaged research", defined as "a wide range of rigorous research approaches and methodologies that share a common interest in collaborative engagement with the community and aim to improve, understand or investigate an issue of public concern, including societal challenges".[24] Community engagement is seen as vital by many universities, and they now even proclaim the virtues of "co-producing" knowledge with communities. This is an agenda driven very much from above, however, as part of the commitment to "innovation", which may be social as much technological. What is interesting is that the turn towards engaged research seems to signal a crisis in confidence in the old technocratic model of scientific diffusion and accepts – even welcomes – the participation of the community (however defined) to meet "societal challenges", defined in practice as the UN's Sustainable Development Goals.

Ethnography – long dominant in the field of anthropology – is not so much a practical method but, rather, an approach to research. Originally it was developed as a way in which Western researchers could gain access to social groups in the colonial territories. They could live with them, observe their cultural interactions and religious rituals and engage in probing conversations. Once back from "the field" (as they called it) they would write up their participant observation notes to produce an ethnography (*ethnos*: people/nation; *grapho*: I write). Today the term "ethnography" covers a multitude of techniques or methods, including participant observation (of which more below) but also in-depth interviews, focus groups, discourse analysis and visual methods such as film, video and photography. Ethnography is defined as "the study of people in naturally occurring settings or 'fields' by means of methods which capture their social meanings and ordinary activities, involving the researcher participating directly in the setting, if not also the activities, in order to collect data in a systematic manner but without meaning being imposed on them externally".[25]

Ethnography can be read as both method (part of the toolkit of techniques we can draw on as researchers) and also as methodology – that is, the broader philosophical framework they fit within: in short, epistemology. From a positivist perspective, it can be criticized for its lack of precision, inability to generalize and failure to meet minimum standards of reliability and validity. There is also a critique from a postmodern/post-structuralist perspective, which questions its naïve realism and its failure to address the crisis of representation. Its epistemological rooting in the "naturalist" tradition (positing natural laws as the rules that govern the structure and behaviour of the universe) has also been queried by the "realist" tradition. Finally, from a Latin American postcolonial perspective, we could argue that ethnography can never escape its colonial origins – the relation with the native "other" despite the transformations and divisions within anthropology over the years.

In the study of Latin American social moments, we have seen the emergence of what is called "transformative ethnography", which seeks to address the tension between theory and practice. Giuseppe Caruso has claimed that "transformative ethnography contributes to knowledge that is nonprescriptive and indirective, involving a process of recognition and adaptation between multiple actors".[26] Ethnographers do not just come in and extract knowledge; they must negotiate the complexities and the tensions within a given social movement – hence the adjective "transformative", as processes of mutual recognition take place. It is also well to bear in mind when thinking about ethnography from a critical perspective that it *"is not and never has been analytically self-sufficient.* Because of its attention to embedded specificity – the very source of its rich and unique knowledge making – ethnography needs history and theory to make sense of what only it can see,"* as Janet Conway puts it.[27] This is certainly something I have found to be the case in the chapters on social movements where both theory and history were ever-present.

Participant observation continues to play a major role in the study of social movements. There is a spectrum of participant observer methods, ranging from the "participant as observer" to the "observer as participant" but with varying degrees of sympathy, detachment, objectivity or subjectivity advocates. This method follows the precepts of what Max Weber called *verstehen*, a German word meaning to "understand in a deep way". In practical terms it may well be the only way to gain access to social groups indicating contestatory or clandestine social movements. It can be said to "give voice" to the participants of social movements, or "actors", as they are called in the literature. The PO method can allow for ambiguity and changes over time and it can study how cultures are constructed and reconstructed. It can provide rich and contextualized accounts deploying a wide range of data to give us what anthropologists call "thick description", and the redefinition of the "depth" of ethnography by the question of the researcher's own identity.[28]

Participant-observation-based research studies are meant to make explicit precisely how they conducted their study so that the reader can get some understanding of how data was gathered. More or less at random, we can take Sonia Alvarez's early work on the women's movement in Brazil to see what is considered best practice in laying out the "personal equation" when doing participant and observation analysis. Alvarez tells the reader how:

> The analysis presented [below] derives from over one hundred interviews with political activists and extended participant-observation in innumerable women's movement meetings. Debates, events, protest actions, and other political activities during November and December of 1981, October 1982 to October 1983, July and August of 1985, and June and July of 1988. The fact that my own social status and organizing experience as a Latina in the US women's movement was analogous to that of many São Paulo's feminists greatly facilitated my access to predominantly middle class-based feminist movement groups and events.
>
> Access to poor and working-class women's groups proved somewhat more difficult as outsiders in general, let alone North American researchers, are generally mistrusted by local social movement groups. In late 1981, I visited several neighborhood women's groups in São Paulo in the company of middle-class feminists, social workers, and female charity workers and decided that the best field strategy would be to follow the activities of one such group quite closely. After explaining the purpose of my research to several such groups, the women's group in Jardim Miriam agreed to have me participate in their ongoing activities in the neighborhood ... [I] have visited the neighborhood and accompanied changing political dynamics there during each of my subsequent field trips. My participation in the Jardim Miriam group also facilitated contacts with other neighborhood women's organizations throughout São Paulo's urban periphery; I regularly traveled with local activists to other neighborhoods and sometimes attended citywide popular meetings in their company.[29]

We obtain an understanding here of precisely how researchers become "participant observers" and what the "research bargain" is – that is, how they are perceived by the social movement under observation. We can interrogate this account, even query some of its assumptions, but it is there for us to critically evaluate. What we cannot say is that today's researchers are always so scrupulous about putting their research process out there for observation.

More recently researchers engaged in participant observation have gone considerably beyond "data collection" in their approaches. One particularly difficult case is described by Kate Hardy in relation to a study of sex workers in Latin America.[30] This study brings to the fore the question of emotions, rarely dealt with in supposedly scientific research processes. Hardy recounts how "throughout the research I was reliant on participant observation, drawing data from the ways in which the women recounted their experiences and spoke to me directly about their feelings, not only in their responses to me. The intersubjective nature of these interactions make it exceedingly difficult to separate this analysis from my own subjective interpretation."[31]

Hardy as researcher also interviewed professionals such as social workers and civil society organizations, and engaged in discourse analysis of the language and images used in the sex workers' pamphlets and literature "to ensure that my own personal experiences and feelings did not overly influence the emergent analysis. That said, recognising, labelling and analysing emotions depends on their refraction through one's own emotional subjectivity, as 'the object is always constructed by the one who observes.'"[32]

Anyone with even a casual acquaintance with Latin American social movement research will have heard of Paulo Freire, liberation theology and participatory action research (PAR) practitioner. This approach is often traced back to the work of Orlando Fals-Borda in Colombia in the late 1960s.[33] Trained in the United States in a quantitative social science approach, Fals-Borda began to find it inadequate to deal with the pressing issues of rural reform in Latin America. Social justice was beginning to come to the fore as a major concern for social researchers; Barrington Moore's[34] comparative historical work, for example, influenced him strongly, and positivist methods within a Cold War political framework were not attractive from that perspective. For Fals-Borda, PAR meant the following.

- Do not monopolize your knowledge nor impose arrogantly your techniques but respect and combine your skills with the knowledge of the researched or grassroots communities, taking them as full partners and co-researchers. That is, fill in the distance between subject and object;
- Do not trust elitist versions of history and science which respond to dominant interests, but be respective to counter-narratives and try to recapture them;
- Do not depend solely on your culture to interpret facts, but recover local values, traits, beliefs, and arts for action by and with the research organizations; and
- Do not impose your own ponderous scientific style for communicating results, but defuse and share what you have learned together, in a manner that is wholly understandable and even literary and pleasant, for science should not be necessarily a mystery nor a monopoly of experts and intellectuals.[35]

PAR was, ultimately, a research philosophy that combined academic knowledge and the wisdom of communities. It was quite clearly overdetermined by the generally effervescent political mood of the post-1968 period. Student radicalism, the war in Vietnam, the French May events of 1968, the Cordobazo of 1969 in Argentina – all these influenced the debate among social scientists. As a Latin American "school", PAR was part of a much broader wave of critical thinking, including the then emerging dependency theory but, above all, the not unrelated work of Freire around *concientização* as a philosophy and practice of popular education. The *Pedagogy of the Oppressed*[36] had a huge influence beyond Latin America in promoting a humanist approach to education and research, which foregrounded the subjective experience of ordinary people. This reflexive-critical approach or method has now diffused across many disciplines, often taking the name of the "bottom-up" method. It can take different forms but it has very much influenced the flavour of non-positivist approaches to social research.

Another influential CBR progenitor is the participatory rural appraisal (PRA) approach pioneered by Robert Chambers, mainly in an African setting. This approach was at first adopted by radical NGOs doing international development work but eventually it was mainstreamed by the World Bank in the 1990s. Chambers, who acknowledges his debt to Freire, promoted a methodology committed to "putting the last first"[37] by drawing out their vision of the world and their needs as rural illiterate communities. Chambers was committed to "the primacy of the personal" and eschewed citing political economy analyses of underdevelopment and its causes. This political vision was rather simplistic, with a set of binary oppositions – core/periphery, white/black, male/female, old/young, teacher/pupil, senior/junior, donor/recipient – determining a simple moral view of the world and how it should be transformed. It is not far-fetched to understand the Chambers perspective as akin to a religious experience, or, as one postcolonial critic put it, a form of "narcissistic samaritanism".[38] Participatory action research becomes a messianic calling, and the path to salvation is centred on "empowerment" of the poor. Participatory research sessions sometimes take on the air of revivalist religious meetings, with great mass fervour bent on discovery of the "truth." Sinners – the more powerful and better off – can admit their sins and see the light. The ascetic selfless facilitator of PRA can exorcise bad thinking and help the "last become the first". It is at least doubtful whether this type of approach to community research will successfully remedy the admitted "democratic deficit" of mainstream top-down approaches. Put simply, no one can "empower" another – or a community, for that matter. If we stand back from the particular Latin American and African contexts – and their distinct local and international interlocutors – we find that the main debate is around the "participation" element in community-based participatory research.

What PAR can provide us as social researchers is an understanding of how research may interact with local community needs and knowledge. It stresses "action" or practice as the best way to test theories, and the validity of this knowledge is seen to be dependent on the extent to which it is "co-produced" with the community. As against the mainstream of the social sciences, it would see research methods as secondary to lived experience, and that, if this is not understood, methods can become a straitjacket on research. I would argue that it is a positive corrective to the Northern research methods textbooks, which tend to be, to put it mildly, quite prescriptive. But I would also urge researchers to bear in mind the warning of a progressive researcher in this tradition, Janet Conway, who asks whether, despite ongoing reflexivity around the role of the researcher, "it is still possible to over identify with the movement we study, that in collapsing the distance between subject and object we remove any space for critical engagement with our interlocutors and collaborators? In other words, do we exhibit a lack of analytic distance that results in accounts that are uncritical of contradictions?"[39]

Identities

The study of social movements means, inevitably, the study of identity: how political identities are formed, mark their differences with others and give meaning to these identities through language. Identities are relational and idents are not fixed. There is always tension between essentialist and non-essentialist perspectives on identity: the first "would suggest that there is one clear, authentic set of characteristics" shared by a group while the second perspective "would focus on differences, as well as common or shared characteristics".[40] The formation of identities may (albeit not necessarily) lead to "identity politics", whereby identity as an oppressed or marginalized group becomes a promoter of political mobilization. This politics is not based on innate or essentialist characteristics; rather, these identities are socially constructed, and they are articulated with other identities in a political manner, not one based on "natural" or biological differences.

One productive way to frame the study of identity is through the approach of "intersectionality", developed in the 1990s by black feminist writer activists.[41] Although it was shaped very much by the US race/class/gender debate, the intersectional approach would lend itself well to frame the study of social movements in Latin America. Intersectionality refers to the way in which different forms of social inequality, oppression and discrimination intersect and become woven into the overall mosaic of identity. Whether it be women, peasants, urban poor or factory workers in Latin America, their identities are formed through intersectionality; they are complex, not simple. It could be argued, as Helma Lutz, Maria Herrera Vivar and Linda Supik do, that intersectionality represents a paradigm shift – "a quantum leap: from the idea of differences between women, via the deconstruction of the category of gender, to the interconnections between different dimensions of inequality".[42]

The intersectionality lens may also help us transcend the division in social movement theory and research between the "politics of redistribution" and the "politics of recognition".[43] Identity politics without a politics of class (to put it simply) will not be transformative. Nira Yuval-Davis, on the race/ethnicity/gender interface, provides clues on how intersectionality could open up new research strategies. As Yuval-Davis argues, the apparent dichotomy "between recognition and redistribution differences needs to be encompassed in an inter-sectional analysis that would be sensitive to the differential constructions of the same social category as an intersected social location and as a mode of social identification".[44] This approach would open up our research, for example, in rela-tion to indigenous communities in Latin America, which have been characterized by a somewhat artificially opposed cultural/identity frame versus an economic/class one in Latin America.

When it comes to providing a methodology for the study of how political iden-tities are formed, one increasingly influential method is that of discourse analysis. There are several, quite distinct variants of discourse analysis, and their cap-acity to be operationalized (used in empirical research) varies. Foucault's theory of discourse is immensely sensitizing in terms of power/knowledge dynamics but is not immediately "applicable" to social movement research – though see Gavin Kendall and Gary Wickham for the case for *Using Foucault's Methods*.[45] A long-standing discourse approach is that of Norman Fairclough's in the context of social linguistics. Fairclough's critical discourse analysis "brings together lin-guistically oriented discourse analysis and social and political thought relevant to discourse and language, in the form of a framework which will be suitable for one on social scientific research".[46] The goal of this approach is to explore the linguistic-discursive dimension of social interactions, and the role they play both in maintaining unequal power relations (such as consumerism or neoliberalism as discourses) or in contesting them through building a counter-hegemony (such as feminism or Buen Vivir as discourses).

In exploring the role of discourse in the making of political identities, it is the approach of Ernesto Laclau that has been most influential in Latin America, even if mainly at a broad theoretical level rather than as an operational meth-odology to date. David Howarth and Yannis Stavrakakis, in introducing this approach, state:

> Discourse analysis refers to the practice of analysing empirical raw materials and information as discursive forms. This mean that dis-course analysts treat a wide range of linguistic and non-linguistic data – speeches, reports, manifestos, historical events, interviews, policies, ideas, even organisations and institutions – as "texts" or "writing" (in the Derridean sense that "there is nothing outside the text").[47]

We note here a difference with Foucault in rejecting a discursive versus non-discursive domain. This is not a form of theoreticism seeking to subsume the empirical case within its precepts but it also, of course, rejects all versions of empiricism and positivism in terms of how it views empirical facts. The theoretical framework is open enough to accommodate research into the complex world of social movements.

In terms of "applying" this methodological approach to the study of social movements in Latin America, I would say the influence has been quite diffuse. It has had a sensitizing effect and, most certainly, its theoretical influence has been huge, not least in this text itself. But, in terms of social movements, we can take Laclau's own studies of Peronism and that of Sebastián Barros and Gustavo Castagnola in one of the edited collections of his "school" as exemplars.[48] Laclau provides a theoretically dense study of Peronism as a prime example of this version of "populism" and argues in relation to the discourse approach that, "from this point of view, the distinction between a movement and its ideology is not only hopeless, but also irrelevant – what matters is the determination of the discursive sequences through which a social force or movement carries out its overall political performance".[49] Barros and Castagnola, for their part, apply this perspective to Peronism between 1955 and 1973 and argue that "a perspective centred on discourse theory can account for the stalemate of Argentine politics without introducing any essentialist assumption – be it an indigenous rationality of the economy or of institutions".[50] By focusing on the formation of political identities (through a discourse-based approach), we can thus avoid all forms of structural determinism typical of a traditional Marxism.

Empirical sociology has, since the 1950s, been dominated by the survey paradigm. Whereas early sociologists and the Chicago School in the United States in the 1920s focused on interpreting social problems, the new approach was deemed more scientific. Large-scale surveys and random sampling (to ensure reliability) became de rigueur. But Daniel Bertaux and Paul Thompson note that "increasingly, as its methodological sophistication has intensified … it has narrowed its interests to hypothesis which a survey can test".[51] Measuring and testing are not necessarily the best way to understand social processes, even though there is still an argument for their inclusion in the repertoire of the social movement researcher. What we have seen since the 1970s is the emergence of a new (or rediscovered) interpretative social science focused on interpretation. One variant is the life story/life history/oral history methodology, which helps us bring to the surface people's perceptions and the multi-layered complexity of cause and effect in human lives.

Bertaux and Thompson, pioneers of life history and oral history approaches respectively, write that "years of working with life histories … have made [the] complex tangles of causality and self-determination familiar to us, leaving us increasingly dissatisfied with the simpler notions of causality which underlie much empirical sociology".[52] The life history/oral history approach is not a naïve one, believing that some "truth" will be captured from participants. There is usually a triangulation (cross-checking) process with other methods, and validation is also sought by taking the readings back to the individual and social group respondents. The histories/interviews are amenable to many different readings; subaltern, gender, linguistic and psychoanalytical perspectives have emerged. A key methodological point that the practitioner needs to bear in mind is that of "saturation", which involves modifying the research questions as results come in until a point is reached when new cases simply confirm what has been already learnt. This plays a similar control role to random sampling in survey research.[53]

In Latin America the study of social movements has only relatively recently engaged with the methodologies of oral sources. Pablo Pozzi, who has promoted the use of oral history, describes its rise as "a revaluing of the oral as against the empire of 'the written' ... A move towards a more democratic history and a movement of renewal and political engagement."[54] Since the 1990s a journal of oral history in Latin America has been produced, and its influence has spread to other disciplines. Oral history in Latin America has had a particular influence in the area of gender studies. John French and Daniel James comment with regard to one collection on women and work that, although "few would today subscribe to the naïve fiction that oral history allows the analyst to achieve direct or unmediated access to the thoughts, feelings, desires and aspirations of those they study ... it does, however demonstrate the many ways that oral history can be used to deepen our understanding of the complex nature of individual and collective consciousness and identity".[55]

One particular deployment of oral history in Latin America has been that carried out with the Andean indigenous communities. In particular, we can note the work of Aymara/Bolivian researcher Silvia Rivera Cusicanqui, whose concept of *historia oral* (oral history) has been used to promote a better understanding of the multiscalar forms of resistance that indigenous people have gone through since the advent of the colonial era.[56] Rivera Cusicanqui argues that oral forms of indigenous history provide a privileged space in which to uncover tactics of the colonial order, and that by viewing it through the eyes of the oppressed history it loses its chronological/linear perspective and becomes a dialectic cycle of oppression and resistance. We can transfer this approach to the study of contemporary multiculturalism and the growing NGOization of civil society activism. Rivera Cusicanqui is also very critical of what she calls the political economy of knowledge and, in particular the development of the niche academic market of postcolonial studies.

The individual, or life history, approach has also gained traction in the study of Latin American social movements in recent years. A good example is the work of

Javier Auyero, which reconstructs two local uprisings in Argentina through the life history of two women activists.[57] Auyero talks at length to the two women about their actions, thoughts and feelings during two sharp encounters with the state, "thereby illuminating the continuity between their life stories (i.e. their trajectories not merely as activists but as workers, wives, lovers, mother, etc.) and their experience of these contentious episodes".[58] Structural causes of episodes in Argentina's economic and political history are matched by the struggle for dignity and respect by individuals. Other sources are drawn on as well such as other interviews with participants, newspaper reports, court proceedings and government enquiries. Like all successful research strategies, a multiplicity of methods helps provide a holistic view of a social movement in action.

Politics

This section deals with what was once known as the ethics of research, and something that was placed before the "ethics committee" of the institution the researcher belonged to. These committees sought to ensure that the researcher was keeping within ethical guidelines devised by a given profession or higher education institution whose declared purpose was to protect vulnerable individuals or groups. Today they might also take much interest in data protection issues, given the importance of data privacy. Although these processes may be of value, we really need to situate research ethics within the wider domain of the politics of research, not least as the so-called "ethics committees" act in a political manner to determine what constitutes permitted research methods and what does not. We are here in a very Foucauldian terrain of power-knowledge, and not one simply defined by Western notions of ethics.

The ethics and politics of working on/with social and human societies are complex. They highlight the contradictions of engaged or activist research in particular. What the ethics panels and communities have created in the Northern universities is a bureaucratic exercise that has ignored the complexity of this research. The checklists and consent forms and the emphasis on the "gate-keeper" to the communities subject to research address only a very small part of the research process. As Kevin Gillen and Jenny Pickerill write, "Too often ethics are deemed something doctoral students need to overcome and much reflection and writing on ethical dilemmas is by early career academics."[59] Yet most experienced researchers readily acknowledge that, once they are immersed in the research process, things turn out to be much more complex than they imagined when designing the research project. The politics of research and epistemological vigilance is clearly not a one-off exercise at the start of research or something experienced researchers can take for granted.

Proclaiming the virtues of the "activist scholar" does not, of course, in itself generate a passport for political legitimacy. On the contrary, it may well exacerbate the usual methodological problems when there is at least a well-established social protocol between the researcher and the researched. In fact, it has some parallels with the debate around covert research and to the extent to which it is "permissible" to gather data under the pretence of neutrality and then publicize it. With sympathetic researchers we come against a different problem from a methodological point of view. Thus, Judith Hellman, a progressive researcher, questions whether over-identification with the social movement being researched (in this case the Zapatistas) might reduce the ability to "ask the hard question" and produce robust research.[60] In the study of Latin American social movements there have, indeed, been many cases of researchers producing what are essentially uplifting stories, rather than rigorous research that reflects the complexity and contradictions inherent in most social movements.

Perhaps the first question any researcher needs to confront today is that of "positionality"; that is to say, the stance of the researcher in terms of the social-political context of a study. It requires centring the researcher, a figure once taken for granted or assumed to be not problematic. Clearly, the positionality of a researcher affects every element of his or her relation with a given community. Sam Halvorsen discusses his own positionality in terms of the epistemic expropriation of Southern social movement knowledge.[61] Extractivism is not just about natural resources in Latin America but also about knowledge. As Halvorsen puts it, "My experience has been that we are forced to live contradictory and dislocated existences as producers of knowledge." He goes on to say that the tendency towards "epistemic expropriation in the context of working with southern knowledge ... require[s] ongoing critical reflection".[62] The reality is that this research process will be fraught, and choices will need to be made by any researcher with critical consciousness.

Birke Otto and Philipp Terhorst, reflecting on their own research into social movements, argue that, "by problematizing the relationships between activist researchers and subaltern positions, we do not intend to reinvent the wheel, but endeavour to point out some of the challenges that the activist researcher may encounter".[63] These are predictable, in a sense. They come to "the field" with different backgrounds, access to resources and decision-making capacity. At one level, it is impossible to translate the subaltern experience into a conventional Western academic product. There may well be two different social practices and languages. Activist researchers can even deepen the original unequal relationship by creating relations of dependence. Clearly, "positionality" is an integral element of the research process, and not only as a preliminary but also as an ongoing critical reflection. Participants in a research process are shaped by society and culture, but so also is the researcher. It need not be a drawback to good research but it needs to be foregrounded, with epistemological vigilance exercised at all stages of the research process and, of course, when writing up and reporting on the research.

In reviewing the literature on Latin American social movements for the purpose of this chapter, I was struck by the extent to which some "engaged" researchers took upon themselves the role of a political advisor. It put me in mind of what Michel Foucault calls the "clinical gaze".[64] Power and control over the body of the individual is handed over to the clinicians in most Western societies. The "clinical gaze", for Foucault, separates the body – or symptoms – from the identity of the person. Bearing in mind that knowledge has the power to make itself true (one has only to think of neoliberalism, once a small, discredited economic school), clinical findings are used as a form of power. The "clinical gaze" provides medicine with the power to regulate deviance and disorder, guided by a vision of normalization. Now the "external gaze" of the social movement researcher can also be subject to power/knowledge relations, and the temptation to become a judge of what is deviant and what is "normal" or expected behaviour from his or her own political standpoint.

It is not a question of arguing for an unattainable, or not even desirable, ethical or methodological neutrality, here. Rather, it is recognizing, as Bourdieu and colleagues do, that, "if, as [Gaston] Bachelard says, every chemist has to struggle with the alchemist within himself [*sic*], then every sociologist has to fight the social prophet that his audience wants him to be".[65] Setting aside the sexist language, the point here is relevant to self-proclaimed radical North American writings on Latin American social movements. The social movement literature, especially since the wave of progressive government after 2000, is replete with advice and recommendation from Northern researchers. They decry the reformist "betrayal" by these governments and demand that social movements be more "revolutionary". But a sociologist is not a social prophet. The task of the sympathetic researcher is to analyse movements, bring in a comparative angle when relevant and disseminate the self-understandings of the movement and its participants to a wider audience. It is not to act as a proxy *comandante*, or as what in Ireland are known as the "long rifles", who urge militancy and sacrifice from afar.

Increasingly in Latin America there is a turn towards the "decolonial option" when it comes to articulating a power-knowledge position. There is now a great deal written on Southern knowledge and subaltern epistemologies,[66] and even on the project for "decolonizing methodologies".[67] Western methodologies for research on indigenous peoples and the once colonized lands have a view of history that is both totalizing and linear. As Linda Smith puts it, this research "through imperial eyes" "assumes that Western ideas ... are the only ideas possible to hold, certainly the only rational ideas, and the only ideas which can make sense of the world, of reality, of social life and of human beings".[68] Indigenous methodologies in Latin America would include the Freirean approach and a whole cluster of new visions of knowledge arising from the Buen Vivir/Sumak Kawsay philosophy, translated into the domain of research methodology.

For the emerging decolonial school in Latin America, "it is necessary to detach oneself from the hegemonic and Eurocentred matrix of knowledge", as Anibal Quijano puts it.[69] The Western paradigm of rationality/knowledge is not the only one; alternatives are emerging based on the decolonizing of knowledge, and new interpretative tools and methodologies are now available for the researcher. Arturo Escobar has been a pioneer in this regard, as shown in his statement that it is now possible "in refracting modernity through the lens of coloniality [to] engage in a questioning of the spatial and temporal origins of modernity, thus unfreezing the radical potential for *thinking from difference* and towards the construction of alternative local and regnal worlds".[70] And it is in social movement research, in particular, that this new epistemology has most purchase, not least as it dovetails with recent advances in feminist and critical race research methodologies.

Finally, then, in terms of articulating a politics of research, we could start with Antonio Gramsci's famous slogan (borrowed from the novelist Romain Rolland) of "pessimism of the intellect, optimism of the will", though I tend to reverse it in my own mind in order to foreground optimism. The categories may be suspect from an epistemological perspective – optimism/pessimism and intellect/will are unsustainable binary oppositions – but the spirit of the advice is clear enough. Ana Dinerstein has recently written eloquently on the "hope" element, leaning on the philosophy of Ernst Bloch.[71] For Dinerstein, "the art of organising hope offers not only a political tool to resist and reject capital as a form of society, but to anticipate alternative social relations, socialites and practices".[72] In terms of research methodology, the principle of realism (as I read Gramsci's "pessimism") needs to be matched by an openness to the potential of the social movements we research and their imagination of alternative futures.

GUIDE TO FURTHER READING

Given the rapidly changing nature of this field of research, it is essential to keep up with the journals that cover Latin America, such as *Latin American Perspectives* (http://latinamericanperspectives.com), *Bulletin of Latin American Research* (https://www.slas.org.uk/publications), *Journal of Latin American Studies* (http://larrlasa.org), *Latin American Research Review* (http://onlinelibrary.wiley.com/journal/15482456), *Latin American Politics and Sociology* (www.cambridge.org/core/journals/journal-of-latin-american-studies/latest-issue) and *Latin American and Caribbean Ethnic Studies* (www.tandfonline.com/toc/rlac20/current). The social movement journals, such as *Social Movements Studies* (www.tandfonline.com/toc/csms20/current) and *Interface* (www.interfacejournal.net), also – occasionally – cover Latin American social movements. A major portal always worth consulting, with country- and theme-specific sections, is LANIC, the Latin American Network Information Center (http://lanic.utexas.edu).

Latin America

Paul Almeida and Allen Cordero Ulate (eds), *Handbook of Social Movements across Latin America* (New York: Springer, 2015). An encyclopaedic review of the social movements covered in this book, plus others such as religious movements and student protest, from a wide range of perspectives and disciplines.

Sonia Alvarez, Jeffrey Rubin, Millie Thayer, Gianpaolo Baiocchi and Agustín Laó-Montes (eds), *Beyond Civil Society: Activism, Participation and Protest in Latin America* (Durham, NC: Duke University Press, 2017). A wide-ranging collection, with a number of important contributions on Brazil, from a perspective within/beyond the civil society discourse.

Ana Dinerstein, *The Politics of Autonomy in Latin America: The Art of Organising Hope* (London: Palgrave Macmillan, 2015). A key "autonomist" text that takes up Ernst Bloch's notion of "hope" to analyse some contemporary social movements in Latin America, particularly the movements in Argentina around 2001/2.

Arturo Escobar and Sonia Alvarez (eds), *The Making of Social Movements in Latin America: Identity, Strategy, and Democracy* (Boulder, CO: Westview Press, 1992). A pioneering text in the "new social movement" tradition bringing together Latin American and international scholars covering a wide range of movements.

Paula Klachko and Katu Arkonada, *Desde abajo, desde arriba: de la resistencia a los gobiernos populares: escenarios y horizontes del cambio de época en America Latina* (Buenos Aires: Prometeo, 2016). A review of many of the iconic social movements since 2000, with the overarching aim of interpreting Marxist "class struggle" potential.

Ronaldo Munck and Kyla Sankey (eds), two-volume special issue of *Latin American Perspectives*: "Social Movements in Latin America" (2020). A wide range of country-specific and movement-focused articles set in context by the editors.

James Petras and Henry Veltmeyer, *Social Movements and State Power: Argentina, Brazil, Bolivia, Ecuador* (London: Pluto Press, 2005). Although it is very much within an orthodox Marxist perspective that somewhat overdetermines its findings, this book is insightful and good on peasant movements. From a critical engaged Marxist perspective, it examines the interface between social movements and progressive governments in Bolivia, Ecuador and Venezuela since 2000.

James Petras and Henry Veltmeyer, *The Class Struggle in Latin America: Making History Today* (London: Routledge, 2017). An update of *Social Movements and State Power*, as above.

Geoffrey Pleyers, *Movimientos sociales en el siglo XXI: perspectivas y herramientas analíticas* (Buenos Aires: CLACSO, 2018). A broad survey of the social movement literature from an alter-globalization perspective (and influenced by Alain Touraine), with some focus on Latin America, particularly Mexico.

Gary Prevost, Carlos Campos and Harry Vanden (eds), *Social Movements and Leftist Governments in Latin America: Confrontation or Co-optation?* (London: Zed Books, 2012). An introductory survey of the main progressive governments in the first phase, from 2000 to 2010, which serves as a useful opening read.

Federico Rossi and Marisa von Bülow (eds), *Social Movement Dynamics: New Perspectives on Theory and Research from Latin America* (London: Routledge, 2015). Set in the context of the North American resource mobilization theory, it covers the interaction between what it calls "contentious" and "routine" politics in a number of countries.

David Slater (ed.), *New Social Movements and the State in Latin America* (Amsterdam: CEDLA, 1985). A very early collection that marked the melding of new social movement theory and the Latin American social movements of the late 1970s and early 1980s. Influential contributions by Ernesto Laclau, Tilman Evers and Maxine Molyneux.

Richard Stahler-Sholk, Harry Vanden and Glen Kuecker (eds), *Latin American Social Movements in the Twenty-First Century: Resistance, Power, and Democracy* (Lanham, MD: Rowman & Littlefield, 2008). A collection of essays that originally appeared in *Latin American Perspectives* covering the early phases of the turn to the left.

Maristella Svampa, *Del cambio de época al fin de ciclo: gobiernos progresistas, extractivismo y movimientos sociales en América Latina* (Buenos Aires: EDHASA, 2017). A wide-ranging political study focused on the interplay between the post-2000 progressive governments, their extractivist policies and the new wave of social movement activation.

Workers

Charles Bergquist, *Labor in Latin America: Comparative Essays on Chile, Argentina, Venezuela, and Colombia* (Stanford, CA: Stanford University Press, 1986). Deals with the historical formation of the working class in these countries, focused on the extraction industries key to economic development.

Ruy Braga, *A política do precariado: do populismo à hegemonia lulista* (São Paulo: Boitempo, 2012). A Brazilian take on the concept of the precariat that shows the limitations of the Northern focus of the dominant debates. Well integrated into the broader debates on Latin American labour studies.

James Brennan, *The Labor Wars in Córdoba, 1955–76: Ideology, Work, and Labor Politics in an Argentine Industrial City* (Harvard, MA: Harvard University Press, 1994). Focused on the interaction between society and the workplace, this book sets the Cordobazo of 1969 in its full social context, and not just the direct political causes.

Enrique de la Garza Toledo (ed.), *Sindicatos y nuevos movimientos sociales en América Latina* (Buenos Aires: CLACSO, 2005). Focused on the interaction between trade unions and some of the "new" social movements, this collection contains useful case studies on Bolivia, Argentina, Colombia and Venezuela at new conjunctures.

John French and Daniel James (eds), *The Gendered Worlds of Latin American Women Workers: From Household to Factory to the Union Hall and the Ballot Box* (Durham, NC: Duke University Press, 1997). Deals with women workers, mainly historically, in Argentina, Brazil, Chile and Mexico, with a strong emphasis on oral history and life history approaches.

Julio Godio, *Historia del movimiento obrero Latinoamericano*, 3 volumes (Buenos Aires: Educator, 1980). A wide-ranging narrative history with particular emphasis on the political tendencies within the labour movement, from anarchism to populism. Needs to be complemented by more recent monographs but provides an overview.

Daniel James, *Resistance and Integration: Peronism and the Argentine Working Class, 1946–1976* (Cambridge: Cambridge University Press, 1988). An early example of a social history approach rather than a political history of labour. The book needs to be complemented with more recent texts, though it is easily accessed through an internet trawl.

Sian Lazar, *The Social life of Politics: Ethics, Kinship, and Union Activism in Argentina* (Stanford, CA: Stanford University Press, 2017). This text focuses on the details of the personal and family life of a union activist and how these shape their community of practice as drivers of a vibrant labour movement and active citizenship.

Jörg Nowak, *Mass Strikes and Social Movements in Brazil and India: Popular Mobilisation in the Long Depression* (London: Palgrave Macmillan, 2019). An explicitly Third World take on strikes that does not assume a Western model of industrial relation and focuses on the support of kinship structures, local communities and social movements to mount successful strike actions, even when trade unions were weak or non-existent.

Paul Posner, Viviana Patroni and Jean Mayer (eds), *Labor Politics in Latin America: Democracy and Worker Organization in the Neoliberal Era* (Gainsville, FL: University Press of Florida, 2018). Set in the context of the labour market reform demanded by neoliberal globalization, this collection shows its impact in terms of labour flexibilization and the weakening of the trade unions in Argentina, Brazil, Chile, Mexico and Venezuela.

Marieke Riethof, *Labour Mobilization, Politics and Globalization in Brazil: Between Militancy and Moderation* (London: Palgrave Macmillan, 2019). A useful narrative account of Brazilian trade unions from 1964 to 2019, set in the economic and political context of the period.

Ian Roxborough, *Unions and Politics in Mexico: The Case of the Automobile Industry* (Cambridge: Cambridge University Press, 2009). Against the conceptual wisdom of the corporatist straitjacket paradigm, this book shows union politics to be more complex and even autonomous than assumed.

Gay Seidman, *Manufacturing Militance: Workers' Movements in Brazil and South Africa, 1970–1985* (Berkeley, CA: University of California Press, 1994). A close read, through a political economy lens, of the relationship between capitalist development and the rise of the new labour movement in Brazil, usefully compared to South Africa.

Saúl Escobar Toledo, *Los trabajadores en el siglo XX: sindicato, estado y sociedad en México: 1907–2004* (Mexico City: UNAM, 2006). A narrative labour history of Mexico that provides a basic but well-informed overview.

Marisa von Bülow, *Building Transnational Networks: Civil Society Networks and the Politics of Trade in the Americas* (Cambridge: Cambridge University Press, 2010). A detailed review of the complex alliances put in place by the labour and other social movements to defeat the Free Trade Area of the Americas project.

Francisco Zapata, *Autonomía y subordinación en el sindicalismo latinoamericano* (Mexico City: El Colegio de Mexico, 1993). A wide-ranging study of Latin American unions focused around the complex interplay between autonomy and subordination to the state.

Peasants

Armando Bartra, *Los herederos de Zapata: movimientos campesinos posrevolucionarios en México, 1920–1980* (Mexico City: Ediciones Era, 1985). From one of the best historians in Mexico, this is a very broad text of peasant movements since Zapata, to be complemented by a trawl of regional and period-specific histories.

Saturnino Borras, Marc Edelman and Cristóbal Kay (eds), *Transnational Agrarian Movements: Confronting Globalization* (Malden, MA: Wiley-Blackwell, 2008). This collection brings agrarian movements for social change into the domain of the globalization paradigm, showing how "local" movements can also be global ones.

Tom Brass, *Latin American Peasants* (London: Cass, 2003). A collection of historical essays with considerable focus on Brazil. Criticizes the subaltern school and its supposed emphasis on non-class identity.

Annette Desmarais, *La Vía Campesina: Globalization and the Power of Peasants* (London: Pluto Press, 2009). Shows how peasants and small-scale farmers can organize collectively in defence of their interests and contribute to the global debates around food security. Online follow-up research readily available.

Carmen Deere and Frederick Royce (eds), *Rural Social Movements in Latin America: Organizing for Sustainable Livelihoods* (Gainsville, FL: University Press of Florida, 2009). At the intersection of peasant and sustainability studies, this collection covers many of the most significant rural social movements through gender, ethnicity and transitional lenses.

Marc Edelman, *Peasants against Globalization: Rural Social Movements in Costa Rica* (Stanford, CA: Stanford University Press, 1999). From a critical cultural anthropology perspective, this book tells the history of how small-scale farmers in Central America responded to the devastation wrought by free market neoliberalism in the 1990s.

Pablo González Casanova, *Historia politica de los campesinos latinoamericanos*, 3 volumes (Mexico City: Siglo XXI, 1985). From one of Mexico's major political scientists, this is a wide-ranging work, useful for an overview of the political history of the peasantry in Latin America.

Cristóbal Kay and Leandro Vergara-Camus (eds), *La cuestión agraria y los gobiernos de izquierda en América Latina: campesinos, agronegocio y neodesarrollismo* (Buenos Aires: CLACSO, 2018). A wide-ranging and theoretically informed review of the so-called "agrarian question" in Latin America today, focused on the deleterious impact of agribusiness on the peasantry.

Wilder Robles and Henry Veltmeyer, *The Politics of Agrarian Reform in Brazil: The Landless Rural Workers Movement* (London: Palgrave Macmillan, 2015). From a traditional Marxist perspective, this book unravels the development of capitalism in rural Brazil and the genesis of the MST, perhaps the most significant rural social movement in Latin America since the Mexican Revolution.

Ben Selwyn, *Workers, State and Development in Brazil: Powers of Labour, Chains of Value* (Manchester: Manchester University Press, 2012). A political economy take on class dynamics and capitalist development in north-eastern Brazil, showing how workers in the grape export sector have used their associational power to contest untrammelled capitalist rule.

Leandro Vergara-Camus, *Land and Freedom: The MST, the Zapatistas and Peasant Alternatives to Neoliberalism* (London: Zed Books, 2014). Set in the broader context of counter-globalization movements, these two major rural social movements are analysed in considerable detail from a political economy perspective.

Leon Zamosc, *The Agrarian Question and the Peasant Movement in Colombia: Struggles of the National Peasant Association, 1967–1981* (Cambridge: Cambridge University Press, 1986). Although it is restricted to one peasant movement and now of mainly historical interest, this book is one of the better, more analytical treatments of the Colombian peasant movements.

Community

Madeleine Adriance, *Promised Land: Base Christian Communities and the Struggle for the Amazon* (New York: SUNY Press, 1995). A useful analysis of the CEBs in Brazil and their interaction with other social issues/movements, such as the struggle for the Amazon.

Leonardo Avritzer, *Democracy and the Public Sphere in Latin America* (Princeton, NJ: Princeton University Press, 2002). A study opposed to imported theories of elite democracy constructed from above, this book demonstrates the vitality of the public sphere and the participation of local communities in the construction of democracy in Brazil.

John Cameron, *Struggles for Local Democracy in the Andes* (Boulder, CO: First Forum Press, 2010). A political-power-based study of the way peasant and indigenous communities engage with and construct local democracy, and its impact on political identities.

Graciela Di Marco and Héctor Palomino (eds), *Reflexiones sobre los movimientos sociales en la Argentina* (Buenos Aires: Jorge Baudino Ediciones, 2004). A collection of essays and debates on the massive community-based mobilizations in Argentina in 2001 and 2002, written close to the events and with a strong analytical frame.

Arturo Escobar, *Territories of Difference: Place, Movements, Life, Redes* (Durham, NC: Duke University Press, 2008). An engaged piece of research from a decolonial perspective of the Afro-Colombian communities of the Pacific coast, showing the complex interactions and political struggles.

Chris Hesketh, *Spaces of Capital/Spaces of Resistance: Mexico and the Global Political Economy* (Athens, GA: University of Georgia Press, 2017). An interdisciplinary multi-level take on social movements in Chiapas and Oaxaca, stressing the production of space and the role of indigenous communities in articulating resistance.

Elizabeth Jelin (ed.), *Los nuevos movimientos sociales*, vol. 2, *Mujeres, rock nacional, derechos humanos, obreros, barrios* (Buenos Aires: Centro Editoriale América Latina, 1995). Part of the rise in interest in the "new" social movements in the 1980s, this volume examines the human rights, labour and community (*barrio*) movements with strong activist engagement.

David Lehman, *Struggle for the Sprit: Religious Transformation and Popular Culture in Brazil and Latin America* (Cambridge: Polity, 1996). The "preferential option for the poor" taken by the Catholic Church is examined closely, in particular its relationship with poor communities.

Gerardo Otero (ed.), *Mexico in Transition: Neoliberal Globalism, the State and Civil Society* (London: Zed Books, 2004). A wide-ranging survey of how globalization impacts on Latin American civil society and how it resists in various ways, based on community and territory.

Mariano Plotkin, *Mañana es San Perón: A Cultural History of Peron's Argentina* (Washington, DC: SR Books, 1993). A rare book on the cultural and symbolic dimensions of Perón's version of populism and how it became rooted in Argentina's popular communities.

Alejandro Velasco, *Barrio Rising: Urban Popular Politics and the Making of Modern Venezuela* (Berkeley, CA: University of California Press, 2015). A detailed ethnography of one popular neighbourhood in Caracas, its divisions and its struggles, and its emblematic role in the Caracazo and thus, indirectly, in the rise of Chavez.

Raúl Zibechi, *Territories in Resistance: A Cartography of Latin American Social Movements* (Oakland, CA: AK Press, 2012). This book reports from the front lines of a range of social struggles, with a strong emphasis on territoriality as a new site of contestation.

Women

Sonia Alvarez, *Engendering Democracy in Brazil: Women's Movements in Transition Politics* (Princeton, NJ: Princeton University Press, 1990). An early "classic" on women and politics in Latin America. Needs to be updated by following articles and chapters by this author in subsequent years.

Sonia Alvarez, Claudia de Lima Costa, Verónica Feliu, Rebecca Hester, Norma Klahn and Millie Thayer (eds), *Translocalities/Translocalidades: Feminist Politics of Translation in the Latin/a Américas* (Durham, NC: Duke University Press, 2014). Informed by recent theoretical trends – Afro, queer, indigenous and feminist – this collection explores the politics of translocations and breaks with the old story of immigrating and assimilating from a complex positionality perspective.

Emilie Bergmann, Janet Greenberg, Gwen Kirkpatrick, Francine Masiello, Francesca Miller, Marta Morello-Frosch, Kathleen Newman and Mary Pratt, *Women, Culture and Politics in Latin America: Seminar on Feminism and Culture in Latin America* (Berkeley, CA: University of California Press, 1990). A theoretically sophisticated take on the relations between gender, culture and politics in Latin America, based on a largely historical analysis around literature and journalism.

Alba Carosio, *Feminismo y cambio social en América Latina y el Caribe* (Buenos Aires: CLASCO, 2012). A result of the CLASCO (Latin American Social Science Council) gender working group, this is a wide-ranging collection, covering many countries, and setting the debate in terms of the political changes brought about by the turn to the left after 2000.

Silvia Chant with Nikki Craske, *Gender in Latin America* (London: Latin America Bureau, 2003). This introductory text cuts across universalizing gender stereotypes and shows how households, poverty, sexuality, family and migration play out in Latin America in unique ways.

Nikki Craske and Maxine Molyneux (eds), *Gender and the Politics of Rights and Democracy in Latin America* (London: Palgrave Macmillan, 2002). Framed by a rights perspective, this volume exemplifies the international feminist perspective of the 1990s as applied in Latin America.

Natalia de Souza, "When the body speaks (to) the political: feminist activism in Latin America and the quest for alternative democratic futures", *Contexto Internacional* 41:1 (2019).

Jane Jaquette (ed.), *Feminist Agendas and Democracy in Latin America* (Durham, NC: Duke University Press, 2009). A useful overview of the women's movements in Latin America from diverse perspectives. Deals with women and the formal political system, the legal dimension of women's rights and the increasingly important international dimension.

Karen Kampwirth (ed.), *Gender and Populism in Latin America* (University Park, PA: Pennsylvania State University Press, 2010). A thorough gendered take on populism and its political regimes, covering Argentina, Brazil, Venezuela, Nicaragua, Ecuador and Mexico.

Gaby Küppers, *Compañeras: Voices from the Latin American Women's Movement* (London: Latin American Bureau, 1993). Valuable direct testimony from activists.

Francesca Miller, *Latin American Women and the Search for Social Justice* (Hanover, NH: University Press of New England, 1991). A historical review from 1890 to 1990, covering early suffrage-oriented feminism through to the influence of international feminism in Latin America during the 1980s.

Maxine Molyneux, *Women's Movements in International Perspective: Latin America and Beyond* (London: Palgrave Macmillan, 2001). A collection of essays on Argentina, Nicaragua and Cuba set in the context of the wider debate around gender and citizenships, and the author's take on "women's interests".

Conceicao Paludo and Dawn Vendereia, *Género, classe y proyeto popular: comprender mais para lutar melhor* (Passo Fundo: Gráfica Batistel, 2001). An activist or engaged perspective that demonstrates the fluid articulation between gender and class politics in Brazil and the unique importance of constructing a popular project.

Sarah Radcliffe and Sallie Westwood (eds), *"Viva": Women and Popular Protest in Latin America* (London: Routledge, 1993). A good reflection on women's roles in the formal and informal economies and the centrality of gender, class and ethnicity in constructing the national in the 1990s.

Virginia Vargas, "Latin American feminisms and their translation to the new millennium (a personal political reading)", in Fernanda Begel (ed.), *Key Texts for Latin American Sociology*

(Los Angeles: Sage, 2019). An invaluable account by a leading feminist, who traces the contemporary movement back to its origins and does not shy away from critical appraisal.

Indigenous

Isabel Aninat, Verónica Figueroa and Ricardo González (eds), *El pueblo mapuche en el siglo XXI: propuestas para un nuevo entendimiento entre culturas en Chile* (Santiago de Chile: Centro de Estudios Públicos, 2017). A broad review of political rights, interculturalism and socio-economic inequality in relation to the Mapuche people in the south of Chile/Argentina. Far less researched than the Andean countries to the north and a distinct minority indigenous population under great pressure.

Edwin Cruz, *Movimientos indígenas, identidad y nación en Bolivia y Ecuador: una genealogía del estado plurinacional* (Quito: Abya Yala, 2012). A meticulous account of the shift from neoliberal multiculturalism to the plurinational state in the Andean countries after the rise of the progressive governments. Well grounded in local debates sometimes missed by international researchers.

Silvia Rivera Cusicanqui, "Ch'ixiakax utxiwa: a reflection on the practices and discourses of decolonization", in Fernanda Begel (ed.), *Key Texts for Latin American Sociology* (Los Angeles, CA: Sage, 2019). A clear outline of the indigenous knowledge perspective and also a critique of the appropriation of the decolonial approach in the Northern academy.

Héctor Díaz-Polanco, *Indigenous Peoples in Latin America: The Quest for Self-Determination* (Boulder, CO: Westview Press, 1997). Based on the Mexican experience, this text takes an anthropology plus political economy perspective to explain the rise of indigenous self-determination politics in the 1990s.

Álvaro García Linera, *Plebeian Power: Collective Action and Indigenous, Working-Class and Popular Identities in Bolivia* (Chicago: Haymarket Books, 2014). Critical sociologist as well as prominent politician Álvaro García Linera provides an engaged questioning of class and communal politics in contemporary Bolivia.

Charles Hale, *Mas que un Indio – More than an Indian: Racial Ambivalence and Neoliberal Multiculturalism on Guatemala* (Santa Fe, NM: School of American Research Press, 2006). A Guatemala-based study from a cultural anthropology perspective that unpacks the significance of "neoliberal multiculturalism" and unsettles Northern preconceptions of any racist politics.

Neil Harvey, *The Chiapas Rebellion: The Struggle for Land and Democracy* (Durham, NC: Duke University Press, 1998). A wide-ranging and detailed account of the "backstory" to the rise of the Zapatistas in the 1990s, in terms of ethnic and class conflict in Chiapas since the Conquest and, in particular, the rise of peasant and indigenous organizations in the 1970s.

Carmen Martínez (ed.), *Repensando los movimientos indígenos* (Quito: FLACSO, 2009). Latin American and international scholars come together to critically examine some of the main issues surrounding indigenous social movements in the Andean countries, not least the relation between class and "cultural" factors.

Thomas Olsen, *International Zapatismo: The Construction of Solidarity in the Age of Globalization* (London: Zed Books, 2005). Set at the interface of a Latin American social movement and the transnational of the Zapatista experience.

Donna Van Cott, *From Movements to Parties in Latin America: The Evolution of Ethnic Politics* (Cambridge: Cambridge University Press, 2005). A political science approach (and vocabulary) treating institutions, party systems and social movements in Bolivia, Ecuador and Peru to provide a useful comparative perspective.

Kay Warren, *Indigenous Movements and Their Critics: Pan-Maya Activism in Guatemala* (Princeton, NJ: Princeton University Press, 1999). An anthropological take on indigenous politics in Guatemala in the period of the peace process (1987 to 1996), following a largely indigenous guerrilla insurgency in the 1980s and its contribution to a multicultural democracy.

Jeffrey Webber, *Red October: Left-Indigenous Struggles in Modern Bolivia* (New York: Haymarket, 2012). From an orthodox Marxist perspective, this text provides an overview of the social struggles that culminated in the election of Evo Morales as president of Bolivia.

Deborah Yashar, *Contesting Citizenship in Latin America: The Rise of Indigenous Movements and the Postliberal Challenge* (Cambridge: Cambridge University Press, 2005). Based on a study of indigenous social movements in Bolivia, Ecuador and Peru, this book illuminates the complex interaction of the state, ethnic cleavages and citizenship.

Environmental

Kiran Asher, *Black and Green: Afro-Colombians, Development, and Nature in the Pacific Lowlands* (Durham, NC: Duke University Press, 2009). An ecological focus on the Black Pacific in Colombia, this text provides a useful overview set in the context of development theory of how social movements have emerged.

Anthony Bebbington (ed.), *Minería, movimientos sociales y respuestas campesinas: una ecología política de transformaciones territoriales* (Lima: Instituto de Estudios Peruanos, 2007). Focused on the Andean countries, this text provides a theoretically informed survey of political ecology and social responses from peasant movements.

Evan Berry and Robert Albro (eds), *Church, Cosmovision and the Environment: Religion and Social Conflict in Contemporary Latin America* (London: Routledge, 2018). Explores the emerging relationships between various communities of faith, the state and popular mobilizations around environmental issues. Introduces ecclesiastical articulation of environmental rights and justice.

Jeremy Campbell, *Conjuring Property: Speculation and Environmental Futures in the Brazilian Amazon* (Seattle: University of Washington Press, 2015). A political economy perspective on land politics, environmental policy and violence in one of the front lines of the global sustainability conflict.

Helen Collinson, *Green Guerrillas: Conflicts and Initiatives in Latin America and the Caribbean: A Reader* (London: Latin American Bureau, 1996). An introduction to the diverse ways in which environmental issues intertwine with the human rights of urban and rural communities.

Gian Delgado-Ramos, *Ecología política de la minería en América Latina: aspectos socioeconómicos, legales y ambientales de la mega minería* (Mexico City: UNAM, 2010). Focused on Mexico but also covering Central America and parts of South America, this book shows the impact of large-scale mining on communities and their resistance.

David Goodman and Michael Redclift (eds), *Environment and Development: The Politics of Sustainability* (Manchester: Manchester University Press, 1991). An early but still essential overview of the plunder of natural resources in Latin America and the relatively recent concern with sustainability.

Eduardo Gudynas, *Derechos de la naturaleza: ética biocéntrica y políticas ambientales* (Montevideo: Tinta Limón, 2000). A critical Latin American environmentalist perspective, distinct from Marxism and engaged with the Buen Vivir movement from a political ecology perspective.

Carlos Larrea, *Post-crecimiento y buen vivir: propuestas globales para la construcción de sociedades equitativas y sustentables* (Ecuador: Friedrich-Ebert-Stiftung, 2014). Part of the growing literature on Buen Vivir as a post-growth environmentally sustainable development philosophy. There is now a vast literature on this topic available on line.

Salvador Schavelzon, *Plurinacionalidad y vivir bien/buen vivir: dos conceptos leídos desde Bolivia y Ecuador post-constituyentes* (Quito: Ecuador Abya-Yala, 2017). An anthropological take on the Buen Vivir discourse in the Andean countries, set in the context of the changes in nature and the emergence of new visions for sustainability that are also politically viable.

Maristella Svampa and Mirta Antonelli (eds), *Minería transnacional, narrativas del desarrollo y resistencias sociales* (Buenos Aires: Biblos, 2009). Covering Argentina from a critical engaged social movement perspective, this text gives great insight into the anti-extractivist movement.

Henry Veltmeyer and James Petras, *The New Extractivism: A Post-Neoliberal Development Model or Imperialism of the Twenty-First Century?* (London: Zed Books, 2014). Written from an orthodox Marxist anti-imperialist perspective, this text seeks commonality across the Andean countries, Argentina and Mexico towards a "new extractivism" as a development model.

Research methods

This is a subject with a plethora of publications, so I will just list some indicative texts directly useful to a social movement researcher.

Robert Chambers, *Revolutions in Development Inquiry* (London: Routledge, 2008). A summative volume by a pioneer in participatory methods in a development context. He argues that these can not only empower local people but also provide more rigorous knowledge than traditional methods.

Donatella della Porta (ed.), *Methodological Practices in Social Movement Research* (Oxford: Oxford University Press, 2014). This is, far and away, the best text to access up-to-date guides on all the relevant research methodologies, from interviews to social surveys and from historical research to discourse analysis.

Vandana Desai and Robert Potter (eds), *Doing Development Research* (London: Sage, 2006). A practical, hands-on review of development research methodologies, which at times overlap with social movement research, such as the various participatory approaches. Covers ethics, "working in different cultures", indigenous knowledge and the various interviewing techniques.

Jeffrey Juris and Alex Khasnabish (eds), *Insurgent Encounters: Transnational Activism, Ethnography, and the Political* (Durham, NC: Duke University Press, 2013). A radical take on the ethnographic approach from a networked perspective. Various researcher-activists explain "how they did it" and present their political reflections.

Xochitl Leyva *et al.* (ed.), *Prácticas otras de conocimiento(s): entre crisis, entre guerras* (Buenos Aires: CLASCO, 2018). A wide-ranging and representative presentation of various subaltern epistemologies from Latin America. Vital reading before dipping into the more "practical" methodology toolboxes.

Thalia Mulvihill and Raji Swaminathan, *Critical Approaches to Life Writing Methods in Qualitative Research* (New York: Routledge, 2017). A survey of how "life writing" permeates the methods of ethnography and lifelong history. It introduces new methodological tools useful to social movement research.

NOTES

1 Introduction

1. M. Diani, "The concept of social movement", *Sociological Review* 40:1 (1992).
2. R. Munck, "Reaction and globalization: nationalists, patriots and Jihadists", in *Globalization and Contestation: The New Great Counter-Movement* (London: Routledge, 2007).
3. J. Cortázar, *Rayuela* (Buenos Aires: Seix Barral, 1970), 3–5, 116.
4. F. Fox Piven and R. Cloward, *Poor People's Movements: Why They Succeed, How They Fail* (New York: Vintage, 1977), 20.
5. B. Moore, *Injustice: The Social Bases of Obedience and Revolt* (London: Routledge, 1978), 82–3.
6. *Ibid.*, 188.
7. See V. Mantouvalou, "Are labour rights human rights?", *European Labour Law Journal* 3:2 (2012).
8. A. Gramsci, *Selections from the Prison Notebooks* (London: Lawrence & Wishart, 1971).
9. See R. Munck, *Rethinking Latin America: Development, Hegemony, and Social Transformation* (London: Palgrave Macmillan, 2013).
10. M. Castells, *The City and the Grassroots: A Cross-Cultural Theory of Urban Social Movements* (Berkeley, CA: University of California Press, 1983).
11. See E. Silva, *Challenging Neoliberalism in Latin America* (Cambridge: Cambridge University Press, 2009).
12. J. Petras and H. Veltmeyer, *Social Movements and State Power: Argentina, Brazil, Bolivia, Ecuador* (London: Pluto Press, 2005).
13. S. Alvarez, "Latin American feminisms 'go global': trends in the 1990s and challenges for the new millennium", in S. Alvarez, E. Dagnino and A. Escobar (eds), *Cultures of Politics/Politics of Cultures: Re-Visioning Latin American Social Movements* (Boulder, CO: Westview, 1998), 306.
14. In M. von Bülow, *Building Transnational Networks: Civil Society and the Politics of Trade in the Americas* (Cambridge: Cambridge University Press, 2010), 11.
15. G. Prevost, C. Campos and H. Vanden (eds), *Social Movements and Leftist Governments in Latin America: Confrontation or Co-optation?* (London: Zed Books, 2012).
16. See G. di Marco and H. Palomino (eds), *Reflexiones sobre los movimientos sociales en Argentina* (Buenos Aires: Ediciones Baudino, 2005).
17. M. Foucault, *The History of Sexuality*, vol. 1 (London: Penguin Books, 1979), 95.
18. *Ibid.*, 112.
19. J. Rouse, "Power/knowledge", in G. Gutting (ed.), *The Cambridge Companion to Foucault* (Cambridge: Cambridge University Press, 2003), 112.
20. Foucault, *The History of Sexuality*, vol. 1, 87.
21. *Ibid.*
22. *Ibid.*, 86.
23. See J. Bidet, *Foucault with Marx* (London: Zed Books, 2016).

24. K. Polanyi, *The Great Transformation: The Political and Economic Origins of Our Time* (Boston: Beacon Press, 2001 [1944]), 60.
25. *Ibid.*, 146.
26. *Ibid.*, 76.
27. *Ibid.*, 186.
28. S. Gill, "Gramsci, modernity and globalization", paper prepared for conference "Gramsci and the Twentieth Century", Cagliari (1977); see www.internationalgramscisociety.org/resources/online_articles/articles/gill01.shtml.
29. Polanyi, *The Great Transformation*, 159.
30. *Ibid.*, 164.
31. *Ibid.*
32. *Ibid.*, 160.
33. B. Jessop, "Polanyi on the social embeddedness of substantively instituted economics", research paper (Lancaster: Department of Sociology, Lancaster University, 2003).

2 Theories

1. See T. Kuhn, *The Structure of Scientific Revolutions* (Chicago: University of Chicago Press, 1962).
2. M. Foucault, *Power*, vol. 3, *Essential Works of Foucault 1954–1994*, ed. J. Faubion (London: Penguin Books, 2000), 75, 341.
3. M. Olson, *The Logic of Collective Action: Public Goods and the Theory of Groups* (Cambridge, MA: Harvard University Press, 1971).
4. See, for example, S. Tarrow, *Power in Movements: Collective Action, Social Movements and Politics* (Cambridge: Cambridge University Press, 1944).
5. Piven & Cloward, *Poor People's Movements*, 139.
6. *Ibid.*, 162.
7. J. Foweraker, *Theorizing Social Movements* (London: Pluto Press, 1995), 35.
8. A. García Linera, *Plebeian Power: Collective Action and Indigenous, Working-Class and Popular Identities in Bolivia* (Chicago: Haymarket Books, 2015).
9. J. Cohen, "Strategy or identity: new theoretical paradigms and contemporary social movements", *Social Research* 52:4 (1985).
10. See A. Touraine, *The Post-Industrial Society: Tomorrow's Social History: Classes, Conflicts, and Culture in the Programmed Society* (New York: Random House, 1971); and A. Gorz, *Farewell to the Working Class: An Essay on Post-Industrial Socialism* (London: Pluto Press, 1987).
11. A. Touraine, *The Voice and the Eye: An Analysis of Social Movements* (Cambridge: Cambridge University Press, 1985).
12. G. Arrighi, T. Hopkins and I. Wallerstein, *Antisystemic Movements* (London: Verso, 1989), 97, emphasis in original.
13. T. Evers, "Identity: the hidden side of new social movements in Latin America", in David Slater (ed.), *New Social Movements and the State in Latin America* (Amsterdam: CEDLA, 1985), 49–60.
14. M. Castells, *The Information Age: Economy, Society and Culture*, vol. 3, *End of Millennium* (Oxford: Blackwell, 1998), 95.
15. D. Clawson, *The Next Upsurge: Labor and the New Social Movements* (Ithaca, NY: ILR Press, 2003), 196.
16. Foweraker, *Theorizing Social Movements*, 27.
17. F. Calderón, A. Piscitelli and J. Regna, "Social movements: actors, theories, expectations", in A. Escobar and S. Alvarez (eds), *The Making of Social Movements in Latin America: Identity, Strategy, and Democracy* (Boulder, CO: Westview Press, 1992), 34.

18. See Escobar & Alvarez, *The Making of Social Movements in Latin America*; and Alvarez, Dagnino & Escobar, *Cultures of Politics/Politics of Cultures*.
19. García Linera, *Plebeian Power*, 305.
20. See J. Aricó, *Marx y America Latina* (Mexico City: Alianza Editorial Mexicana, 1980).
21. H. Vanden and M. Becker (eds), *José Carlos Mariátegui: An Anthology* (New York: Monthly Review Press, 2011), 130.
22. G. Esteva, "The hour of autonomy", *Journal of Latin American and Caribbean Ethnic Studies* 10:1 (2015).
23. Gramsci, *Selections from the Prison Notebooks*.
24. E. de Ípola and J. Portantiero, "Lo nacional popular y los populismos realmente existentes", *Nueva Sociedad* 54 (1981).
25. E. Laclau, *On Populist Reason* (London: Verso, 2005), 107.
26. *Ibid.*, 136.
27. T. Wickham-Crowley and S. Eckstein, "The persisting relevance of political economy and political sociology in Latin American social movement studies", *Latin American Research Review* 50:4 (2015), 32.
28. N.-L. Sum and B. Jessop, *Towards a Cultural Political Economy: Putting Culture in Its Place in Political Economy* (Cheltenham: Edward Elgar, 2015).
29. Escobar & Alvarez, *The Making of Social Movements in Latin America*.
30. M. Keck, "Weaving social movements back in", in F. Rossi and M. von Bülow (eds), *Social Movement Dynamics: New Perspectives on Theory and Research from Latin America* (Farnham: Ashgate, 2015), 223.
31. *Ibid.*

3 Workers

1. C. Bergquist, *Labor in Latin America: Comparative Essays on Chile, Argentina, Venezuela, and Colombia* (Stanford, CA: Stanford University Press, 1986), vii.
2. D. James, *Resistance and Integration: Peronism and the Argentine Working Class, 1946–1976* (Cambridge: Cambridge University Press, 1988), 121.
3. M. Atzeni and J. Grigera, "The revival of labour movement studies in Argentina: old and lost agendas", *Work, Employment and Society* 33:5 (2019).
4. R. Antunes, M. Aurelio Santana and L. Praun, "Chronicle of a death foretold: the PT administrations from compromise to the coup", *Latin American Perspectives*, 2018; doi: https://journals.sagepub.com/doi/pdf/10.1177/0094582X18807210.
5. *Ibid.*, 92.
6. I. Roxborough, "Urban labour movements in Latin America since 1930", in L. Bethel (ed.), *Latin America: Politics and Society since 1930* (Cambridge: Cambridge University Press, 1998), 232.
7. *Ibid.*, 257.
8. D. Bacon, "With López Obrador in, workers have the confidence to walk out", American Prospect (6 February 2019); https://prospect.org/world/lopez-obrador- in-workers-confidence-walk.
9. Von Bülow, *Building Transnational Networks*, 25, emphasis in original.
10. See M. Anner, *Solidarity Transformed: Labor Responses to Globalization and Crisis in Latin America* (Ithaca, NY: Cornell University Press, 2011).

4 Peasants

1. L. Vergara-Camus, *Land and Freedom: The MST, the Zapatistas and Peasant Alternatives to Neoliberalism* (London: Zed Books, 2014), 85.

2. P. McMichael, *Food Regimes and Agrarian Questions* (Halifax, NS: Fernwood, 2013).
3. J. Petras and H. Veltmeyer, "Peasant-based socio-political movements in Latin America", in J. Petras (ed.), *The New Development Politics: The Age of Empire Building and New Social Movements* (Farnham: Ashgate, 2003).
4. P. Freire, *Pedagogy of the Oppressed* (London: Penguin Books, 1980).
5. T. Flores, "Vertical inequality, land reform and insurgency in Colombia", *Peace Economics, Peace Science and Public Policy* 20:1 (2014), 27.
6. L. Zamosc, *The Agrarian Question and the Peasant Movement in Colombia: Struggles of the National Peasant Association, 1967–1981* (Cambridge: Cambridge University Press, 2015).
7. Petras & Veltmeyer, "Peasant-based socio-political movements in Latin America", 100.
8. C. Kay, "Rural development: from agrarian reform to neoliberalism and beyond", in R. Gwynne and C. Kay (eds), *Latin America Transformed: Globalization and Modernity* (London: Arnold, 1999), 284.
9. See B. Loveman, *Struggle in the Countryside: Politics and Rural Labor in Chile, 1919–1973* (Bloomington, IN: Indiana University Press, 1976).
10. P. Silva, "The state, politics and peasant unions in Chile", *Journal of Latin American Studies* 20:2 (1988), 436.
11. *Ibid.*, 437.
12. Kay, "Rural development", 288.
13. S. Barrientos, *Women and Agribusiness: Working Miracles in the Chilean Fruit Export Sector* (Basingstoke: Palgrave Macmillan, 1999).
14. P. Rosset, "Evolution of the struggle for land and territory in La Vía Campesina International", in R. Munck and R. Delgado Wise (eds), *Reframing Latin American Development* (London: Routledge, 2018), 167.
15. A. Desmarais, *La Vía Campesina: Globalization and the Power of Peasants* (Halifax, NS: Fernwood, 2007).

5 Community

1. Foweraker, *Theorizing Social Movements*, 4.
2. L. Grueso, C. Rosero and A. Escobar, "The process of black community organizing in the southern Pacific coast region of Colombia", in Alvarez, Dagnino & Escobar, *Cultures of Politics/Politics of Cultures*, 205.
3. E. Soja, *Thirdspace: Journeys to Los Angeles and Other Real and Imagined Spaces* (Oxford: Blackwell, 1996).
4. R. Zibechi, *Territories in Resistance: A Cartography of Latin American Social Movements* (Oakland, CA: AK Press, 2012), 8.
5. A. Escobar, *Territories of Difference: Place, Movements, Life, Redes* (Durham, NC: Duke University Press, 2008), 64.
6. J. Gibson-Graham, *Postcapitalist Politics* (Minneapolis: University of Minnesota Press, 2006), xxxiv, emphasis in original.
7. G. Baiocchi, "Participatory budgeting and the long history of participation in Brazil", in S. Alvarez *et al.* (eds), *Beyond Civil Society: Activism, Participation and Protest in Latin America* (Durham, NC: Duke University Press, 2017), 32.
8. L. Kowarick, "The pathways to encounter: reflections on the social struggles in São Paulo", in D. Slater (ed.), *New Social Movements and the State in Latin America* (Amsterdam: CEDLA, 1985), 85.
9. F. Betto, *O que é Comunidade Eclesial de Base?* (São Paulo: Editora Brasiliense, 1981), 77.
10. N. Vink, "Base communities and urban social movements: a case study of the metalworkers' strike 1980, São Bernardo, Brazil", in Slater, *New Social Movements and the State in Latin America*, 108.

11. E. Dagnino, "Culture, citizenship, and democracy: changing discourses and practices of the Latin American left", in Alvarez, Dagnino & Escobar, *Cultures of Politics/Politics of Cultures*.
12. L. Avritzer, "Civil society in Brazil: from state autonomy to political interdependency", in Alvarez *et al.*, *Beyond Civil Society*, 60.
13. P. Loureiro and A. Saad-Filho, "The limits of pragmatism: the rise and fall of the Brazilian Workers' Party (2002–2016)", *Latin American Perspectives* 46:1 (2019), 77.
14. I. Velez-Torres and D. Varela, "Between the paternalistic and the neoliberal state: dispossession and resistance in Afro-descendant communities of the Upper Cauca, Columbia", *Latin American Perspectives* 41:6 (2014), 22.
15. U. Oslender, "Another history of violence: the production of 'geographies of terror' in Columbia's Pacific Coast region", *Latin American Perspectives* 35:5 (2008), 88.
16. K. Asher, *Black and Green: Afro-Colombians, Development, and Nature in the Pacific Lowlands* (Durham, NC: Duke University Press, 2009), 201.
17. Proceso de Comunidades Negras, "Renacientes"; https://renacientes.net/quienes-somos.
18. Grueso, Rosaro & Escobar, "The process of black community organizing", 213.
19. Escobar, *Territories of Difference*.
20. *Ibid.*, 165.
21. D. García Delgado and J. Silva, "El movimiento vecinal y la democracia: participación y control en el Gran Buenos Aires", in E. Jelin (ed.), *Los nuevos movimientos sociales*, vol. 2, *Mujeres, rock nacional, derechos humanos, obreros, barrios* (Buenos Aires: Centro Editoriale América Latina, 1985), 64.
22. J. Holloway, *How to Change the World without Taking Power* (London: Pluto Press, 2002).
23. G. Esteva, "The meaning and scope of the struggle for autonomy", *Latin American Perspectives* 28:2 (2001), 130.
24. A. Dinerstein, *The Politics of Autonomy in Latin America: The Art of Organising Hope* (London: Palgrave Macmillan, 2014).
25. M. Modonesi, *Subalternity, Antagonism, Autonomy: Constructing the Political Subject* (London: Pluto Press, 2014), 125.
26. J. Hellman, "The study of new social movements in Latin America and the question of autonomy", in Escobar & Alvarez, *The Making of Social Movements in Latin America*, 54.
27. *Ibid.*
28. *Ibid.*, 56.

6 Women

1. V. Schild, "New subjects of rights? Women's movements and the construction of citizenship in the new democracies", in Alvarez, Dagnino & Escobar, *Cultures of Politics/Politics of Cultures*, 92.
2. M. Molyneux, "Mobilisation without emancipation? Women's interests, state and revolution in Nicaragua", in Slater, *New Social Movements and the State in Latin America*, 240.
3. Alvarez, "Latin American feminisms 'go global'".
4. G. Di Marco, "Social movement demands in Argentina and the construction of a 'feminist people'", in Alvarez *et al.*, *Beyond Civil Society*, 120.
5. *Ibid.*, 130.
6. S. Alvarez, *Engendering Democracy in Brazil: Women's Movements in the Transition Politics* (Princeton, NJ: Princeton University Press, 1990), 135.
7. *Ibid.*, 173.
8. F. Macaulay, "Women and politics", in J. Buxton and N. Phillips (eds), *Developments in Latin American Political Economy: States, Markets and Actors* (Manchester: Manchester University Press, 1999), 96.

9. M. García Castro, "Engendering powers in neoliberal times in Latin America: reflections for the left on feminisms and feminisms", *Latin American Perspectives* 28:6 (2001), 17.

10. See www.ine.gov.ve.

11. M. Fox, "Women and Chavismo: an interview with Yanahir Reyes", NACLA (25 June 2013); https://nacla.org/article/women-and-chavismo-interview-yanahir-reyes.

12. *Ibid.*

13. *Ibid.*

14. See Venezuelanalysis, "Feminist struggles in Venezuela: an interview with Comadres Púrpuras (part II)" (1 November 2018); https://venezuelanalysis.com/analysis/14127.

15. S. Motta, "'We are the ones we have been waiting for': the feminization of resistance in Venezuela", *Latin American Perspectives* 40:4 (2013), 40.

16. S. Fernandes, "Barrio women and popular politics in Chávez's Venezuela", *Latin American Politics and Society* 49:3 (2008), 107.

17. N. Steinbach, M. Navarro and S. Alvarez, "Feminism in Latin America: from Bogota to San Bernardo", in Escobar & Alvarez, *The Making of Social Movements in Latin America*.

18. *Ibid.*, 256.

19. Schild, "New subjects of rights?", 68.

20. Alvarez, "Latin American feminisms 'go global'", 306.

7 Indigenous

1. C. Martínez Novo (ed.), *Repensando los movimientos indígenas* (Quito: FLACSO, 2009), 17.

2. D. Yashar, "Democracy, indigenous movements, and the postliberal challenge in Latin America", *World Politics* 52:1 (1999).

3. R. Burbach, M. Fox and F. Fuentes, "Bolivia's communitarian socialism", in *Latin America's Turbulent Transitions: The Future of Twenty-First-Century Socialism* (London: Zed Books, 2013), 86.

4. L. Farthing, "An opportunity squandered? Elites, social movements and the government of Evo Morales", *Latin American Perspectives* 46:1 (2019), 225.

5. J. Webber, "From left-indigenous insurrection to reconstituted neoliberalism in Bolivia: political economy, indigenous liberation, and class struggle", in J. Webber and B. Carr (eds), *The New Latin American Left: Cracks in the Empire* (Lanham, MA: Rowman & Littlefield, 2013), 184.

6. *Ibid.*, 185.

7. P. Klachko and K. Arkonada, *Desde abajo, desde arriba: de la resistencia a los gobiernos populares: escenarios y horizontes del cambio de época en Buenos Aires* (Buenos Aires: Prometeo, 2016), 7.

8. D. Van Cott, *From Movements to Parties in Latin America: The Evolution of Ethnic Politics* (Cambridge: Cambridge University Press, 2005), 103.

9. *Ibid.*, 113.

10. M. Becker, "Pachakutik and indigenous political party politics in Ecuador", in R. Stahler-Sholk, H. Vanden and G. Kuecker (eds), *Latin American Social Movements in the Twenty-First Century: Resistance, Power, and Democracy* (Lanham, MD: Rowman & Littlefield, 2008), 179.

11. E. Cervone, "Los desafíos del multiculturalismo", in Martínez Novo, *Repensando los movimientos indígenas*, 211.

12. V. Silva, "The return of the state, new social actors, and post-neoliberalism in Ecuador", *Latin American Perspectives* 43:1 (2016), 17.

13. N. Harvey, *The Chiapas Rebellion: The Struggle for Land and Democracy* (Durham, NC: Duke University Press, 1998).

14. *Ibid.*, 8.

15. A. Gilly, "Chiapas and the rebellion of the enchanted world", in D. Nugent (ed.), *Rural Revolt in Mexico: US Intervention and the Domain of Subaltern Politics* (Durham, NC: Duke University Press, 1998), 319.
16. Vergara-Camus, *Land and Freedom*, 286.
17. C. Fuentes, "Chiapas: Latin America's first post-communist revolution", *New Perspectives Quarterly* 11:2 (1994); M. Castells, *The Information Age*, vol. 2, *The Power of Identity* (Oxford: Blackwell, 2004); A. Touraine, "Marcos: el democrata armado", *La Jornada Semanal* (22 December 2001).
18. Gilly, "Chiapas and the rebellion of the enchanted world", 312.
19. *Ibid.*
20. Cited in T. Olesen, *International Zapatismo: The Construction of Solidarity in the Age of Globalization* (London: Zed Books, 2005), 184.
21. *Ibid.*, 3.
22. J. Hellman, "Real and virtual Chiapas: magical realism and the left", in L. Panitch and C. Keys (eds), *Socialist Register 2000: Necessary and Unnecessary Utopias* (London: Merlin, 2000), 175.
23. J. Paulson, "Peasant struggles and international solidarity: the case of Chiapas", in Panitch & Keys, *Socialist Register 2000*, 286.
24. See Enlace Zapatista, "Palabras para todos los que forman parte en las filas del Ejército Zapatista de Liberación Nacional" (1 January 2003); https://enlacezapatista.ezln.org.mx/2003/01/01/comandante-david-palabras-para-todos-los-que-forman-parte-en-las-filas-del-ejercito-zapatista-de-liberacion-nacional.
25. Olesen, *International Zapatismo*.
26. J.-P. Sartre, foreword to F. Fanon, *Wretched of the Earth* (London: Penguin Books, 1969).

8 Environmental

1. See K. Hicks and N. Fabricant, "The Bolivian Climate Justice Movement: mobilizing indigeneity in climate change negotiations", *Latin American Perspectives* 43:4 (2016).
2. E. Gudynas, "Extractivism: tendencies and consequences", in Munck & Delgado Wise, *Reframing Latin American Development*, 65.
3. R. Munck (ed.), *Water and Development: Good Governance after Neoliberalism* (London: Zed Books, 2017).
4. W. Morales, "Social movements and revolutionary change in Bolivia", in Prevost, Campos & Vanden, *Social Movements and Leftist Governments in Latin America*, 56.
5. S. Spronk and J. Webber, "Struggles against accumulation by dispossession in Bolivia: the political economy of natural resource contention", in Stahler-Sholk, Vanden & Kuecker, *Latin American Social Movements*, 86.
6. Zibechi, *Territories in Resistance*.
7. Webber, "From left-indigenous insurrection to reconstituted neoliberalism in Bolivia", 83.
8. Cited in P. Terhorst, M. Olivera and A. Dwinell, "Social movements, left governments, and the limits of water sector reform in Latin America's left turn", *Latin American Perspectives* 40:4 (2013), 57.
9. *Ibid.*, 65–6.
10. Becker, "Pachakutik and indigenous political party politics in Ecuador", 176.
11. A. Acosta, "From the ghost of development to utopias", in H. Fagan and R. Munck (eds), *Handbook on Development and Social Change* (Cheltenham: Edward Elgar, 2018).
12. S. Caria & R. Domínguez, "Ecuador's Buen Vivir: a new ideology for development", *Latin American Perspectives* 43:1 (2016), 29.

13. A. Acosta, "The Yasuní–ITT initiative, or the complex construction of utopia", in D. Bollier and S. Helfrich (eds), *The Wealth of the Commons: A World beyond Market and State* (Amherst, MA: Levellers Press, 2012).

14. *Ibid.*

15. M. Le Quang, "The Yasuní–ITT initiative: toward new imaginaries", *Latin American Perspectives* 43:1 (2016), 197.

16. A. Borón, "'Buen Vivir' and the dilemmas of the Latin American left", Climate and Capitalism (31 August 2015); https://climateandcapitalism.com/2015/08/31/buen-vivir-and-dilemmas-of-latin-american-left.

17. E. Viola, "The ecologist movement in Brazil (1974–1986): from environmentalism to ecopolitics", *International Journal of Urban and Regional Research* 12:2 (1988), 221–2.

18. A. Alonso, V. Costa and D. Maciel, "The formation of the Brazilian environmental movement", Working Paper 259 (Brighton: Institute of Development Studies, University of Sussex, 2005), 21.

19. J. Damask, "Evolution of the environmental movement in Brazil's Amazonia", research report (Gland, Switzerland: World Wide Fund for Nature, 1998).

20. S. McCormick, "The governance of hydro-electric dams in Brazil", *Journal of Latin American Studies* 39:2 (2007).

21. K. Hochstetler, "The evolution of the Brazilian environmental movement and its political roles", in D. Chalmers *et al.* (eds), *The New Politics of Inequality in Latin America: Rethinking Participation and Representation* (Oxford: Oxford University Press, 1997), 192.

22. Acosta, "The Yasuní–ITT initiative".

23. R. Ramírez, "Socialismo del Sumak Kawsay: o biosocialismo republicano", in *Los nuevos retos de América Latina: socialismo y Sumak Kawsay* (Quito: Secretaría Nacional de Planificación y Desarrollo, 2010).

24. S. Radcliffe, "Development for a postneoliberal era? Sumak Kawsay, living well and the limits of decolonization in Educator", *Geoforum* 43:2 (2012).

9 Ways forward

1. M. Thayer and J. Rubin, "Uncontained activism", in Alvarez *et al.*, *Beyond Civil Society*, 335.

2. F. Jameson, "Cognitive mapping", in C. Nelson and L. Grossberg (eds), *Marxism and the Interpretation of Culture* (London: Macmillan, 1988), 355.

3. See K. Lynch, *The Image of the City* (Cambridge, MA: MIT Press, 1960).

4. A. Toscano and J. Kinkle, *Cartographies of the Absolute* (Alresford: Zero Books, 2015), 69–70.

5. M. Svampa, *Del cambio de época al fin de ciclo: gobiernos progresistas, extractivismo, y movimientos sociales en América Latina* (Buenos Aires: Edhasa, 2017), 35.

6. M. Hardt and A. Negri, *Multitude* (New York: Penguin Books, 2004).

7. M. Green, "Gramsci cannot speak: presentations and interpretations of Gramsci's concept of the subaltern", in M. Green (ed.), *Rethinking Gramsci* (Abingdon: Routledge, 2011), 75.

8. Touraine, *The Voice and the Eye*, 68.

9. Foucault, *Power*, 269.

10. Rouse, "Power/knowledge", 112.

11. For example, M. Fuentes and A. Frank, "Ten theses on social movements", *World Development* 17:2 (1989).

12. Svampa, *Del cambio de época al fin de ciclo*, 40, emphasis in original.

13. S. Radcliffe, "Civil society, social difference and politics: issues of identity and representation", in Gwynne & Kay, *Latin America Transformed*, 218.

14. R. Debray, *Revolution in the Revolution?* (London: Penguin Books, 1967).

15. Holloway, *How to Change the World without Taking Power*.
16. G. Almeyra, *La protesta social en Argentina (1990–2004)* (Buenos Aires: Ediciones Continente, 2004), 81.
17. S. Alvarez *et al.*, "Interrogating the civil society agenda: reassessing uncivil political activism", in Alvarez *et al.*, *Beyond Civil Society*, 7.
18. For example, J. Castañeda, "Latin America's left turn: there is more than one pink tide", *Foreign Affairs* 85:3 (2006).
19. E. Thompson, *The Making of the English Working Class* (London: Penguin Books, 1970), 5.
20. *Ibid.*, 11.
21. G. Stedman Jones, *Languages of Class: Studies in English Working Class History* (Cambridge: Cambridge University Press, 1983), 19.
22. *Ibid.*, 76.
23. Laclau, *On Populist Reason*, 154.
24. C. Mouffe, *For a Left Populism* (London: Verso, 2018), 56.
25. See Munck, *Rethinking Latin America*.
26. Laclau, *On Populist Reason*, 127.
27. Svampa, *Del cambio de época al fin de ciclo*, 44.
28. Laclau, *On Populist Reason*, 74.
29. F. Jameson, *Archaeologies of the Future: The Desire Called Utopia and Other Science Fictions* (London: Verso, 2007), 50.

10 Methodological appendix

1. B. Carlsen and C. Glenton, "What about N? A methodological study of sample-size reporting in focus group studies", *BMC Medical Research Methodology*, 2011; doi: 10.1186/1471-2288-11-26.
2. S. Da Silva, P. Tamás and J. Kampen, "Articles reporting research on Latin American social movements are only rarely transparent", *Social Movement Studies* 17:6 (2018), 746.
3. R. Munck *et al.* (eds), *Higher Education and Community-Based Research: Creating a Global Vision* (London: Palgrave Macmillan, 2004).
4. Touraine, *The Voice and the Eye*, 14.
5. A. Melucci, *Nomads of the Present: Social Movements and Individual Needs in Contemporary Society* (London: Hutchinson, 1989), 239.
6. A. Melucci, *Challenging Codes: Collective Action in the Information Age* (Cambridge: Cambridge University Press, 1996).
7. S. Motta, "Notes towards prefigurative epistemologies", in S. Motta and A Nilsen (eds), *Social Movements in the Global South: Dispossession, Development and Resistance* (London: Palgrave Macmillan, 2011).
8. *Ibid.*, 181.
9. P. Bourdieu, J.-C. Chamboredon and J.-C. Passeron, *The Craft of Sociology: Epistemological Preliminaries* (Berlin: de Gruyter, 1991), 36.
10. *Ibid.*, 39.
11. P. Berger and T. Luckmann, *The Social Construction of Reality: A Treatise in the Sociology of Knowledge* (New York: Anchor Books, 1966), 11.
12. A. Bryant and K. Charmaz, *The Sage Handbook of Grounded Theory* (London: Sage, 2011).
13. A. Mattoni, "The potentials of grounded theory in the study of social movements", in D. della Porta (ed.), *Methodological Practices in Social Movement Research* (Oxford: Oxford University Press, 2014), 23.
14. K. Charmaz, "Grounded theory as an emergent method", in S. Hesse-Biber and P. Leavy (eds), *Handbook of Emergent Methods* (New York: Guilford Press, 2008).
15. Bourdieu, Chamboredon & Passeron, *The Craft of Sociology*, 38.

16. Moore, *Injustice*; T. Skocpol, *States and Social Revolutions: A Comparative Analysis of France, Russia and China* (New York: Cambridge University Press, 1979).

17. D. Ritter, "Comparative historical analysis", in della Porta, *Methodological Practices in Social Movement Research*, 99–100.

18. D. della Porta, "Comparative analysis: case-oriented versus variable-oriented analysis", in D. della Porta and M. Keating (eds), *Approaches and Methodologies in the Social Sciences: A Pluralist Perspective* (Cambridge: Cambridge University Press, 2008), 206.

19. P. McMichael, "Incorporating comparison within a world-historical perspective: an alternative comparative method", *American Sociological Review* 55:3 (1990).

20. F. Cardoso and E. Faletto, *Dependencia y Desarrollo en América Latina* (Buenos Aires: Siglo XXI, 1969); F. Cardoso and E. Faletto, *Dependency and Development in Latin America* (Berkeley, CA: University of California Press, 1979).

21. R. Collier and D. Collier, *Shaping the Political Arena: Critical Junctures, the Labor Movement, and Regime Dynamics in Latin America* (Notre Dame, IN: University of Notre Dame Press, 2002).

22. Bergquist, *Labor in Latin America*.

23. Vergara-Camus, *Land and Freedom*; C. Hesketh, *Spaces of Capital/Spaces of Resistance: Mexico and the Global Political Economy* (Athens, GA: University of Georgia Press, 2017).

24. Campus Engage, *Engaged Research: Society and Higher Education: Addressing Grand Societal Challenges Together* (Dublin: Campus Engage, 2016).

25. J. Brewer, *Ethnography* (Milton Keynes: Open University Press, 2000), 6.

26. G. Caruso, "Transformative ethnography and the World Social Forum: theories and practices of transformation", in J. Juris and A. Khasnabish (eds), *Insurgent Encounters: Transitional Activism, Ethnography and the Political* (London: Verso, 2013), 238.

27. *Ibid.*, 229; J. Conway, "Ethnographic approaches to the World Social Forum", in Juris & Khasnabish, *Insurgent Encounters*, 291, emphasis in original.

28. C. Geertz, "Thick description: towards an interpretive theory of culture", in *The Interpretation of Cultures: Selected Essays* (New York: Basic Books, 1973).

29. S. Alvarez, *Engendering Democracy in Brazil: Women's Movements in Transition Politics* (Princeton, NJ: Princeton University Press, 1990), 17.

30. J. Hardy, "Dissonant emotions, divergent outcomes: constructing space for emotional methodologies of development", *Emotion, Space and Society* 5:2 (2012).

31. *Ibid.*, 114.

32. *Ibid.*, 115.

33. O. Fals-Borda and M. Rahman, *Action and Knowledge: Breaking the Monopoly with Participatory Action-Research* (Lanham, MD: Rowman & Littlefield, 1991).

34. B. Moore, *Social Origins of Dictatorship and Democracy: Lord and Peasant in the Making of the Modern World* (Boston: Beacon Press, 1966).

35. Fals-Borda & Rahman, *Action and Knowledge*, 23.

36. Freire, *Pedagogy of the Oppressed*.

37. R. Chambers, *Whose Reality Counts? Putting the First Last* (London: Intermediate Technology Publications, 1997).

38. I. Kapoor, *The Postcolonial Politics of Development* (London: Routledge, 2008), 63.

39. Conway, "Ethnographic approaches to the World Social Forum".

40. K. Woodward, "Concepts of identity and difference", in K. Woodward (ed.), *Identity and Difference* (Milton Keynes: Open University Press, 1997).

41. See P. Grzanka (ed.), *Intersectionality: A Foundations and Frontier Reader* (Boulder, CO: Westview Press, 2014).

42. H. Lutz, M. Herrera Vivar and L. Supik, "Framing intersectionality: an introduction", in H. Lutz, M. Herrera Vivar and L. Supik (eds), *Framing Intersectionality: Debates on a Multi-Faceted Concept in Gender Studies* (Farnham: Ashgate, 2011), 9.

43. N. Fraser, "Rethinking recognition", *New Left Review* 3 (2000).

44. N. Yuval-Davis, "Beyond the recognition and re-distribution dichotomy: intersectionality and stratification", in Lutz, Herrera Vivar & Supik, *Framing Intersectionality*, 165.
45. G. Kendall and G. Wickham, *Using Foucault's Methods* (London: Sage, 1999).
46. N. Fairclough, *Discourse and Social Change* (Oxford: Polity, 1994).
47. D. Howarth and Y. Stavrakakis, "Introducing discourse theory and political analysis", in D. Howarth, A. Norval and Y. Stavrakakis (eds), *Discourse Theory and Political Analysis: Identities, Hegemonies and Social Change* (Manchester: Manchester University Press, 2000), 5.
48. S. Barros and G. Castagnola, "The political frontiers of the social: Argentine politics after Peronist populism (1955–1973)", in Howarth, Norval & Stavrakakis, *Discourse Theory and Political Analysis*.
49. E. Laclau, *New Reflections on the Revolution of Our Time* (London: Verso, 1990), 23.
50. Barros & Castagnola, "The political frontiers of the social", 35.
51. D. Bertaux and P. Thompson, "Introduction", in *Between Generations: Family Models, Myths, and Memories* (Oxford: Oxford University Press, 1993), 5.
52. *Ibid.*, 42.
53. D. Bertaux, "From the life history approach to the transformation of sociological practice", in D. Bertaux (ed.), *Biography and Society: The Life History Approach in Social Sciences* (London: Sage, 1981), 220.
54. P. Pozzi, "Oral history in Latin America", *Oral History Weekly* 73 (6 June 2012).
55. J. French and D. James (eds), *The Gendered Worlds of Latin American Women Workers: From Household and Factory to the Union Hall and Ballot Box* (Durham, NC: Duke University Press, 1997), 298.
56. S. Rivera Cusicanqui, "El potencial epistemologico y teórico de la historia oral: de la logica instrumental a la descolonización de la historia", *Voces Recobradas: Revista de Historia Oral* 8:21 (2006).
57. J. Auyero, *Contentious Lives: Two Argentine Women, Two Protests, and the Quest for Recognition* (Durham, NC: Duke University Press, 2003), 298.
58. *Ibid.*, 4.
59. K. Gillen and J. Pickerill, "The difficult and hopeful ethics of research on, and with, social movements", *Social Movement Studies* 11:2 (2012), 139.
60. Hellman, "Real and virtual Chiapas".
61. S. Halvorsen, "Cartographies of epistemic expropriation: critical reflections on learning from the South", *Geoforum* 95 (2018).
62. *Ibid.*, 17.
63. B. Otto and P. Terhorst, "Beyond differences? Exploring methodological dilemmas of activist research in the global South", in Motta & Nilsen, *Social Movements in the Global South*, 210.
64. M. Foucault, *The Birth of the Clinic* (London: Tavistock, 1973).
65. Bourdieu, Chamboredon & Passeron, *The Craft of Sociology*, 25.
66. B. Sousa Santos, *Epistemologies of the South: Justice against Epistemicide* (London: Routledge, 2014).
67. *Ibid.*, 56.
68. L. Smith, *Decolonizing Methodologies: Research and Indigenous Peoples* (London: Zed Books, 1999).
69. A. Quijano, "Coloniality of power, Eurocentrism and Latin America", *Nepantla: Views from South* 1:3 (2000).
70. Escobar, *Territories of Difference*, 37–8, emphasis in original.
71. Dinerstein, *The Politics of Autonomy in Latin America*.
72. *Ibid.*, 224.

INDEX

agency
    of the Argentinian trade unions, 33
    role in social movements, 2
    working-class formation, 122
Almeyra, Guillermo, 119
Alonso, Angela, 107
Alvarez, Sonia, 27, 78, 79, 83, 84,
    120, 135–6
Amerindian peoples. *See also* indigenous
    movements
    agrarian communism, 23
    autonomy theory and, 24–5
    Buen Vivir philosophies, 99
    within *indigenismo*, 23–4
Argentina
    autonomist movement, 69
    collapse of neoliberalism, x
    community organizations, 66, 68–9
    Cordobazo, 32, 67, 75
    feminism in, 75, 76–7
    human rights movements in, 32
    labour movements under
        Kirchnerism, 32–3
    labour movements under military
        dictatorship, 32
    labour movements under Perón, 30–2
    Madres de Plaza de Mayo, 8, 27, 32, 75
    Ni una menos, 76
    Peronism, 31, 67, 75, 115
    piqueteros, ix, 5, 10, 27, 69
    place-based social movements, 59
    post-neoliberal governments, x
    Qué se vayan todos, 59, 71
    rise of Mauricio Macri, xi, xii
    rise of the right, xi, xii
    sociedades de fomento, 67
    vecinazos uprisings, 68
    women's movements, 76–7
    working-class labour insurgency, 32
Asher, Kiran, 65

autonomy
    concept of, 24–5, 70
    critiques of, 70–1
    and global liberal feminism, 83, 115
    indigenous movements and, 70, 92
    liberal readings of, 119–20
    pedagogy and, 48
    of the *piqueteros*, 69
    subaltern class development, 117
    and the Zapatista movement, 69

Baiocchi, G., 61
Becker, Mark, 91, 104
Bergquist, Charles, 29
Bolivia
    Buen Vivir philosophies, 110
    contrasted with Ecuador, 92
    environmental movements, 101–4
    forms of indigenous movement, 87
    gas war in El Alto, 89, 101–2
    gasolinazo, 88, 102
    government–social movement clashes, 102
    indigenous movements, 85, 101, 102
    Movement towards Socialism (MAS), 87,
        88, 101
    new wave of indigenous movements, 87
    post neoliberal governments, x, xi, 121
    social movements under Evo Morales'
        government, 87–9
    water wars, 87, 89, 101, 102
Bolsonaro, Jair, xi, 79
Bourdieu, Pierre, 129–30, 131, 145
Brazil. *See also* Landless Workers
    Movement (MST)
    anti-dam movement, 108–9
    Central Única dos Trabalhadores (CUT),
        34, 35, 48
    Church support for community
        organizations, 61–2
    civil society, 62